John J McAfee

Kentucky Politicians

Sketches of Representative Corncrackers and Other Miscellany

John J McAfee

Kentucky Politicians
Sketches of Representative Corncrackers and Other Miscellany

ISBN/EAN: 9783337077686

Printed in Europe, USA, Canada, Australia, Japan

Cover: Foto ©Suzi / pixelio.de

More available books at **www.hansebooks.com**

KENTUCKY POLITICIANS.

SKETCHES

OF

Representative Corn-Crackers

AND

OTHER MISCELLANY.

BY

JOHN J. McAFEE.

"O wad some power the giftie gie us
To see oursel's as ithers see us."

Press of
The Courier-Journal Job Printing Company, Louisville, Ky.
1886.

ENTERED ACCORDING TO ACT OF CONGRESS, IN THE YEAR 1886, BY
JOHN J. McAFEE,
IN THE OFFICE OF THE LIBRARIAN AT WASHINGTON.

DEDICATION.

This Book is dedicated to the Honorable gentlemen

whose names grace its pages,

as a

token of my honest admiration and esteem.

Its merit lies in the fact of its sincerity and fidelity to truth.

As such a memento it is

offered to them by the hand of Friendship.

JOHN J. McAFEE.

Louisville, Ky.

Preface.

This work consists of biographical notes of Kentucky politicians, sketches of representative Corn-Crackers, and miscellany; reminiscences of the past forty years, army experiences, glimpses of Southern life; a reliable account of how the great Cavalryman, General John H. Morgan, was killed; a eulogy on General U. S. Grant; bits of philosophy, and distinctively a compilation of historical facts in the lives of the leading young men of our State who have reflected credit on Kentucky by their independence, their courage, and their genius. It also contains the history of their ancestry—tells who they were, their places of nativity, their Alma Mater, and a list of the public offices they have held.

As a book of accurate reference, and the means by which one can easily acquaint himself with the experiences of those lofty spirits who opened up Kentucky while yet a wilderness, the home of the savage and the wolf, I bespeak an indulgent recognition of whatever merit it may possess.

The Author.

Contents.

BIOGRAPHICAL SKETCHES.

Hon. Robert T. Albritton	7
General David Rice Atchison	10
Hon. J. C. S. Blackburn	17
Hon. W. O. Bradley	20
Hon. W. C. P. Breckinridge	25
Judge Eli H. Brown	29
Colonel John Mason Brown	32
Hon. Joshua F. Bullitt, Jr.	36
Hon. Robert A. Burton	41
Hon. John G. Carlisle	44
Hon. Asher Graham Caruth	48
George M. Davie, Esq.	52
Hon. Henry C. Dixon	57
General Basil W. Duke	61
Judge Fontaine T. Fox	65
General Parker W. Hardin	68
Hon. Thomas F. Hargis	73
Hon. Thomas H. Hays	77
Hon. John K. Hendrick	81
General Fayette Hewitt	85
Hon. James R. Hindman	89
Judge Wm. B. Hoke	92
Hon. William L. Jackson, Jr.	95
Hon. Richard A. Jones	98
Hon. Lafayette Joseph	101
Hon. J. D. Kehoe	105
Judge William Lindsay	109
Hon. Emmet G. Logan	113
Hon. James B. McCreary	118
Hon. Thomas E. Moss	121
Hon. W. C. Owens	124
Judge M. H. Owsley	128
Hon. P. Booker Reed	131
Hon. John S. Rhea	135
Hon. Henry Hamilton Skiles	138
Hon. James W. Tate	146
Hon. William Preston Taulbee	149
Judge Reginald Heber Thompson	153
The Thompson Brothers	156
Colonel Sterling B. Toney	160
Hon. Henry Watterson	164
Hon. Albert S. Willis	168
Hon. Leander Cobb Woolfolk	172
Colonel Bennett H. Young	176

MISCELLANEOUS SKETCHES.

Views of Louisville as a .... a Home	183
A .... on General	185
A .... Proposition to act as Umpire	188
.... in Saddle	191
.... of Long Ago	197
February 22d	202
General U. S. Grant	206
General John H. Morgan	210
How to Better One's Self	218
Kindness	221
Notable Characters	224
Our Dead—Preserve their Memories	230
Our Happiest Days	232
Our Sacred Past	234
Remarks on the Death of Hon. James A. McCampbell	241
The Blue and the Gray	243
The Future	246
The Ingratitude of the Masses	249
The Thirst for Office	251
Thoughts about Boys	254
Truth—a Lost Art	257

HON. ROBERT T. ALBRITTON.

The noblest aspiration of the human heart is, or ought to be, the desire to be and to do right, and to deserve the encomiums of our fellowmen. Every one who lives up to this high ideal, according to his best ability, has triumphed over the lesser ills of life, which great minds ignore. If from such a man the careless world should withhold the praise he seeks, and to which *per se* he is entitled, it is a wrong, whose perpetration may never be offset by any amount of good in another direction. If, on the contrary, he should receive the meed of praise which his upright and manly course merits, his happiness, his pride, and his ambition being assured, his emulation to rise to a still nobler plane of well-doing is forever awake. Such a man, born to the luck of appreciation among his fellowmen, is the gentleman whose biography engrosses my mind and pen to-day—Robert T. Albritton. His father, John Albritton, Esq., was a gentleman of great probity and excellence, whose ancestors were among the first settlers of North Carolina, but uniting his life with that of Miss Conway, of Virginia, one of the brightest and prettiest belles of her day and time, the two young people, at an early period in the history of Kentucky, came to this State and settled down with the full intention of "growing up with the country." Among the lady's male ancestors on the Conway side of the house are several who have distinguished themselves for bravery and ———, and whose names stand high in the communities in which they lived. Among them was Miles W. Conway, who was a member of the convention of 1792, which met in Danville to form the first constitution of Kentucky. Another, Preacher Conway, is mentioned in the State Annals as having said in Boston that "President Lincoln would like to have God on his side, but he *must* have Kentucky." Still another belonged to Captain James Harrod's company, which, in 1780, kept watch over the Falls, in what is now Jefferson and Shelby counties.

Hon. Robert Albritton was born in the county of Graves on the 11th day of April, 1844. He was educated in the schools of the county of his nativity, where his scholastic course was as thorough, if not more so, than those attained by other young men whose parents could not consider them "finished" and ready for the battle of life unless they matriculated at "Princeton" or "William and Mary," or some other equally well-known college or university.

Now, it is a fact that Graves county was formed in 1823 out of a part of Hickman county. It was named in honor of Major Benjamin Graves, who was an amiable, shrewd, and intelligent man. He resided in Fayette county, following the peaceful pursuit of agriculture, finding his purest enjoyment in studying nature in her varying moods, and learning from her how to fill his barns and glean rich harvests of golden grain; but, for all that, he several times represented Fayette county in the Legislature of his State. When the United States declared war against Great Britain, in the year 1812, Benjamin Graves was among the first to volunteer his services in defense of his country's rights. He received the appointment of major in Colonel Lewis' regiment, and a more gallant officer, a more active and vigilant soldier never led a charge or fought for freedom. He was killed in the memorable battle of Raisin, and his life-blood ebbed away and mingled in its flow with the bluest blood in the States.

When the tocsin of war was sounded twenty-five years ago, the record stands that A. R. Boone (being a member of the General Assembly) was expelled from the House of Representatives on December 21, 1861, "because directly or indirectly connected with giving aid and comfort to the Confederate army and repudiating and acting against the Government of the United States and the Commonwealth of Kentucky."

From which facts it will be seen that Graves county has her heroes, whose chivalry stands second best to none in the world; and every Kentuckian who fought for the "Lost Cause," in memory of the gallant daring and hard fighting, the endurance and the privations involved in that struggle, should "take off his hat" to the historic name of "Boone," made doubly dear to him by this incident.

He was not alone in his sympathy with the Southern movement.

Robert T. Albritton was certainly in harmony with him, for he was among the first of the young and impulsive patriots who espoused the "cause" and rallied to the battle-cry of "Dixie." He was made captain of Company "H," of the Eighth regiment of Kentucky infantry, serving through the entire war with that courage and efficiency common to the soldiers of Kentucky, it matters not in what armies they fight. The people of the South keep sacred the remembrance of the service of Kentucky soldiers in the days of old, and this young and chivalrous officer "acted well his part." No matter how fierce and desperate the battles in which his regiment was engaged, young Albritton came out of them with "flying colors." One day, however, a cloud drifted across his "lucky star," and he was taken prisoner. For seven months he languished at Camp Morton. It is only among those who endured the martyrdom of prison life for the cause of liberty, national independence, and States' rights that a comprehensive view of such suffering can be obtained.

At the close of the war, Captain Albritton returned to his home, rejoiced to find his old-time friends and associates had lost none of their good feeling for him on account of the internecine struggle. Since then he has taken an active part in politics. He has been twice elected sheriff of his county. He was twice chosen chairman of the congressional committee of his district, and in August, 1885, he was elected State Senator from the district composed of the counties of Graves, Fulton, and Hickman. He is considered one of the strongest and soundest solons of the General Assembly. He is a man of great dignity of character; he commands respect, and yet there is nothing austere about him. He is genial, companionable, and courageous as a lion.

In 1877, he married the charming daughter of Irvin Anderson, Esq. He was well known to the representative men of the State in ante-bellum days as the highest and noblest type of a Kentucky gentleman. Greater praise than this no man need aspire to gain.

Mr. and Mrs. Albritton have quite an interesting family of children, who bid fair to do honor to their excellent parents in moral worth and intellectual brilliance.

GENERAL DAVID RICE ATCHISON.

Full a century and a half ago there was born in the shadows of the hills of Hanover county, Va., a child destined to sway his fellow-beings with his convincing eloquence and the powerful influence of his shining example, as it seldom falls to the lot of one mortal to assert himself above others unless backed by the marvelous strength of noble birthright, of trained armies, or the significance afforded by countless thousands of dollars. None of these aids were his. His parents were poor, obscure, and unobtrusive, but in this little child of theirs glowed the spark of genius. Nothing afforded him enjoyment equal to that derived from the sweet stories of the Gospel. He would rise early on Sunday morning, put a piece of clap-bread (a species of oatmeal-cake rolled thin and baked hard) in the bosom of his hunting-shirt, and travel thirteen miles on foot to hear President Davison preach. The minister, noticing a little ragged boy sitting near the door so regular in his attendance, detained him. On examination, he found that he was a pious boy, with fine tastes. He put him under his supervision, and gave him what in those days was esteemed a first-rate education. He was converted under the preaching of President Edwards, and studied theology under Rev. John Todd. He graduated at Princeton College, New Jersey. His name was David Rice, but, in the familiar parlance of those who loved and revered him, in later days he was known only by the title of "Father Rice." In the struggle for National Independence, he took a warm and zealous part, and esteemed it commensurate with the dignity of his clerical profession to address the people at county meetings and recite their grievances, while he urged measures for their suppression. In the year 1783 he came to Kentucky. He was then fifty years old, and was the third Presbyterian minister who crossed the mountains. He identified his fortunes with those of the brave spirits who had, in the face of long odds, established an infant colony amid the trackless wilds of a new country, dark with unguessed dangers. His influence was everywhere felt. He came among the hardy pioneers like a sweet south wind, infusing peace into their souls and good will toward their fellowmen. He gathered the Presbyterians into regular congregations at Danville, at Shawnee Run Church, near the spot where Shakertown now stands, and at McAfee Station. Previous to his arrival in Kentucky, marriages were all solemnized by magistrates, but subsequent to that event the people made it a point to procure the services of clergymen. At McAfee's Station, on the 3d of June, 1784, he united two glad hearts in the bonds of love and unity, and on the next day, the 4th instant, preached the funeral sermon of Mrs. James McCown, whose maiden name was McAfee, the first sermon ever preached on the banks of Salt river.

David Rice was not ornate in his delivery. As a theologian, he was plain, practical, and earnest. His judgment was sound, his disposition conservative, and his deportment exemplary. He spent much of his time in prayer. When in the pulpit, his manner was most solemn and impressive. His intercourse with society was dignified and grave, but never austere. He was one of the patriarchs of Presbyterianism in Kentucky. Besides his active duties as a minister, and the organization of many churches, he was always zealous in advancing the cause of education. He was the first teacher in the Transylvania Seminary, and was also for several years the Chairman of its Board of Trustees.

The public esteemed him with immeasurable regard, and, as evidence of the hold he had upon the affection of the people, of high and low degree, he was elected a member of the convention which met in Danville in 1792 to frame a State Constitution. He exerted his influence on that memorable occasion, but without success, for the inserting of an article providing for the gradual extinction of slavery in Kentucky. He was a great man—a good man. He tried to do right under all circumstances, to be frank and fair with his fellowmen, and he gathered his reward in their universal homage. In *personnel* he was slender, tall, and active, possessed of great vigor and alertness, and in his old age he looked like a picture of Time smiling serenely beneath the snow-crown of many winters. He died in Green county on the 18th of June, 1816, in the eighty-third year of his age. His last words were, "Oh! when shall I be free from sin and sorrow?"

To perpetuate his name, many of the old-time people of a century ago adopted the name of "Rice" as a family Christian name. It was so with the McAfees, the Atchisons, the Welches, and many others. Indeed, the name of David Rice will never die while the echoes live among the Cumberland mountains that fortify the southern borders of Kentucky. Among his near lineal descendants are the children of John Welch, of Jessamine county, who married Miss Bettie Rice. They have several distinguished children—Rev. Thomas Rice Welch, now Consul-General to Canada; Judge William Rice Welch, of Illinois, and Doctor John C. Welch, a distinguished surgeon, now resident in Nicholasville, Ky. Genius never dies; she but takes on new colors and constantly renews her youth at the fountain of immortal fame; but on none of those who have been honored by wearing the title of this great man, David Rice, has the sign-manual descended as visibly as it did upon the brow of David Rice Atchison, the subject of this sketch, and the most prominent man among those who stood like giants amid the political battles of the past, and who survived the splendor of an eminently successful political life, as a superb oak might daringly rear its emerald crest to the blue dome, though civilization had felled a forest around it. He stood a link between the past and present, until the other day he fell as the monarch of the wood might fall—conquered by age alone.

David Rice Atchison was born in Fayette county, Ky., south-east of Lexington, August 11, 1807. His father, William Atchison, Esq., was a gentleman of great wealth, a profound thinker, and almost a zealot in his unbounded religious enthusiasm as a Presbyterian. His mother was Miss Catherine Allen, whose ancestral line might be traced back amid the pine forests of the grand old State of North Carolina. From his early years it was impressed upon the mind of young Atchison that his parents desired that he should become a Presbyterian minister. The fact of his bearing so great a name as "David Rice" would, with many lads, have been the best stimulus to excite religious enthusiasm, and so bias the bent of his inclination for a life-pursuit; but it had no influence over this brilliant young scion of a splendid race other than to   his character all inclinations toward wildness, and to early impress him with the conviction that, if not a minister of the Gospel, he must be something great to repay his parents for the keen disappointment he inflicted by a choice of career varying from their fervent individual desire.

He was educated at Transylvania University, Lexington, Ky. While there he formed the acquaintance of another young Kentuckian who became his classmate and his life-long friend, and whom he met years afterward in the United States Senate—the one representing the State of Mississippi, the other Missouri. This was Jefferson Davis. Neither war nor its vicissitudes ever had the power to sever a friendship begun in the springtime of their lives.

At the age of twenty-two, David Rice Atchison removed to Liberty, Clay county, Mo., and began the practice of law. Success was not slow to welcome him. From 1831 to 1838 he served with distinction in the State Legislature. After this, when but thirty-three years old, he was appointed Judge of the Circuit Court. In the same year he was appointed by Governor Reynolds a Senator of the United States, to fill the unexpired term of Dr. L. F. Linn, made vacant by the death of that worthy gentleman. For fourteen years—from 1841 to 1855—he served in the Senate of the United States.

No man, among all the luminaries gathered at the capital, could outrival him, whether as prominent factor or conspicuous actor. At the time of the Kansas and Nebraska troubles, David Rice Atchison was the leader and chief adviser of the pro-slavery party. He received the credit of framing the bill repealing the Missouri Compromise. He was superbly educated, and allied to his natural genius, his knowledge of law, and his fine analytical mind and parliamentary finish, his magnificent stature and elegant manners rendered him a central figure of attraction even among the Titans of those days— Clay, Webster and Calhoun, Seward, Sumner and Hale, Douglas, Benton and Davis, and scores of others scarcely less able or brilliant. He was frequently chairman of important committees, and wherever he appeared commanded respect and won admiration.

When but thirty-eight years of age he was President *pro tempore* of the Senate of the United States. At forty-six, by the death of Wm. R. King, Vice-President of the United States, he became, being President of the United States Senate, Acting Vice-President of the United States. It was while holding the latter position, in 1849, that the event occurred which made him President of the United States for one day. The term of President Polk expired with the 3d day of March, 1849, and the 4th of March in that year falling upon Sunday, President-elect Taylor was not willing to take the oath of office upon that day. The latter's inauguration did not, therefore, take place until noon on Monday, March 5, 1849. David Rice Atchison, being then the presiding officer of the Senate, and having the natural succession to the presidency, if there was no president or vice-president at the time, was practically the President during Sunday, the 4th.

Many important measures came up in the fourteen years he was in office: Texas and California were admitted into the Union; the Wilmot Proviso; the compromise measures of 1850; the Kansas embroglio, and the permanent questions of finance, banks, currency, and revenue, all of which are forever unsettled matters for national controversy, whose adjustment involves all the wisdom and patriotism that can be brought to bear upon them. No matter what the subject for national consideration, while he had a voice in public affairs, David Rice Atchison was true to his convictions and faithful to his party, to his State, and to his friends. It is generally conceded that he was the most popular senator of his day and time among his compeers, whether of his own or the opposing party. He was a man of such magnificent culture, of such generous impulses, so brilliant, so moral, so manly and upright, that men crowned him with not only their admiration but their affections. Yet amid all the brilliance of his prominent public life he found time to love God and worship Him. He was a firm believer in the Bible, and often asserted that he found it impossible to be otherwise, although at one time he had tried to doubt it. And so it was that the seeds of "peace on earth, good will to men," sown by David Rice, in the pioneer days, in the hearts of his fellow-statesmen, brought in a golden harvest after many years. The world had offered this young man, David Rice Atchison, the allurements of earth; it had endeavored to beguile his conscience with sounding brass and tinkling cymbals, but all to no purpose; the holy lessons learned at his mother's knee were more potent than the sophistries of the world, and his individual needs were best satisfied by the adaptability of the Gospel to the requirements of his contemplative mind—requirements which led him along the same path that Shakespeare, Milton, Bacon, Webster, Clay, and others had passed, through the shadows of doubt to the effulgent goal of conviction.

When the late civil war began, David Rice Atchison, who was in warm sympathy with the South, helped to organize the Confederate forces in his vicinity, and was in several engagements, in which he bore himself with courtly courage. His rank was that of a general, but at the time of his enlistment his health was frail, and to his deep regret he was forced to send in his resignation.

Hoping to be able, through perfect quiet and rest from his public labors, to recuperate his health, General Atchison retired to his farm near Gower, in Clinton county, Mo., living in private, calm and undisturbed, but his hope was vain. He never again entered the arena of public life. He was seventy-nine when he died, beloved and mourned by a large concourse of friends and relations. In presence he was over six feet high, splendidly built, a man every inch of him. He has passed through the Valley of the Shadow, but the reputation he has left with the nation is a priceless heritage which will continue to halo the past with its golden splendor like the undying glory of a never-setting sun.

Among his nearest relatives left in this State, after he moved to Missouri, born in the same county, was the Hon. Samuel Ayers Atchison, the eminent lawyer, who died in Louisville in 1869. This latter gentleman was twice wedded. His first wife, an elegant lady, was the sister of Governor James T. Morehead. Among her children was the brilliant young lawyer, Samuel Atchison, who died in this city in 1880, lamented by his friends, and mourned by those who knew him best, as one whose like would not soon be looked upon again. He had a magnificent mind, and stepped to the front rank at the chancery bar as if he had an imperial title.

BENJAMIN F. ATCHISON, ESQ.

Mr. Atchison's second wife was Miss Eliza Love, a lady of great refinement and intelligence, who is still living at the age of eighty years in full possession of her faculties. Of this marriage was born, in Louisville, Ky., June 20, 1852, an only child, Benjamin F. Atchison, Esq., a lawyer of that city, whose capacity and talents justify the highest hopes of eminence in his profession. After graduating at a Kentucky college in 1870, he studied law, and matriculated in the law department of the University of Louisville, graduating therefrom in 1873. The directness of his course, his fine common sense, his prudent habits, and excellent judgment have heretofore attracted the attention of the people more than that undoubted genius with which his intimate associates know that he is gifted. His wit is delicate and polished, his manner genial and delightful, his observation accurate and keen. His skill in cross-examination, rare in one so young, attests his acquaintance with the motives and character of men. While not appearing to the world a book-worm, his learning is solid and extensive, and his memory allows no treasure he has toiled for to escape. All these qualities are based upon the strong foundation of integrity and sincerity. He is at his best when confronted by unexpected difficulties in the trial of his causes; and he has that presence of mind in such dangers which is the surest test of self-reliance and the consciousness of powers which he always holds well in hand. He is one of those modest, unassuming men with lofty and fixed purposes in life, who do not culminate prematurely, but whose mental stature keeps steady pace with his years, and who will never disappoint the highest expectations of those who understand his admirable character, and those expectations are very high.

This gentleman several years ago married Miss Minnie Warren, daughter of L. L. Warren, the devout Presbyterian, whose worth as a man was coequal with that of David Rice, who lived for his people and his God. Warren Memorial Church, in this city, is a monument to his religious convictions and munificent philanthropy, which will survive the sweep of many a storm and the gathering dust of ages.

John Atchison, Esq., of Bowling Green, Kentucky, and Dr. Thos. A. Atchison, of Nashville, Tennessee, a distinguished surgeon, who reached the pinnacle of his profession and retired to the walks of private life, possessed alike of great wealth and influence, are the only near relatives in this section, besides Benjamin F. Atchison, Esq., of the great David Rice Atchison, whose fame as a jurist, soldier, scholar, statesman, citizen, lifts a column of glory to the skies, to whose splendor many men may turn their eyes, yet scarcely see another in the nineteenth century equaled by accumulated chronicles of deeds as noble, as faithful, as imperishable. General Atchison lived and died a bachelor.

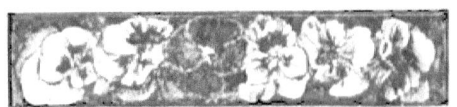

HON. J. C. S. BLACKBURN.

Kentucky's Senator in Congress, Hon. J. C. S. Blackburn, is a man of remarkable eloquence, having at his command a vocabulary of astonishing dimensions, which he puts to fluent use. His voice is full, rich, resonant, and, when he is upon the hustings advocating the rights of the great national and now victorious Democratic party, it rings like a silver clarion, easily filling any auditorium to its boundaries with its harmonious utterances. He was born in the county of Woodford in the year 1838. He is the youngest son of a large family of children, the eldest of which is ex-Governor Luke P. Blackburn, who is an old and highly-respected citizen of Louisville, Ky., ripe in years and full of honors. Judge Joseph H. Lewis, of the present Court of Appeals in Kentucky, is a brother-in-law. Ex-Mayor Morris, of Chicago, was another. The most estimable wife of the last-named gentleman survived him many years, and died in this city in 1884. She was an inveterate Southerner—Southern in heart and in soul, and during the war, of all the ladies in Chicago she was the most active and untiring in her kind and tender ministrations to the Southern prisoners at Fort Douglas. Her name, through the eloquent praise of those whose incarceration she brightened with the light of her Christian charities, in many households of the Southland, became like a strain of familiar music. If it be true that God loves a cheerful giver, her high and noble soul has long ere this received the merited reward of "Well done, good and faithful servant." She possessed all the attributes of the pioneer matrons, whose heroic deeds aided much in opening up the country and establishing civilization as a permanence this side of the Alleghanies. They could not be commended too highly. They were true to every lofty impulse which graces the name of woman, and, with their firm and practical views of life, they made the rough, crude homes of the early settlers dear and comfortable to them as though beautified by every art and exhibition of luxurious designs that belong to modern times. Their guerdon lies in the knowledge, which is our herison, that civilization has spread mile on mile into the far West, spanning rivers and tunneling mountains; like electricity, forcing its way wherever it listeth, until in the waste places the lily blends its fragrance with the erubescent rose; and where trackless wilds once baffled the piercing rays of the sun, the jarring tumult of presses that never pause and the rush and whirl of busy cities are now heard; and the hamlets, with their varied sounds of honest labor, tell that the march of progression has not slackened its pace. All these changes are monuments reared to the memory of the good and true, who lived and struggled and died, leaving the rich heritage to us that we now, as a nation, enjoy. And yet how few pause in this busy life to pay homage to those whose meritorious deeds won the respect of the world, which goes ringing down the centuries. Mrs. Morris was a typical daughter of those famous American women who have helped to make the imperishable history of the country. Yet, with them to-day, wrapt in a gloom profound, we know that she is lowly lying, deaf alike to the homage of the world or the friends who loved her, and that the only consolation to the trusting soul is the thought that God gaveth and it is He who taketh away. The women of the Blackburn family are celebrated for their courage and their noble charities. They have never been daunted by either war or epidemic in the intelligent dispensing of alms to those who merit the mercy of the noble-hearted. Wealth to them is meaningless if hoarded up for sordid purposes.

Senator Blackburn graduated at Centre College, Danville, Ky., and in the law at Lexington, Ky. He is, strictly speaking, of indigenous growth, not only in point of birth and education, but also by marriage and in manner. His wife, an exceedingly handsome, elegant, and accomplished lady, is the daughter of the late Kentucky centenarian, Doctor Christopher Columbus Graham, who, at the time of his death, was probably the best known man in the State. During his life he was universally honored, and his death brought general gloom to the country in which he lived, and throughout whose borders he was so well and favorably known. Senator Blackburn was in the Southern army, and after the close of the war, in 1865, he swung his shingle out to the people of Arkansas as a practicing attorney at law with Judge R. H. Thompson, now of this city, as his partner. All the time pining for his native State, he returned to Woodford county in 1867; and in 1871, after a stormy canvass, he was elected to the Legislature, and, upon its organization, was chosen Chairman of the Committee on Railroads. He was re-elected in 1873, and was made Chairman of the Committee upon the Judiciary. In 1874, he was elected to the Congress of the United States, and continually succeeded himself until elected by the Legislature of 1883-'84 to the United States Senate, taking his seat March 4, 1885. Mr. Blackburn has made for himself a reputation as a bold and logical debater that is national, having measured lances with General Butler, President Garfield, and other Republican luminaries while a member of Congress, and each time having covered himself with glory at the intellectual jousts; and this, too, at a time when the country at large was overwhelmingly Republican. In those dark days, when the future fate of the Democratic party hung trembling in the balance of existence, the South and West stood greatly in need of the invaluable services of just such a debater as Blackburn, and never in a single instance has he proved recreant to a nation's trust in his courage, his intelligence, or his fidelity. The Republican party had grown arrogant and aggressive, and it was eminently necessary that they should be met in national councils with such valor and logic as Blackburn—and Blackburn alone—possessed. To say that he has covered himself with glory and nobly served his constituents is to do him a simple justice.

In physique he is very attractive, being a man of mark among a multitude. He is five feet eleven inches in height. His movements are quick, but full of a subtle grace and elasticity. His hair is a rich brown, his eyes are of a glinting blue in color, and wearing usually an expression which indicates great firmness of opinion and steadfastness of purpose in whatever cause he espouses. Honest principle, incorruptible and imperishable, is the groundwork of his character. His friends love him and bestow upon him a steadfast devotion that is admirable, and Kentuckians generally hold him in high esteem, and expect much of him in his new field of service to the nation.

HON. WILLIAM O'CONNELL BRADLEY.

Madison was a county of Virginia, one of nine established by the General Assembly of that State out of Kentucky county, afterward called Kentucky district, before the separation of Kentucky, and her admission into the Union June 1, 1792. It was formed (the seventh in order) out of a part of Lincoln county, and it was named in honor of James Madison, afterward President of the United States.

Mr. Madison was born March 5, 1751, in a town on the south side of the Rappahannock, in Virginia, called Port Royal. The home of his parents, however, was in Orange county, where he always resided. Mr. Madison received the very best education the country afforded, having graduated at Princeton College during the presidency of the celebrated Dr. Witherspoon. When he left college he studied law; not, however, with the view of adopting it as a profession. In 1776 he was elected to the Legislature of Virginia. At the succeeding county election he was not returned, but when the Legislature assembled he was appointed a member of the Council of State, which place he held until he was elected to Congress in 1779. While a member of the Council of State he formed an intimate friendship with Patrick Henry and Thomas Jefferson, which endured as long as life lasted. He continued in Congress during the years 1780, 1781, 1782, and 1783, being a leading, active, and influential member of that body, and in all its deliberations filling a prominent part. In the years 1784, 1785, and 1786, he was elected a delegate to the State Legislature. In 1786 he was a member of the convention at Annapolis, which assembled preliminary to the convention at Philadelphia, which formed the Federal Constitution. He was a member of that convention also, and assisted in framing the present Constitution of the United States. He continued a member of the old Congress by reappointment until its expiration in 1786. On the adoption of the Constitution, he was elected to Congress from his district, and continued a member from 1789 till 1797. He was the author of the celebrated resolution against the alien and sedition laws passed by the Virginia Legislature in 1798. When Mr. Jefferson was elected President, he appointed Mr. Madison Secretary of State, in which office he continued during the eight years of Jefferson's administration. In 1809, on the retirement of Mr. Jefferson, he was elected President, and administered the government during a period of eight years. At about sixty years of age he retired from public life, and ever afterward resided on his estate in Virginia, with the exception of about two months while at Richmond as a member of the convention in 1829, which sat there to remodel the Constitution of the State. His farm, his books, his friends, and his correspondence were the sources of his enjoyment and occupation during the twenty years of his retirement. On the 28th of June, 1836, he died, as serene, philosophical, and calm in the last moments of his existence as he had been in all the trying occasions of his life. When they received intelligence of his death, the Congress of the United States adopted a resolution appointing a public oration to commemorate his life, and Hon. John Q. Adams was selected to deliver it.

In honor of President Madison then, this county in Kentucky was named, and it does honor to his memory. It is the largest of the blue-grass counties. Its surface is diversified; the western is broken and quite hilly, the central part is generally undulating, the eastern portion lies well, but it is not so rich and productive as other portions of it.

Madison county felicitates herself in many respects beyond the prosperity of her citizens, the beauty of her scenery, and her illustrious history. She is rich in curiosities and objects of interest, calculated to inspire the tourist, the dreamer, and the student. She possesses the first of so many things, that to be well acquainted with Madison county argues a general comprehensive knowledge of the State. The first road or trace, called "Boone's trace," was cut from the Long Island, on Holston river, not far from the place of treaty, to Boonesborough, on the Kentucky river. The first contest between the whites and Indians on Kentucky soil occurred on Saturday morning, March 25, 1775, in what is now Madison county, about fifteen miles south of the Kentucky river. The first fort was established here, the first ferry, the first marriage in Kentucky took place at Boonesborough, the first store in Kentucky, the first schools were also opened and started in this same locality, and many more such incidents and deeds and civilized accomplishments originated in Madison county. She has produced soldiers, statesmen, jurists, orators, and divines whose origin any land might be proud to claim ; but there is not one cause above another, and has never been, about which she has reason to feel a deeper glow of pride than the fact that Robert McAfee Bradley was born (and reared within her borders) on March 27, 1808, and died in Lancaster, August 31, 1881. He was a great land lawyer — he had been schooled and trained in the experiences of land litigation, of which there seemed no end in Kentucky for many years. His practice was extensive and successful. He was eloquent, witty, and magnetic. He was fearless, and cool, and composed as an Oriental. He never sought and never

ROBERT McAFEE BRADLEY.

desired to fill public office. His profession was his pride, his ambition, and his delight. Beyond it and his family ties, he took interest in the cause of temperance and the development of intelligence through the dissemination of knowledge in public schools. Popular education was his dream, and to the last it commanded his interest and his attention. His wife's maiden name was Miss Ellen Totten. She was born in 1815, in Garrard county, Ky., and was the worthy and exemplary wife so gifted and good a man deserved to possess. She was a noted beauty and belle in her youth. They were blessed with five children, four daughters and one son. The daughters were all married happily, bearing respectively the names of Batchelor, Newell, Morrow, and Mayes. The son, William O'Connell Bradley, also married Miss Margaret R. Duncan, of Garrard county. Robert McAfee Bradley's father and grandfather were both Revolutionary soldiers, who served their country with honor and distinction. He, himself, was as thoroughly known as a lawyer as any man in Central Kentucky. His ability was not only acknowledged, but his charities were great, and he had many admirers and friends in all classes of society. He was the author of a book which bears the humorous title of "Granny Short's Barbecue," which was published in this city by Messrs. Bradley & Gilbert. He was a singularly-eloquent man, and if the subjoined quotation bears me not out in my assertion, then do I admit I know not the quality of eloquence. Demosthenes, Cicero, Patrick Henry, Webster, Tom Marshall, and all or any of those great minds of the past or the present age, whose silver tongues have inspired the hearts of men to cherish, honor, and love truth, never surpassed the grandeur of thought, the felicity of expression, and the nobility of sentiment contained in the utterances of Mr. Bradley, when he felt that right was might, in his plea for justice at the hands of his fellowmen. It was in one of his great land suits; forty witnesses had been summoned by the defense, and testified that a certain survey had been made but ten years, when the plaintiff in the case contended that it was made thirty years previous to the time asserted by the opposing parties in interest. The evidence Mr. Bradley introduced were blocks cut from identified corner-trees on which the annulations showed since the marks had been made. Confronting the jury with one of these blocks in his outstretched hand, with an air of inexpressible dignity and conscious power, he said: "I rely not upon the testimony of man, the frail creature of an hour. Influence, money, hope, or fear may corrupt him or warp his judgment. I offer the testimony of the Most High. Since these trees were marked by the surveyor's tomahawk, year by year, with His own immortal finger, He has drawn a line indicating the passing time. Tempest or sunshine, rain or storm, that invisible hand heeded not, as with unerring certainty it recorded the fleeting years amid the stillness of the forest. No money can change, no power warp this testimony. Not all the waters of the ocean can wipe it out. God placed it there, and there it must remain as long as those majestic trees lift their heads toward the clouds. Here are thirty lines drawn by the Divine hand. Which will you believe, the evidence of God or man?" Was it a wonder the jury found for the plaintiff? What heart could remain cold, what mind be obdurate in the presence of such convincing eloquence?

And with such a father could it be otherwise than that the son should develop into a magnificent man who commands the respect and admiration of the world, and the affection and confidence of the community in which he resides? William O'Connell Bradley does this and more. But let his clear cut record on the tablets of fame speak for him, do him the justice, and win for him the praise my pen may not weave into a laurel wreath for his ambitious young head. He was born near Lancaster, in Garrard county, March 18, 1847. He enlisted in the Federal army at fourteen years of age; at seventeen, with the down of manhood scarce darkening on his lip, by a special act of the Legislature he was admitted to the practice of law, taking rank soon after before the Court of Appeals as a brilliant speaker and a profound lawyer. In politics he is a Republican. In 1870, he was elected county attorney of Garrard. In 1872, he was nominated for Congress, and after a brilliant canvass was defeated, his district being Democratic. In 1876, he was re-nominated, and again sustained defeat owing to a similar cause, but this time by a reduced majority. In 1878, and again in 1882, he declined the nomination for Congress; and in 1879, declined a nomination for attorney-general of the State of Kentucky. The cause of so doing was ill-health. In 1880, he was a delegate to the Chicago National Convention. It was in this convention the Hon. Roscoe Conkling, of New York, placed the name of that illustrious soldier and statesman, General U. S. Grant, in nomination for a third term to the Presidency of the United States, claiming "Appomattox" as the platform of the National Republican party. The young and gifted Kentuckian, William O. Bradley, was unanimously chosen by the delegates of that convention to second the nomination. He did so, thundering forth such a storm of eloquence that he attracted the attention and won the admiration of that body, composed, as it was, of gifted men of national reputation. As a logician Mr. Bradley has scarcely a peer in his native State. His oratory is ornate, his argumentative qualities finished and convincing, and his acumen at once polished and profound. He was a member of the National Republican Committee for Kentucky. In 1884, he was a delegate at large and chairman of the Kentucky delegation in the Chicago National Convention which nominated James G. Blaine, of Maine, for the presidency of the United States. In this convention Mr. Bradley made a ringing speech against the proposition from Massachusetts and Indiana to reduce the electoral strength of the South.

Before he was eligible he received the complimentary vote of his party in the Legislature for United States Senator. In 1884, he was chosen by President Arthur to prosecute the Star-route thieves. The attorney-general of the United States refusing to allow a full and impartial prosecution, Mr. Bradley promptly retired from the case. His sense of justice, his pure love of equity revolts at unfairness and he never gives it countenance. Mr. Bradley was the first politician in Kentucky who took active ground for national aid to education. This he did in his canvass for Congress in 1872.

HON. W. C. P. BRECKINRIDGE.

It is my honest belief that greatness is hereditary, and that those who have through generations cultivated aristocracy of muscle seldom leave to their posterity those intellectual attributes that entitle them to an entrance in the charmed circle swayed only by the aristocracy of mind. That is the true dividing line which, from time immemorial almost, has separated social classes. It may be that the origin of the difference began away back in the dim distance of the sacred past, when learning was not so generally disseminated as it is now; but, be this surmise based upon veritable facts o merely erroneous suggestions, the inalienable truth remains that we usually find our great men and great women had great ancestors. I do not mean by this assertion to draw the bar sinister across the escutcheon of any living being in our republic, or any other country under the sun, for to do this would be to fly in the face of a grand array of brilliance and beauty, of genius and talent, as displayed among what we call "self-made people;" but even among them it will usually be found that they take pride in tracing back their divine gifts to this or that ancestor who had an aspiration to elevate themselves, not only in this world's goods, but intellectually. We do not expect, when we sit down under the vine and fig-tree planted years ago, to gather thorns and thistles. And we are not disappointed. It may be that this inherent greatness does not display itself in every generation, but it is there, and extreme situations will invariably evolve it. The field that has lain fallow for a season yields richer crops when they plow open its furrows again, and on the same natural principle suppressed greatness in one generation adds to the brilliance of the next. It is only in individual cases where the phœnix Genius arises from the ashes of her splendor without waiting for the torch-bearer of Fate to find the vital spark and give it air. But we all alike admit that only from acorns can the oaks—mighty monarchs of the forest—spring into life. The errant winds of chance may blow these acorns hither and yon, but wherever they take root they are oaks, and as such hold sway and yield their grateful shade to lesser things seeking shelter beneath them.

From which dissertation—taken in connection with the honored name which illumines the preface of my sketch to-day—may be deduced my conviction that Hon. William Cabell Preston Breckinridge, in whom concenters the greatness of more than one distinguished family, could not well avoid being what he is—"The silver tongued orator of the West." He is the present member in Congress from the celebrated "Ashland District," which has so long been famous in the annals of the country, rendered so by the illustrious men who preceded him in representing it in the National Councils. It would be futile to enumerate them or their brilliant speeches and acts in order to excite interest in the minds of a Kentucky public. Their names have passed into the history of the State, and belong to the nation's archives. We have no need to blush in comparing their love of country and their noble achievements in her honor, whether enacted upon the hustings or in the nation's forum, with the intellectual spirits that once gave glory and fame to Greece, and whose eloquence still seems to haunt the Parthenon at Athens, though the lips that framed the words have long since turned to dust. Kentuckians know full well that the clarion voice of W. C. P. Breckinridge will give forth no uncertain sound, and that when he speaks his utterances will be remembered.

He was born on the 28th day of August, 1837, near Baltimore, Md., his father, Rev. Robert Jefferson Breckinridge, being at that time pastor of the Second Presbyterian Church of Baltimore. Having been prepared at Transylvania University, he entered the junior class at Centre College, September, 1853, and graduated there April 26, 1855. He studied in the office of the celebrated Madison C. Johnson, of Lexington, Ky., and was graduated in the law department of the University of Louisville, Ky., on February 27, 1857. Everywhere he was regarded as a young man of brilliant promise; it had been said from his earliest years that he had given signs and assurances of uncommon mental endowments. And so it was that much was expected of him; nor has he yet disappointed those who love and admire him and watch with the deepest interest his growing greatness. During the war between the States, Colonel Breckinridge had his opinions, and he staunchly abided by them. He became captain of Company "I," Second Kentucky (Morgan's) Cavalry, on July 17, 1862, which position he filled with great credit to himself and to the entire satisfaction of his superior officers, until he abandoned it to become major of Breckinridge's Battalion, September 17, 1862, and later on colonel of the Ninth Kentucky Cavalry, on December 17, 1862. His record as a soldier is dear to the heart of every Confederate who struck a blow, like Marco Bozzaris, "For God and his native land." The civil struggle brought to an end, he returned to Lexington, Ky., and practiced law with brilliant success until elected to the Forty-ninth Congress of the United States on November 4, 1884, where he continued to gather laurels, his genius and his ability giving him a rank second to none. He was re-elected to the Fiftieth Congress on the 2d of November, 1886. Colonel Breckinridge has been twice married. His first wife was Miss Lucretia Clay, daughter of Hon. Thomas Clay, and granddaughter of Henry Clay. This lovely lady lived but a brief while subsequent to her marriage. His second wife was the daughter of Doctor John R. Desha, deceased, of Lexington, Ky., a physician of prominence and ability. Her name is poetical enough for her to have been born under the skies of the Orient, and musical as the inceptive song of a nightingale—"Issa." They have several charming children, among them a beautiful daughter, who is admiringly mentioned whenever she appears in Washington society.

Colonel Breckinridge's mother was a lady of whom he was justly proud. She was Miss Sophronisba Preston, who was born at the Salt Works, then in Washington, now in Smythe county, Va. To say she belonged to so noble a family as the Virginia Prestons is like granting her a royal patent on all that was gracious and kind. His father, the Rev. Robert Jefferson Breckinridge, was born March 8, 1800, at Cabell's Dale, Fayette county, Ky., and died at Danville, Ky., December 27, 1871. He was the seventh child and fourth son of Hon. John Breckinridge and Mary Hopkins Cabell, and connected, through his grandmother, Letitia Preston Breckinridge, with the Prestons, of Virginia, Kentucky, and South Carolina, and with the Marshalls, Browns, and other distinguished families of Kentucky. He was the most distinguished clergyman of his day, and wielded a potent influence in both Church and State affairs. He was royal in birthright and finished in scholarship. Like Lord Byron, he had traveled wherever civilization had left its imprint upon the sands of time, and his discourses were fuller of poetry and eloquence than the romances of Scheherezade. He took an active interest in everything around him, from the products of the field to the minerals of the earth. History glows with his acts. He was accounted the giant of the family, intellectually. His genius was certainly of the highest order. His education was profound. His will knew no bounds. He was an enthusiastic Union man in the late war, and brought his widespread influence to bear upon all who listened to his convincing arguments to uphold the Union "though the heavens fell." Wherever he appeared he was a power, and oftener the controlling spirit.

The name of Breckinridge, like those of Cæsar, Cromwell, Napoleon, is imperishable. It shines like a star on the scroll of American fame, and dates back to the Reformation. The ancestors of this splendid clan of people took part in the memorable defense of Londonderry in the seventeenth century. They were, on the paternal side of the house, what was then called "Scotch-Irish"—that is, they were Presbyterians from the North of Ireland then, but originally from Scotland. After the restoration of Charles II. they were hotly persecuted in Ayreshire, their original seat, and were driven thence into the highlands of Braedlabane, where they spent half a century. Thence they removed to Ireland, and thence early in the last century into Virginia. They were a persecuted remnant of the Scotch Covenanters, who suffered long and heroically in defense of liberty and reformed religion, and their courage, intelligence, and fidelity they left as birthrights to their descendants, than which they could not hold greater or nobler possessions.

JUDGE ELI H. BROWN.

The county of Meade was formed in 1823, and named in honor of Captain James Meade, who fell in the battle of the river Raisin. And it was in this county that Eli H. Brown was born on the 13th of November, in the year of our Lord 1841. He is the fifth son of John Mc. Brown, Esq., who was born in Nelson county, Ky., in 1799, and his mother was Miss Minerva Murray, of Washington county, Ky., the daughter of Colonel John Murray, of that county. She was born in the year 1808. Their ancestry were among the early settlers of Virginia and Pennsylvania, distinguished for valor, intrepidity, and intellectual superiority. Eli Brown was educated at the academy of Hawesville, Hancock county, Ky. He studied law with George W. Williams, Esq., then a resident of that town, but now residing in Owensboro, Ky. He could not have been in better training, for Mr. Williams was regarded at that time as the ablest chancery lawyer in that section of the State.

Mr. Brown entered upon the practice of his profession in good faith at Hawesville, Ky., in February, 1862, but he was soon elected

City Judge of Hawesville, which place he occupied from 1862 to 1864. This term of office having expired, he was then elected county attorney, which position he held through the term of eight years, which "carried him over" to 1872. After a time he removed to Owensboro, Ky., and entered into a copartnership with his old preceptor, George W. Williams, Esq. In the Greeley campaign Mr. Brown was made elector for the Second Congressional district. Samuel E. Smith, Esq., of Greenville, Ky., was the elector for the Republicans, and their joint discussions in the Greeley and Grant campaign excited much interest, and everywhere over the district attracted great crowds to listen to their flow of wit and eloquence.

Samuel E. Smith was the gentleman who, in 1867, contested the seat of Kentucky's gifted and brilliant John Young Brown. When their claims were presented to Congress neither was allowed to take the seat, and the Second Congressional district was without representation that session, Mr. Brown's loyalty not being acceptable to a Republican Congress, notwithstanding his large majority of the vote of the district.

Mr. Eli H. Brown also acted as Commonwealth's Attorney *pro tem.* under Judge Martin H. Cofer, deceased, during which time he gave universal satisfaction in the performance of his official duties. Mr. Brown has always endeavored to avoid politics.

In October, 1878, he removed to Louisville, Ky., and entered upon the practice of law, forming a co-partnership with his relative, David M. Rodman, Esq. They make a strong and popular firm, and have always enjoyed a fine clientage.

In February, 1870, Mr. Brown was married to Miss Nannie W. Dorsey, of Nelson county, Ky., a lady of wealth and culture. They have four children to cheer and adorn their home, full of brightness and beauty and promise.

In his person Judge Brown forms the connecting link between three distinguished families born and reared in Kentucky—the Hustons, the Murrays, and the Allens. They need no encomiums pronounced by me. Their names stand prominently upon the records of the State from the year 1799 down to the present day, as lawyers, politicians, and soldiers. No matter what the position, they reflected credit upon it and themselves. General Thomas Crittenden, ex-governor of Missouri; Governor Eli Murray, of Utah, and Judge John Allen Murray, of Breckinridge county, Ky., are among the younger members of these remarkable families, all congenial "Corn-crackers," born and reared in Kentucky and educated in her institutions of learning and research. And certainly they compare favorably with any specimens of the Anglo-Saxon race to be found in any country and with specimens of any other civilized and enlightened people on the face of the globe.

Judge Brown is a man of fine stature and commanding appearance. He has great conversational adaptability, and possesses many warm and admiring friends who take pride in his success in life, and out of true personal regard advance his interests whenever they can. When a man can command fidelity in his friends one may well repose faith in his intrinsic merits.

COLONEL JOHN MASON BROWN.

When in thoughtful mood I scan the pages of histories and biographies, and search annals and records of Kentucky and Kentucky's great men, I feel like a bibliomaniac burrowing amid antiques, quite forgetful that the sun of to-day is shining, and that the march of progression continues from ocean to ocean, until suddenly the name of some one of our great departed brings to mind a similar name worn fairly and nobly by a descendant who has taken his place in the niche God meant for him to fill, and it shines like a golden link in the long chain of circumstances binding the present to the past; and then I realize the salient truth that while that blood courses in the veins of descendants, valor, integrity, and genius are the natural heritage of well-born Kentuckians.

Especially is this true when I gather data from the name of "Brown." In every noble enterprise, in every struggle for the right, in peace and in war, from the first revolutionary war to the last civic struggle, these scions of a noble house have been leading men in the State, and some of them in the nation. Well may the heart beat faster with pardonable pride, and the flush of gratified feeling glow upon the cheek to read the family record. James Brown, Esq., was the first secretary of State; John Brown, Esq., was our first delegate to Congress. He was a representative to the Virginia Legislature from Kentucky, and was elected a delegate by that body and took his seat with the other representatives from Virginia. He was an eminent lawyer of Kentucky, possessed of talent, influence, and popularity. He made his mark as a man of spirit and genius, and contended for Kentucky's right to be independent from Virginia with a fervor and a determination which brought about controversy and animadversion, but eventually attained for Kentucky her independence and a market for the products of her exuberant soil. He was the first United States Senator from Kentucky; and three times he filled that place before the people, winning from President Madison, one of the profoundest statesmen and purest patriots this country has ever produced, an encomium which is the crown jewel in all the splendor of his fame. He said: "I was in intimate friendship with Mr. Brown when we were associated in public life, and I always regarded him, while steadily attentive to the interests of his constituents, duly impressed with the importance of the Union and anxious for its prosperity." So fell, like a castle builded with cards a rude breath might destroy, the foolish fiction about Spanish intrigues. It was blown away like dust from a great and glorious name belonging to an honorable and noble-minded gentleman, who had conferred the highest distinction on his State and country by a judicious display of ability and resolution and a staunch adherence to the rights of his constituents as free men and American citizens. Ben Gratz Brown was another member of this fine clan of people. He was half-brother to Colonel John Mason Brown. He was United States Senator from 1860-'67 from Missouri. He was also governor of Missouri from 1870-'74, and in the electoral college, in session at Frankfort on December 4, 1872, his name was put in nomination for President of the United States, and vice-president, also, in proof that, although the State of Missouri was wedded to him, Kentucky was proud of her son, and, in her estimation, he belonged to the whole country, and would grace with wisdom and probity and prudence the highest position within the gift of the people. Judge Mason Brown was secretary of the Commonwealth from 1855 to 1859. He was a profound thinker, a just judge, a true patriot. He was popular, efficient, and, when at the age of sixty-seven he departed this life, on January 27, 1867, in Frankfort, Ky., he left friends and citizens to deplore his death, and to aver that they would not soon look upon his like again.

Orlando Brown, another distinguished member of the family, was one of the most scholarly and elegant men Kentucky ever produced. For many years he was the editor of the Frankfort *Commonwealth*. He was also secretary of State under Governor Crittenden for a time, and was commissioner of Indian affairs under President Taylor.

And so, growing, as it were, root and branch, fiber and blossom, in the heart of Kentucky, this great people have made a name woven through and through Kentucky's integral fame as a State, and have taken precedence, in communities in which they resided, for dignity, genius, and ability.

John Mason Brown, the subject of my sketch, is the oldest son of Judge Mason Brown, and his mother's maiden name was Miss Mary Yoder, of Spencer county, Ky. John Mason was born in Frankfort, Ky., on the 26th of April, 1837. He was educated at Yale College, and graduated from that institution in 1856. He studied law with Thomas M. Lindsay, Esq., of Frankfort, Ky., and entered upon the practice of his profession in St. Louis, Mo., in 1858. The years 1859-'60 he spent in the West among the Indians. The spirit of adventure and unrest had seized him, and the roving, nomadic life not only afforded him pleasure through its novelty, and the outdoor existence invigorated his already splendid constitution, but his experiences widened his knowledge of men and expanded his views regarding the Western world.

In 1862, he returned to Kentucky and entered the Federal army as major of the Tenth Kentucky Cavalry. In 1863, he was promoted to the colonelcy of the Forty-fifth mounted infantry, which position he continued to hold; a portion of the time, however, he commanded the Second brigade in the Fifth division of the Twenty-third Army Corps. The services of his command were devoted to the Army of the West, where they were in constant requisition.

At the close of the internecine struggle, he was mustered out of the service, and re-entered upon the practice of his profession at Lexington, Ky., as the partner of Madison C. Johnson, Esq., which firm continued until 1873, when he removed from Lexington to the city of Louisville, Ky., at which point he entered upon a copartnership with W. F. Barrett (who was his brother-in-law). In 1882, he and George M. Davie, Esq., formed a copartnership, and in 1885 the name of Judge Alex. P. Humphrey was added to the firm, and it stands to-day " Brown, Humphrey & Davie." The brilliance, erudition, and probity embraced in the trio of names I have hitherto mentioned under the sketch of George M. Davie, Esq., and the merit and genius of the three gentlemen are too well known to require repetition here.

Colonel John Mason Brown delivered the oration on the anniversary of the battle of Blue Lick Springs, the 19th day of August, 1882, and he was also the orator of the centennial anniversary of the city of Frankfort, Ky., October 6, 1886. These two orations were remarkable for their historic research and forensic display, and were enjoyed by assembled thousands of Kentuckians and others. In 1869, he was united in the holy bonds of matrimony to Miss Mary O. Preston, of Lexington, Ky., daughter of General William Preston, and brilliant and elegant as are all the ladies of the Preston family.

They have four children, charming and promising, who are the delight of their hearts and home.

JOSHUA F. BULLITT, JR.

June is the most beautiful month of all the year. Even denizens of cities admit the fact, and with tenfold force are its enchantments enhanced with those who live "afar from the mad'ning crowd."

And why should it not be so, when their senses are regaled with breeze-loads of fragrance and eye-fills of beauty; when the trees fling out their green banners, and Mother Earth puts on her holiday gown of emerald velvet, embossed with rainbow-tinted flowers; when the throats of birds are full of golden and silver notes, sweeter than the gurgling of Egyptian flutes; when rippling tides grow pellucid, and Dame Nature, wandering on sloping shores, over bloom-broidered meads, or climbing heights whose eternal solitudes remain undisturbed by the foot of man, wears ever a serene and tender smile?

To-day, everywhere we may hear the jarring thunder of presses that never pause, and the ring of the hammer on the anvil; we may see edifices reared like palaces on either hand; but how many of us pause to remember that over a century ago this State was a howling wilderness, and that the possessions we now enjoy were gained for us by our forefathers, and that too at the cost of many lives? How many of us pause amid the rush and hurry of every-day life to remember, when we look into the faces of some of our fellow-citizens, that their ancestors gathered around the camp-fires, and stemmed the Ohio in birchen bark canoes, struggled, died, but to the last were ever upheld and aspiring that the rare emprise of this wonderful land—the Indian's hunting ground, Kaintuckee—might be ours? Yet the annals of our State bear the record that Captain Thomas Bullitt, having distinguished himself in the expedition against Fort Duquesne in 1773, in the month of June in that same year took command of a small band of adventurous spirits, in company with Hancock Taylor (both surveyors), and James, George, and Robert McAfee, in company with their brother-in-law, James McCown, took command of another band, and they came down the Ohio together and reached the mouth of Limestone creek, where Maysville now stands, and remained there for two days.

On July 4th and 5th they visited Big Bone Lick, in what is now Boone county, and made seats and tent poles out of the enormous back-bones and ribs of the mastodon which were found there in large quantities.

On July 7th, at the mouth of Levisa or Kentucky river the companies separated, Captain Bullitt going to the Falls, which point he reached on July 8th, pitched his camp above the mouth of the Beargrass creek, and retired at night to a shoal above Corn Island. He surveyed land under warrants of Lord Dunmore below the Falls to Salt river, and up that stream to Bullitt's Lick, in what is now Bullitt county. In August he laid out the town of Louisville on part of the plot of the present city. And so is it that while Kentucky remains a Commonwealth, and Louisville stands incorporated as a city, and while the waters of "the beautiful river" foam and whirl at the falls, the name of "Bullitt" must go sounding on forever, indissolubly knit in with the fibers of memory, and be part and parcel of the one and the other. It is a fit theme for praise and pride, not only to individuals, but to the State at large. And Kentucky history readily accords what is due; for pages are devoted to the achievements of this noble and excellent family. Towns and counties are named for them. We have a Bullitt county, Bullitt's Station, Bullitt's Lick, Bullittsburg, and Bullittsville. And from those early days to the present time we have never been without two or three Bullitts to occupy places of brilliance and prominence in Kentucky. Especially prominent among them were Cuthbert and Thomas Bullitt, the first two gentlemen who embarked in the mercantile business in Louisville. They were distinguished for probity and splendid business qualifications. They became very prosperous, and attained large possessions that were left to their children by way of inheritance.

Alexander Scott Bullitt was another member of this famous family, who was justly popular. His career was marked by intellectual brilliance and personal excellence. His father, Cuthbert Bullitt, of Virginia, was a lawyer of distinction, who practiced his profession with success until he was appointed Judge of the Supreme Court of Virginia, which office he held at the time of his demise. In 1784, six years previous to his father's death, Alexander Scott Bullitt emigrated to Kentucky (it was then a portion of Virginia), and he settled on or near the stream called Bullskin, in what is now Shelby county. The depredations of the Indians in that locality compelled him to seek a less exposed situation, and he came to Jefferson county, where he entered and settled upon the tract of land on which he continued to reside until his death. In 1792 he was elected a delegate to the convention which met in Danville and framed the constitution of Kentucky. After the adoption of the constitution he represented Jefferson county in the Legislature, the first convention of which took place in Lexington, Ky., in a two-story log house on June 4, 1792, and Alexander Scott Bullitt was the first speaker of the Senate in that body politic, a position which he filled acceptably until 1799, when he was again chosen a delegate to amend the constitution. He was chosen president of this convention. The year following, 1800, he was elected lieutenant-governor of the State. He served one term in this capacity. After this the county of Jefferson continued to send him to the Legislature, either as senator or representative, until 1808, when he retired from public life, and resided on his farm in Jefferson county until his death, which occurred on the 13th of April, 1816.

Equally prominent and admired and beloved to an unusual degree is Judge Joshua F. Bullitt, who in March, 1861, was elected judge of the Court of Appeals to fill the unexpired term of Henry C. Wood, deceased. Judge Bullitt is a man of exceeding spirit, brave and fearless in expressing his opinions, who, knowing the right, dares maintain it in the face of overwhelming odds. Certain it is that he waited in the furnace blast the pangs of transformation for the sake of the land he loved and cherished.

On November 22, 1864, as once before on August 11, 1864, by order of General Burbridge, he was arrested, charged with belonging to a secret political society called the "Sons of Liberty," in company with Thomas Jeffries, M. J. Paul, H. F. Kalfus, John Talbott, John Colgan, and John Harris. They were nominally sent off via Memphis, Tenn., into the Southern Confederacy, but really retained in the military prison in that place. Their release was finally secured by the Confederate General N. B. Forrest, in exchange for some Memphis citizens and engineers, captured in one of his raids. On March 1, 1865, he was summoned for trial before the Legislature, to be held on May 23d, same year, on the charge of belonging to a treasonable association. The President was requested to grant Judge Bullitt respite from arrest, that he might return to Kentucky from Canada to attend the trial. Judge Bullitt himself wrote a magnificent letter to Thomas E. Bramlette, then governor of Kentucky, which for dignity, spirit, and manly independence has not its equal in the annals of literature. He had sought refuge in a neutral country from the violence of military rule, and positively refused to return to Kentucky, when months previous her military commander had publicly declared that he should be tried by a military court and executed without any chance of his appeal to the clemency of the President. As a consequence, Governor Bramlette approved the address of the Legislature to him, requesting him to remove from office Hon. Joshua F. Bullitt, one of the Judges of the Court of Appeals (for the Third District and Chief-Justice), formally removed him and declared the office vacant. Thus his case was disposed of without any trial, after he had been arrested, ordered and sent out of the State by the military authorities without opportunity for defense, and was held at bay by threats of an unscrupulous military commander to execute him without chance of clemency.

But time, the healer of all trials and tribulations, brought about changes which proved that Judge Bullitt had never lost the high place he held in the esteem of his fellow statesmen. When the internecine struggle had ceased and military rule was abolished in Kentucky, he returned to his home and lived to welcome in the happy day when the Legislature, by twenty-one to eight in the Senate and forty-three to nine in the House, adopted the resolution freeing him from the accusations of the mock trial of May 23, 1865, and March 1, 1865, and declaring that they considered the whole affair an insult to the honor and dignity of the Commonwealth of Kentucky, a flagrant outrage on his constitutional rights, and a manifest violation of all rules of equality and justice. The proceedings and address in his case were rescinded and declared null and void.

What a record of oppression and outrage, side by side with that of the gallant Captain Tom Bullitt, who came in the splendor of his young manhood and penetrated the unexplored wilds of Kentucky. The commentary on the gratitude of the people is necessarily in the usual line of comment.

Colonel Thomas Walker Bullitt is another member of this illustrious family. He is an eminent lawyer, and has a fine practice at the Louisville bar. He married Miss Annie Priscilla Logan, a descendant of the great Marshall clan, and herself a lady of brilliant ability and extreme loveliness of character. Colonel Bullitt was in Morgan's cavalry during the war, and was for two years a prisoner at Fort Delaware. Patrick Henry was a grand-uncle, and Alexander Scott Bullitt, hitherto cited in this sketch, was his grandfather. His great-grandfather, Colonel William Christian, was killed by the Indians in 1786. W. A. Bullitt, William C. Bullitt, Dr. Henry M. Bullitt, John C. Bullitt, and Thomas W. Bullitt are all, or were all, men who occupied places of high trust, and who were intrinsically men of probity and noble attainments.

Joshua F. Bullitt, Jr., whose name adorns my sketch, is the oldest son of Judge Joshua F. Bullitt, Sr., and Elizabeth R. Smith, both Kentuckians by birth and Kentuckians in character—large-brained and large-hearted, a credit to either sex, and beloved and honored by friends and relatives. Joshua F. Bullitt, Jr., was born in Jefferson county on the 24th day of July, 1856. He was educated in the city schools of Louisville, and later on he matriculated at the Washington and Lee University at Lexington, Va. In 1878 he studied law under his father and Attorney-General James Speed, completing his course at the University of Virginia. In 1879 he entered upon the practice of his profession with his father in Louisville, Ky. In 1884 he was chosen Elector for the Fifth Congressional District, and was elected to the Legislature from Jefferson county in August, 1885, and was on the Committee on the Code of Practice. He was married to Mrs. M. T. Churchill, March 4, 1884. They have one child, a daughter, Miss Mary Cummins Bullitt. Mr. Bullitt is a gentleman of fine attainments, great popularity, and possesses an exceedingly winning address. He is yet young, and the possibilities of his future lie untrodden before him. He has great character, a fine mind, and much energy and perseverance. He can attain whatsoever he chooses to attempt. He has many friends and admirers, who will see that he carries his flag to victory whenever he sounds the tocsin to advance upon the enemy, for they all wish him success and happiness, and a long life and prosperity to him and to those who are dear to him.

HON. ROBERT A. BURTON.

In compiling biographical sketches of the representative men of Kentucky, I have sought in every instance to do justice to each subject under discussion, and to render honor to those to whom honor is due. It is a generally-accepted opinion, however, that those we love and admire are without faults. Be this true or fallacious, I find to-day that I have no language at my command through whose use I could do justice to the Hon. Robert A. Burton as a man and a gentleman, or in which I could express his merits of head and heart. This distinguished Kentuckian was born in the county of Mercer, or that portion of Mercer county which at a later date was divided off and erected under the title of Boyle county, in 1842, and is the ninety-fourth of the State. The place of his nativity was made historic not only by his birth, but by the battle that was fought over the old homestead at Perryville, October 8, 1862. On the 11th day of August, 1834, Robert A. Burton first saw the light of day. He is the third son of John A. Burton, Esq., of Perryville, Ky., who was a gentleman of wealth and great culture, and who was considered the ablest financier in that part of the country, being both a farmer and a banker. At his death, he left a fortune to each of his children, every one of whom was in life and character and ability worthy of descent from so noble a father.

Their mother's maiden name was Louisiana Chandler.

The Burtons and Chandlers at an early day emigrated to Kentucky from Virginia, and the father and mother of R. A. Burton were both born in this State, which was admitted into the Union on the 7th day of June, 1792. Their third son—the subject of this sketch—graduated from the Perryville University in 1856, and was admitted to the Bar in 1860. In 1859, he was elected to the Legislature from Marion county, where he now resides. He had no opposition. During the stormy days of 1860-'61, he remained, and was so considered, a staunch Breckinridge Democrat. Indeed, it was his vote and the vote of Lieutenant-Governor Richard Jacob, from the county of Oldham, that held Kentucky true to the motto graven on the rock contributed to Washington's monument: "Kentucky, the first State admitted into the Union after the adoption of the Federal Constitution, and will be the last to go out."

On the 17th day of May, 1860, Mr. Burton was married to Miss Margaret Lowry, of Jessamine county. She is a lady of great personal beauty, and is possessed of many accomplishments. She is the daughter of James Lowry, Esq., now deceased, who was a wealthy and popular farmer of that county.

In 1862, Mr. Burton was elected judge of Marion county, and in that capacity he served altogether twelve years.

In 1869, he was elected to the Kentucky Senate from the Marion district, defeating the Hon. C. S. Hill for the position. The latter gentleman was an antagonist of no mean ability, having represented the district in the Congress of the United States, and also being a lawyer of great prominence. At the time, Mr. Burton overcame a majority of six hundred; and in 1876 he was chosen a delegate from the congressional district to the national convention which nominated Tilden and Hendricks.

Recently, he was one of the opponents of Hon. Attilla Cox, of Owen county, for the position of Collector of Revenue for the Fifth district of Kentucky, and, although defeated in his aspirations by the appointment of Mr. Cox, that gentleman was graceful and courtly enough to make Mr. Burton one of his deputy collectors, a position which he now holds and will honor.

In *personnel*, Judge Burton is a man of distinguished appearance. He is tall, knitted like an athlete, a perfect type of the old-time aristocratic Kentuckian, kind-hearted, generous, and courtly as a prince.

He stands high in the estimation of the people, and his many warm and true friends cherish for him an affection which knows neither bounds nor estrangement as the years go by. Would to God the State had five hundred thousand citizens like him! Then, indeed, would cease the sorrow and suffering of the indigent, for none can appeal to him in vain for either alms or human sympathy.

He resides on a fine farm in Marion county, surrounded by every elegance and comfort wealth and position and a cultured taste can draw about him. There he lives as luxuriously as a king, without any kingly cares to make his head lie uneasily because of the crown he wears. His crown is a noble manhood; his throne is the hearts of his friends. God bless him!

HON. JOHN GRIFFIN CARLISLE.

Kenton county is one of the newest and smallest in the State of Kentucky and ranks as the ninetieth in order of formation. It was organized in 1840, out of the Western part of Campbell county, as divided by the Licking river. Its area is small, being only from six to twelve miles wide and twenty-five miles long. It is easy of access, with the Lexington pike on the West and the Kentucky Central railroad along its Eastern border. Its bottom lands are rich and very productive; the uplands are undulating, but grow fine wheat, corn, and tobacco. The county is dotted with well-kept gardens and many excellent dairy farms for the supply of Covington and Cincinnati markets. The lands that lie along the Lexington turnpike are said to be of a very superior quality.

The county is, indeed, excellent in everything; its people are intelligent and progressive; its towns are well ordered and thickly populated, wearing that air of thrift and independence which goes hand in hand with success.

The annals of the past bear silent witness of the earliest visitors who set foot on the borders of the Licking river, the date going back to the month of March in the year 1751, when Christopher Gist, in his tour as agent of the Ohio Company, with his small following of white men, crossed the Licking at or near its mouth. From that time down to the present day there have always been men of marked distinction in that locality in the State: Kenton, Taylor, Stephens, Morgan, Morehead, Stephenson, Benton, Sandford, Bright, our own delightful General John W. Finnell, and the central figure of the Democratic party of to-day, on whom the eyes of brave and independent citizens of the Union turn, as the eyes of the wise men of old must have looked upon the splendor of the Star of Bethlehem, recognizing it as the sign of the presence of the Saviour of mankind on this earth: I refer to John Griffin Carlisle, one of the greatest men in America, whose views of public policy have ever been conservative, statesmanlike, and liberal, and in whom all earnest thinkers must recognize the coming saviour of the Democratic party.

John Griffin Carlisle was born in Campbell county, Ky., on the 5th of September, 1835. He received his education in the best schools afforded by the neighborhood in which he lived. At fifteen years of age he, himself, became an instructor of the young, and until he was twenty years old it was his vocation to teach "the young ideas how to shoot." After that time he began the study of the legal profession under the guidance of Ex-Governor John W. Stephenson and Judge William B. Kinkead. In 1857, he became the partner of the latter gentleman, and at once took rank at the bar and in general public estimation as possessing one of the clearest and most analytic minds of any young man in Kentucky. In 1859 to 1861, he was elected to the lower house of the General Assembly of Kentucky. He was condemned, however, in the late civic strife to rest on his laurels, because of the entertainment of certain ardent sentiments incompatible with a dream of promotion in the community he had hitherto had the honor to represent. But the frowns of Fate and Fortune could not withstand the smiling conviction of the ambitious young Kentuckian that he was born to fill a niche in the halls of Fame.

In 1864, Mr. Carlisle was nominated for presidential elector on the Democratic ticket, but this honor he declined to accept. In 1865, he was the Democratic candidate for the State Senate from Kenton county, and was defeated at the polls by his opponent, Mortimer M. Benton, Esq.

Fiat justitia ruat cælum runs the Latin maxim, and it became the watchword of the Democratic party in Kentucky and brought about a different order of public affairs, for in February, 1866, the Senate declared the seat of Mr. Benton vacant, because the election was "neither free nor equal in the sense required in the Constitution, being regulated, controlled, and unduly influenced by armed soldiers in the service of the United States in utter disregard of the law."

Mr. Carlisle was elected to fill the vacancy from 1866 to 1869, and was triumphantly re-elected for another term from 1869 to 1873. He was also a delegate-at-large from Kentucky to the National Democratic Convention at New York, in July, 1868.

In 1871 he resigned his position in the State Senate, which he had so ably and creditably filled—his rulings while Speaker of that body being invariably sustained when appealed from—and accepted the Democratic nomination for lieutenant-governor of the State, to which office he was elected August, 1871, for four years, receiving 125,955 to 86,145 votes cast for the Radical nominee, serving the people of Kentucky in that capacity until 1875. In 1872, for a few months, he was also leading editor of the Louisville *Daily Ledger*. In 1876 Mr. Carlisle was alternate presidential elector for the State-at-large. He was also elected to the Forty-fifth, Forty-sixth, and Forty-seventh Congresses, and was re-elected to the Forty-eighth, Forty-ninth, and Fiftieth Congresses, the last election occurring November 2, 1886. As a Democrat he received no opposition to the Forty-eighth and Forty-ninth Congresses, but the labor movement in the last election not being fully anticipated, he was confronted with a formidable candidate, who was vanquished, however, with eight hundred and odd majority.

Mr. Carlisle was elected Speaker of the House of Representatives December 3, 1883, and re-elected in December, 1885, and so impartial was his ruling, so just, unvaryingly kind, and courteous was his bearing, that at the close of the Forty-ninth Congress the Republican members of that august body presented Mr. Carlisle with a splendid silver service, at the cost of $500, in token of their appreciation and respect for him as a fair and considerate Speaker. Indeed, it is frequently declared that as a parliamentarian he has few equals and no superiors in Europe or America. So clear, forcible, logical, and convincing are his arguments that his following is unusually strong from political and legal standpoints, while socially and intellectually, in the estimation of his many friends, he is invincible.

His dignity is unsullied, and his ability is admitted to be preeminent. His oratory is of the highest order, and as a statesman he is at once bold, brilliant, and sagacious. Should he ever occupy before the American people a place more prominent, but scarcely less brilliant, than he holds to-day, it is prophesied by those who are the closest observers of political events that the emancipation of his party and his country would be lastingly assured. The reins of the government would be held with ability, prudence, and firmness, and the prosperity and advancement of the nation would be more brilliant than at any other time within the history of the United States.

In *personnel* Mr. Carlisle is as strikingly fine and vigorous as he is distinctively grand in intellect and character. He is married, and his wife is one of the noblest and most excellent of her sex. She has long ruled in social circles, and is as popular in society as Mr. Carlisle is popular throughout the entire country.

HON. ASHER GRAHAM CARUTH.

When one pauses to think—unbiased by fancied wrongs or angry passions—of the bonds of good-fellowship and the inalienable ties of consanguinity that hem in and knit together and bind the hearts and the memories, the interests and ambitions, of the people of these United States, from the storm swept prairies and lofty mountain peaks of the North-west, to the lemon and orange groves of Florida and the magnolia bosques of Louisiana and Texas, vocal with the songs of the mocking-birds, and from the Eastern shores, where the waves of the Atlantic lap the creeping sands, to the Golden Gates of California, where the mellow music of the Pacific tide fills all the slumberous air, one realizes how impossible it must ever be—States' rights, party principles, or what not veering opinion and desire—to maintain divided interests and separate national politics in this great, free, and enlightened land!

When we talk of the State of Tennessee we are compelled to revert to the pioneer days when the sons of Virginia and North Carolina made their homes within her borders; when the howling wolf and the tawny savage fought them back step by step. When we think of Kentucky's early days it is the same—and so on through all the States that now go to form one splendid country. Always the same! The brave and enlightened sons of one State sought the solitudes of the wilderness and the sweep of the prairies and the peaks of the mountains to expand the country and open up the way for civilization that the United States might be the foremost nation of the world. One recalls the privations and sufferings of the brave, adventurous spirits long since flown from our midst, and petty and small indeed seem the little spites and political ambitions that sway the multitudes to-day who people the States, where pure suffrage is no longer known and "the powers that be" are blatant of their triumphs. Where is the community of interest that once characterized the nation? Where the brotherly love and the pride of country? The solemn silence that wraps the memories of the past gives never an answer.

These thoughts came into my mind to-day, like the reverberations of harmonious strains when peace, purity, and patriotism filled the nation's heart. Only now and then, sparkling like gems whose brilliance no earthly setting can enhance or destroy, we see again in men of to-day the divine splendor of the spirits that have passed away. They shine with no uncertain light in the pulpit, at the forum, on the hustings, and in the councils of the nation, and whenever they appear they have their following—men do homage to their brilliance and genius as naturally as each planet that revolves in the heavens has its satellites.

Such a man is Asher Graham Caruth, the subject of my sketch, and as such he commands the respect and admiration of his fellowmen. He is the third son of H. C. Caruth and Miss Mary Mansfield. His father was a Tennesseean by birth, but his ancestors came originally from North Carolina. His paternal grandfather was a captain in the Revolutionary War, a fact of which he is very proud. And who that is thoroughly acquainted with the history of that noble State can call the pride vainglory? When we remember that, as early as 1585 to 1589, Sir Walter Raleigh gave his auspices toward the settlement of that splendid land, and that within the borders of the State where roll the waters of the Roanoke are engraven undying records of chivalry and martyrdom and independence; when we recall how savages attacked and massacred the settlers, and how fever and famine set their ravenous teeth on the hearts that the Tuscaroras and Corees had left to beat, and how they would not despair; when we remember the sanguinary conflicts at Guilford Court-house, Brier Creek, Cedar Springs, Fishing Creek, and other places, and that the Mecklenburg Declaration of Independence was made May 20, 1775, so that North Carolina has the honor to have first proposed a separation from Great Britain; I repeat, when we recall all these salient points in history, who shall blame a man for being proud of his ancestral North Carolina line, and who shall so far sink beneath the level of appreciation and pride of State and country as to call that pride—vainglory?

Mr. Caruth's mother came from a race of people whose names are honorably enrolled in the annals of our own State. She was a Mansfield, and through generations Allen county, Ky., has been the chosen place where they rest beneath their own vine and fig trees. One of her relatives, George W. Mansfield, was a member of the convention which framed the present Constitution of Kentucky, assembled at Frankfort, Ky., October 1, 1849. He also served his State in the House of Representatives through the years 1834, 1835, 1836, 1846, and 1850. Another relative, E. D. Mansfield, wrote a most delightful memoir of Dr. David Drake, the distinguished physician, professor, and author who founded and established the Medical College of Ohio at Cincinnati. Still another was one of the Spartan band which was known as "The Forlorn Hope," and which was led by Colonel William Whitley at the battle of the Thames, fought in October, 1813. His address to his band will live in history along with Patrick Henry's sunburst of oratory, "Give me liberty or give me death!" He said: "Boys, we have been selected to second our colonel in the charge (Colonel Richard M. Johnson). Act well your part; recollect the watchword—victory or death!" * * How well they recollected it we all know, as but two were left to recall the incidents of the battle and to bear witness as to who killed Tecumseh. Such incidents shine in the memory like "jewels in an Ethiop's ear" in contrast with the sordid and self-engrossed aspect of modern times.

But I digress. When I leave the present and wander amid the hallowed scenes of the past, I often forget the busy life of to-day. Asher Graham Caruth was born in Scottsville, Allen county, Ky., on the 7th of February, 1844. He was educated in the Louisville High School. In 1864, he was law librarian of Louisville, Ky., and in 1866 he graduated from the University of Louisville, Ky. He entered upon the practice of his profession in Hopkinsville, Ky., at which place he combined with his love of legal lore the qualifications of a popular and able editor, for he founded the *Kentucky New Era*, a delightful paper still in existence in that enterprising and progressive town. In 1871, Mr. Caruth returned to Louisville, where he again practiced his profession, devoting his entire time to the blind Goddess of Justice. He was soon elected attorney of the School Board, and this position he continued to fill until he was elected Commonwealth's attorney in August, 1880, of the Ninth Judicial district. He was the elector of the Fifth Congressional district in 1876. And recently he was re-elected without opposition to the same position, which he filled with exceptional ability and brilliance. On October 9, 1886, he was nominated for Congress from the Fifth Congressional district and elected on the 2d of November following by a majority of one hundred and forty votes. No man enjoys a more sincere and widespread popularity than does Mr. Caruth, and whatever he undertakes to do he does with a dash and vim which are superlatively suggestive of a latent power that he holds in matchless reserve.

As a friend he is fervent and sincere, as an opponent he is to be feared and avoided, for with him there is "no such word as fail."

Mr. Caruth has a brother—George William Caruth—of whom too much can not be said in praise, and of whom I never think save as "the Prince of Gentlemen!" He resides in Little Rock, Ark. Another brother, David Caruth, Esq., of St. Louis, Mo., is a gentleman of prominence, ability, and popularity.

Mr. Caruth married Miss Terry, a lady of great refinement and elegance, well known in society, and the daughter of a prominent commission merchant (now deceased), of this city.

GEORGE M. DAVIE.

In the year 1796 the county of Christian, in the State of Kentucky, was formed and named in honor of Colonel William Christian, a young Virginian, who fought gallantly in Braddock's war, and who attained the reputation of being a brave, active, and efficient officer. When the Indian hostilities ceased, he married the sister of Patrick Henry, and settled himself in Bottetourt county, Virginia. At one time he was a member of the General State Convention, and, on the conclusion of the war, for several years he represented his county in the Virginia Legislature. His reputation for civic talents was equaled only by his peerless military record.

In 1785, Colonel Christian emigrated to Kentucky, and settled on Beargrass. Colonel Floyd had been killed by an Indian in 1783. He had been "chief among the chosen" in that section of the State, and his loss seemed irreparable to the people until Colonel Christian located himself among them. His intelligence, tireless energy, and knowledge of the Indian character gave him the front rank among the pioneers. His presence was greatly needed, but his opportunity to benefit his countrymen was of brief duration in Kentucky. In April of the succeeding year (1786), a body of Indians committed depredations on Beargrass, and escaped to the opposite side of the Ohio river with their usual matchless celerity of movement, and thence made their way leisurely back to their towns. Colonel Christian, at the head of a party of fearless men, went in swift pursuit, overtook them on their homeward route, and gave them battle. The conflict was bloody, the Indian force destroyed, but Colonel Christian fell mortally wounded, as did one of his followers. Colonel Christian was remarkably popular, and his death was long and much regretted. His daughter had married, during the fall preceding his unfortunate "taking off," Alexander Scott Bullitt, Esq., son of the distinguished lawyer, Cuthbert Bullitt, and himself a brilliant and excellent statesman, who served Kentucky as representative, senator, lieutenant-governor, and private citizen, always with distinction, fidelity, and great honor to himself.

Christian county is also made famous in history as the birthplace of Jefferson Davis, ex-president of the Confederate States of America, but that part of Christian in which he was born is now included in Todd county.

We have as a citizen among us a man of kindred genius, spirit, and ability, who also claims Christian county as his birthplace. I refer to George M. Davie, Esq., whose name graces the head-lines of this biographical sketch of "Representative Corn-crackers and Kentucky Politicians;" for, though he has no "war record," being too young to take part in it at the time of the great civil struggle, and though he has attended to his profession rather than politics, he is emphatically a representative of the highest and noblest type of Kentucky manhood, possessing all the fire and fervor of the modern statesman, with the strength, and polish, and soundness of Kentuckians of the old school of gentlemen and scholars, who have given to the State her imperishable fame for chivalry, and oratory, and power. He is the son of Winston J. Davie, Esq., and Miss Sarah A. Phillips. His parents were persons of the highest social position, and of that exclusive and elegant tone that distinguished large slave-holders in the brave days of old. Mr. Davie's grandparents were North Carolinians. His mother was a brilliant and handsome lady, who was a native of Columbus, Georgia, but his father was a Kentuckian, born also in Christian county.

The birth record for the subject of my sketch stands: George M. Davie, March 16, 1848. He is the second child. His education was very "thorough." He attended the best schools the country afforded at Memphis, Tenn., at Centre College, Danville, Ky., and, in 1865, he matriculated at Princeton College, New Jersey, from which institution of learning he graduated with great honor in 1868.

In 1869, Mr. Davie came to Louisville, Ky., and entered upon the study of law with Robert Woolley, Esq., whose brilliant ability and agreeability General Humphrey Marshall often asserted were not excelled by any man in Kentucky, and were equaled by only a few.

In 1870, Mr. Davie, who developed the most remarkable love and adaptability for his chosen profession, received his license. He attended the law school but three months, after which he entered the office of Muir & Bijur. He remained with these gentlemen until 1874, when he became part of the firm, which remained in existence until 1877, after which time it stood "Bijur & Davie" until 1882. The senior partner died, and after his melancholy demise Mr. Davie formed a copartnership with John Mason Brown, Esq., his brother-in-law. They continued to practice their profession in unison until February, 1885, when the name of Judge Alex. P. Humphrey became incorporated in that of the firm. And so it stands at the present time, forming a trio of the most brilliant array of names ever woven together in this or any other State in the Union. For profoundness, ability, and a thorough comprehension of the intricacies and technicalities involved in the profession they have few equals and no superiors.

Mr. Davie on December 5, 1878, was wedded to Miss Margaret Howard Preston, daughter of General William Preston, of Lexington, Ky. Like all the ladies of the "Preston house," Mrs. Davie is superb. No Kentuckian who takes pride in his State and the brilliant records of her best people but feels his heart warm and his blood thrill at thought of this great and excellent family—the Prestons. In the late war their property was confiscated ; they were themselves expatriated, but they boasted of the "blue blood" of royalty in their veins, and they never once shirked the issue of events brought on them by a proud defense and expression of their independent principles and their fearlessly maintained opinions.

General William Preston has attained the highest distinction as statesman, soldier, citizen, envoy extraordinary and minister plenipotentiary to Spain under President Buchanan in 1858.

In 1861, he requested his recall. He had covered himself with glory in his foreign course, having received the warmest encomiums for the same from William H. Seward, the United States Secretary of State. The first battle of Manassas was fought before he returned to the United States, and when he reached Kentucky he immediately began to urge the people to prompt and united resistance to the Lincoln administration. How futile were his attempts, we all know only too well. He entered the Confederate army. He served on the staff of General Albert Sidney Johnston, who fell and expired in his arms at the instant of a glorious assault on the enemy.

He served also on the staff of General Beauregard, but was soon commissioned brigadier-general, in April, 1862. He was at Corinth and Tupelo. He guarded the line of the Tallahatchie and aided in the defense of Vicksburg, the first siege of which was abandoned July 27, 1862, by Admirals Farragut and Porter and the Federal land forces. In October, 1862, he reached Kentucky, but too late to take part in the battle of Perryville. At Murfreesboro, he commanded the right of Breckinridge's division, and in the fatal charge across Stone river he covered himself with the mantle of distinction. He commanded the troops of South-western Virginia in 1863. After the battle of Chickamauga, the enemy retreated to Missionary Ridge, from which point of vantage General Preston dislodged them, storming and gaining the heights and driving the Federal troops pell-mell down the ridge through every avenue of escape to Chattanooga. It was a grand victory, a famous charge, which will rank in history side by side with the ride of the noble Six Hundred,

"All in the Valley of Death."

The Confederate loss in the charge, dead and wounded, was over a thousand men. As a Kentuckian, I am proud to accord the victory to General Preston.

One child has blessed the union of Mr. Davie with the daughter of the brave and distinguished General Preston. He is now five years of age.

Mr. Davie is highly respected in every relation of life. He has been devoted to his profession, and has more than once argued cases before the Supreme Court of the United States with great credit to himself. He has given but small time to politics, but he has been for five or six years the chairman of the Democratic committee of his district.

He has also served as a member of the school board, I believe, during the years 1881 and 1882. Whenever the time comes when he chooses to leave his musty tomes of legal lore and stand before the people as a brave and fearless exponent of their rights in the councils of State or nation, that time will prove him to be a man of nerve, ambition, power, attainment, and accomplishment. He is brilliant, versatile, profound to an unusual and distinguished degree. His friends are many and his admirers are legion.

In personal appearance, Mr. Davie is elegant, faultless, and suave as a courtier, but there is a light in his fine eyes and a firmness in his handsome face which, beyond all grace of manner and blandness of speech, declare the existence of a proud, free soul and a stainless conscience which dares maintain the right and fears to meet no issue.

HON. HENRY C. DIXON.

In the year 1798 Henderson county was formed out of a part of Christian county. It was the thirty-eighth county organized in the State. It was named in honor of Colonel Richard Henderson. Its territory was originally much larger than it is at the present day, for three counties have since been formed from it—Hopkins in 1806, Union in 1811, and Webster in 1860. The land comprised within its borders is remarkable for its fertility. As a corn-growing county Henderson ranks sixth, but as a tobacco region it ranks first. The people who inhabit that chosen country are as versatile in genius and what is termed "native talent" as the land is notable for its fertility. Warmer hearts never beat, lovelier women, cleverer men never lived anywhere on the face of the globe than those that may be found any day, everywhere, in Henderson. But in genuine cleverness in that rare spirit of *bonhomie* which makes a man a welcome guest wherever he appears and missed whenever he goes away—in that overflowing kind-heartedness and generous goodness which has long ago rendered Kentucky famous among States, and her children accounted the "chosen" of the New World, Henry C. Dixon, the subject of this sketch, is the most bountifully blessed of any man I ever met, and, I had almost added, the most to be envied, because of his light and joyous heart. Surely the sun shone and the birds sang the day he was born, for so far he has been surrounded with light and joy and good cheer. September, the loveliest month in all the year—September 19, 1845, so says the family chronicle, this glad spirit came to dwell among us. He is the second son of ex-Senator Archibald Dixon and Elizabeth R. Cabell. His father was a North Carolinian by birth, but by early adoption he became a Kentuckian; for, born in the year 1802, in 1804 his father moved with his family to Kentucky, to Henderson county. He received a general education commensurate with the opportunities afforded the children of pioneers.

Humphrey Marshall, the historian, in his "History of Kentucky," compiled and published in 1812, makes mention of the fact that Captain James Harrod, who settled Harrodsburg, could but imperfectly read or write, in these words: "It was not letters he learned nor books he studied. And, it may be asked, what there can be in the character of such a man that merits the notice of the historian? It is true, indeed, that the knowledge of letters, the perusal of books, and what is called an education, furnishes, enlightens, and enlarges the mind, and brings into action, with multiplied advantages, those qualities, both physical and mental, which nature gives to men. But it can not be affirmed that education creates any new organ or faculty of the soul, or gives a quality not otherwise inherent. Before the establishment of schools, and before the term education was ever known— aye, before letters were invented or books or pens were made, the human heart was the seat of kindness, of generosity, of fortitude, of magnanimity, and all the social virtues. The mind of man, in unison with his feelings, by a primeval decree, taught him justice, the first in importance of human virtues, which it cherished by reflections on the beneficent effects of doing unto others as he would that others should do unto him. This is the precept of nature. Then, without knowing how to read and write, James Harrod could be kind and obliging to his fellowmen, active and brave in their defense, dextrous in killing game, the source of supply, and liberal in the distribution of his spoils. He could be an expert pilot in the woods, and by his knowledge guide his followers to the destined point with equal certainty and safety. In fine, he could be a captain over others less endowed with the useful and benevolent qualities of the heart and of the head. He was always ready to defend his companions and his country. What nobler act of merit be chronicled?"

So with Archibald Dixon. The divine spirit was in him to attain ascendancy over his fellowmen by superior qualities of head and heart. And although, as I have said, his opportunities for intellectual attainments were limited, he made the most of them, and when he left school he studied law, and in 1825 he began to practice his profession. From the inception of his legal career he was successful to the time when, wearied with the accumulated honors of public life, he retired to the privacy of his own vine and fig tree. He represented his county in the Kentucky Legislature in 1830 and 1841, and was State senator in 1836 and 1840. He was elected lieutenant-governor, 1844 to 1848, on the Whig ticket, defeating General W. S. Pilcher by a majority of 11,081, whereas his co-nominee's (Governor Owsley) majority was only 4,624. In 1849, he was a delegate to the convention which formed the present Constitution of Kentucky, and he was defeated by James Guthrie for president of that body by a party vote of forty-eight to fifty. In 1851, as Whig candidate for Congress, he was defeated by Lazarus W. Powell. But in December, 1851, he was elected United States senator over James Guthrie by seventy-one to fifty-eight, to fill the vacancy, 1852 to 1855, caused by Henry Clay's resignation. In this body he was the author of the famous Kansas-Nebraska bill, as accepted by Judge Douglas, repealing the Missouri Compromise act of 1821. In 1862, he was elected to the Border State Convention held in Louisville, where he vainly endeavored to avert the disasters of war by recommending measures of compromise and conciliation. After that he never appeared in public service. He died in 1876.

Is it strange that the son of such a man should show to this generation of Kentuckians the promise of brilliance and ability which his father displayed with such magnificence in the days when intellectual giants were wont to measure lances, whose memories to-day illumine the past with electric and imperishable refulgence? Henry C. Dixon was educated partially in Henderson. Later on he attended the celebrated school of Dr. Sayre in Frankfort, Ky., and finally completed his studies at the University in Toronto, Canada.

He, too, studied law, and was admitted to the bar in 1867. In 1883, he was elected to the State Senate, where he has displayed such ability and has so won all hearts that he has enhanced the good opinions of his constituents, and has made other men wish they were his constituents. He is young yet, and the world is before him to choose, but I risk the prophecy that his name will be handed down to posterity as a "shining light," by which they may find the path which leads to honor and renown—coequal, if not surpassing, the splendid record his father left to him to emulate and to the Commonwealth to cherish among its sacred archives.

John Young Brown, the brilliant orator and statesman, is his brother-in-law, having married his sister, Miss Rebecca Hart Dixon, a most charming and accomplished lady.

Dr. Archibald Dixon, the distinguished physician, now resident in Henderson, is brother to the gentleman whose many noble qualities I delight to record. His great grandfather, Henry Dixon, was a colonel in the revolutionary army, and he is named in honorable memory of him. Henry Dixon, the soldier, fought at the battle of Camden with such gallantry that in the report of the general commanding he received distinguished mention. He fell covered with glory at the battle of Eutaw Springs, which was fought in 1781 on the banks of the small affluent of the Santee river from which it took its title—a title that will go "sounding down the ages" in attestation of the heroism and valor of those who bartered life for the independence and liberty of their country and their descendants.

So is it that the noble names of those who have served their native land and the Commonwealth to which they individually belonged are preserved, and the review of their valorous deeds ever inspires emulous regard in those on whose shoulders their mantles of honor have descended.

Henry C. Dixon will add green leaves to the wreaths of laurel and bay that crown the column of fame erected to the "Dixon" family, and his friends expect as much of him.

He is dignified and urbane in manner, full of wit and humor—the life of the "goodlie companie" wherever it be assembled. He has dark hair and expressive dark eyes. He wears a moustache, but dispenses with other hirsute adornment. If the quotation be acceptable because applicable, one might say of him, in the language of the poet:—

> "None know him but to love him,
> None name him but to praise."

He is unmarried.

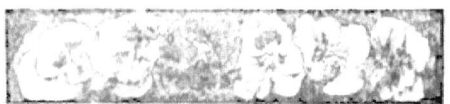

GENERAL BASIL W. DUKE.

The name of the distinguished gentleman which graces the head of this brief sketch vividly recalls the chaotic period of twenty-four years ago, when the rolling drum and ear-piercing fife, with no uncertain sounds, were calling the brave men of the North and South to arms, that they might fight for "God and their native land." Alas! for those by-gone days, when partisan excitement culminated at a degree of intensity of opinion and principle which was never equaled in this country nor surpassed in any other! What a waste and wreck of peace and happiness seems that other time seen by the light of to-day! Then the tramp of the soldier was heard in every city and hamlet in the Union, and everywhere there was the wailing and weeping, the pangs of parting, and the dread of impending disaster consequent upon the disruption of home ties and desolated hearth-stones. The valiant fathers, sons, brothers, and lovers went away as go the waves that have curled and crept upon the shining beach when they glide into the current which sweeps boldly on to the fathomless depths of sea, never again to return upon its course. The mothers, daughters, sisters, and sweethearts kept watch and ward at home, oftentimes as do the lookers-on among the crags who see ships go to wreck upon a stormy ocean, yet are powerless to shield or save. But, despite these sad thoughts, we must admit the salient truth that war, even though its course is marked by devastation, is a great civilizer. The greatest fruit of our internecine strife is the present development of the South, its increasing wealth, its rapidly-growing population and prosperity, and the consequent disappearance of certain unseemly peculiarities which once marred its beauty, even as spots upon the sun's disc mar its splendor. There is no reason now why those who love the South should not anticipate for it a future of brillance not heretofore conceived by the American people. However, it was not to discuss the political or social aspect of the country that I took up my pen, but to pronounce a fitting eulogy upon a brave and efficient officer, in so far as such eulogy could be pronounced in a biographical sketch so brief as I design each of my papers upon prominent Kentuckians to be.

Basil W. Duke is the son of Nathaniel Wilson Duke and Mary Pickett Curry, who was a Virginian. His father was a native of Mason county, Ky. He was a naval officer by education and profession, having served in that department of American service from 1825 to the time of his death, which occurred in 1852.

The subject of this sketch was born in the county of Scott on the 28th day of May, 1837. He was educated partly in Georgetown and partly at Centre College, completing his course in 1854. Immediately thereafter he entered upon the study of the law with Judge Robertson, of Lexington, Ky., who was conceded to be the ablest jurist Kentucky had ever furnished to the bench. In 1856, Mr. Duke completed his law course and removed to St. Louis, where he began the practice of his profession. When the tocsin of war beat its wild alarums he joined the State troops, with the rank of captain. In June, 1861, he returned to Kentucky and married Miss Henrietta H. Morgan, the sister of General John H. Morgan, whose fame is the synonym of chivalry, and whose brilliant deeds as a cavalier rival those of a Bayard or a Knight of King Arthur's Table Round. Subsequent to his marriage, he set out for the South and joined the Confederate army at Bowling Green, Ky. In October, 1861, he was chosen adjutant of Morgan's squadron, and served with that rank until June, 1862, when, upon the organization of the Second Regiment of Kentucky Cavalry, John Morgan was, by concession, made the colonel, and Duke lieutenant-colonel. In October following, Colonel Morgan was promoted to the rank of brigadier-general, and Lieutenant-Colonel Duke was promoted to the colonelcy of the finest cavalry regiment in the Confederate army. Several times, while leading this splendid body of men, he was wounded. His power of physical endurance, through heat or cold, never faltering or knowing dread, was at once the pride and wonder of his regiment, composed of the wealthiest and knightliest sons of Kentucky. He may not have known it, but the soldiers of his command gave him the sobriquet of "The Little Whalebone." His efficiency and endurance was their constant boast. During the campaigns of 1862 and 1863 he wrote a book of tactics, entitled "Duke's Cavalry Drills," showing the versatility of his mind and his remarkable powers of application, allied with indomitable will and unflagging industry.

On the 4th of September, 1864, General Morgan was killed, and Colonel Duke was promoted to the rank of brigadier-general, his commission dating from that sad day. He held the position to the close of the war. On the 10th day of May, 1865, General Duke surrendered his command at Washington, Ga., having been assigned the duty of escorting President Davis and the portable treasury of the Confederate States to that point. After the close of the war General Duke returned to Kentucky, making his home in Lexington. There he wrote the "History of Morgan and his Cavalry." He has contributed many valuable and interesting articles to the popular magazines of the day, clearly establishing his right to be ranked among the ablest of the literati. His talents are varied, and these, combined with his good common sense, enable him to adapt himself to any sphere of life and to be an ornament everywhere he appears. In March, 1868, he removed to Louisville (his present home) and entered upon the practice of law. In August, 1869, he was elected from the city to the Legislature; and after serving one session with great credit to his constituents and to himself, the Congress of the United States refused to remove his disabilities. Learning this, he immediately resigned his seat, and returning to his office resumed the practice of law. In August, 1875, after an excited and hotly-contested canvass with George Wm. Caruth and Hon. Nat Robertson, of Shelby county, both men of eminent ability and lawyers of high reputation, he was elected Commonwealth's attorney of the Louisville district, which position he filled for five years with the most gratifying success. It was the universal comment of the bar that he was the fairest prosecutor who had ever filled the position. He never went outside the proof to convict any one, but his very fairness and his close elucidation of facts made him dangerous to the law-breakers. At the present time the general is the attorney of several railroad companies, and is most admirably adapted to the position of controlling great railroad systems and gathering together the network of their crossing and recrossing as easily as the fair hand of a lady meshes her lace-making. He controls men with the same ease and grace as that same illustrative lady might show in wielding a fine ivory fan upon a state occasion. His manner is dignified and deferential. His figure is slight, his hair brown, his moustache unique, and his eyes are piercing and black as ebony. He is modest and unassuming, claiming nothing, wearing the honors thrust upon him with becoming dignity. To enter more fully than I have done into the genealogy of this distinguished gentleman would bring a long array of State names, for he is allied to some of the grandest families in the Commonwealth—the Marshalls, the Colstons, the Greens, the Warrens, the Picketts, and hosts of others. His private life is peculiarly happy, the domestic side of his character being even more admirable than his public one. He has an interesting wife and several children, one daughter (Miss Currie) being especially distinguished for her brilliance and delicate execution as a violinist.

JUDGE FONTAINE T. FOX.

Judge Fontaine T. Fox, of the city of Louisville, is the fourth son of the venerable Judge Fontaine Fox, of Danville, Ky. The latter gentleman was born in Richmond, Ky., in 1803. His ancestry were Virginians, and his wife was Miss E. J. Hunton, of Charlottesville, Va., she claiming that town as the place of her nativity since 1809. No one who has the honor of a personal acquaintance with this most estimable lady, or who knows her by reputation, but acknowledges her to be the model of refinement and the accepted type of a Christian wife and mother.

No jurist in the State ranks higher in point of integrity and finished attainments in law and literature than does Judge Fox, Sr. A more indulgent parent never lived. He has, with the assistance of his excellent wife, reared and superbly educated a large family of children. A picture of their charming domestic life, if placed on canvas for the eyes of the world to see, would be priceless, and the object of universal envy. Austerity and the cold and cheerless dignities that usually hamper the affectionate relations between parents and children never disturbed the harmonies of their lives. He was always the familiar companion in their household as she was the idol of their heart. When the sons of that household went their devious ways amid the tumult and the traffic of the world, home was the "Mecca" to which their souls journeyed ever, with unabated enthusiasm and a glowing tenderness of sentiment which sent a thrill of pleasure to the hearts of their friends whenever they talked of "mother" and "father," or pictured for their delectation the quiet happiness that reigned around the domestic hearth. A man may well be pardoned for lingering with delight over such a tender theme!

Judge Fox, Sr., is the only survivor of a coterie of distinguished Kentuckians born, reared, and educated in the central part of the State, who were prominent both at the bar and in politics for half a century. Read the brilliant array of names! Joshua F. Bell, Thomas E. Bramlette, John B. Thompson, Beriah Magoffin, and George Dunlap. Whenever either or any one of these gentlemen was announced for a speech at the bar or from the hustings in any county in the State, it was sufficient to insure a rousing crowd who never failed to disperse, after the intellectual treat was over, shouting aloud their enthusiastic applause.

Ah! those by-gone times and those dead-and-gone orators! They were not, as politicans of to-day, taken from the pavement or from the shops and made the leaders of "rings" and "cliques." Their knowledge was imbibed in the old schools of perfection, and their oratory, crisp with the sparkling coruscations of their genius, allied with matchless diction and suavity of address, won for them admirers and friends wherever men sat under the sound of their voices, and the homage paid to their eloquence has been handed down from fathers to sons as family traditions.

Judge Fontaine T. Fox, Jr., was born in the county of Pulaski on the 11th day of June, 1836. In his early life he was extremely delicate. He graduated from Centre College in 1855, in the class of which Dr. H. H. Allen, of Princeton, Kentucky, was the valedictorian. John Young Brown, W. C. P. Breckinridge, and Dr. James Holloway, the distinguished surgeon of that name, a resident of this city, were all graduates of that same class. From 1855 to 1856, Fontaine Fox, Jr., taught school and studied law, never idling away his time, but striving steadily onward toward the goal of his ambitious hopes. In 1866 he received his license and removed to Louisville, where he opened an office and began the practice of his profession. In 1868 he was elected a member of the Board of Alderman, and served with that body from 1868 to 1870. In 1871 he acted as assistant attorney for the city of Louisville. In 1878 he was appointed by Governor James B. McCreary, vice-chancellor, which position he filled with eminent ability until the time of the regular election to take place, when he declined to make a race before the people for the office.

He is the author of a law book of acknowledged merit upon insurance. In addition to this erudite volume, he has contributed articles upon varied subjects to the leading magazines, and has been quoted in the periodicals of England as high authority in pure English literature. His pen is facile, as his genius is versatile.

In 1882 Judge Fox was married to Miss Mary Barton, the accomplished daughter of Prof. S. S. Barton, who taught the Greek and Latin languages and Belles Lettres at Center College during the time the judge was a student at that famous institution. One child, a lovely boy, has been given to Judge and Mrs. Fox to bless their marriage, and to stimulate them to win laurels for him in the great battle of life. Gentle, affectionate, intellectual, and refined, their domestic life can but repeat the happiness Judge Fox, to the writer's knowledge, enjoyed in his boyhood's home.

In 1885 Judge Fox was nominated on the Prohibition ticket for the office of State treasurer, and by his active canvass and classic speeches (which would have charmed the ears of Pittacus himself!), made in various portions of the Commonwealth, he received the largest vote of any man who has ever run upon that ticket in Kentucky—a ticket which is fast winning favor even in a corn-cracking State, which has probably manufactured more whisky in proportion to its population than any other State in the Union. For twenty years it has been a boasted product with Kentuckians, but the judge never "smiles" with them in their boast.

In personal appearance he is the thoughtful, grave student. Extremely neat in his attire, of bland address and pleasant voice, he is at all times the thoroughbred gentleman. His friends are many, and if he has faults they are so few that even the censorious forget to count them.

GENERAL PARKER W. HARDIN.

To speak or write of one to whom we are endeared by association or relationship is to do so *con amore*. My self-appointed task—to add my mite of praise to the universal voice that cries "Evoe" to the distinguished men who perpetuate the fame of Kentucky in the nation—becomes a delight when I undertake to render a biographical sketch of General Parker W. Hardin. The tie of relationship and the bond of association at the bar and in society have endeared the name and the wearer of it to my heart for many a year. And my intimate knowledge of the charm of his domestic life enhances my appreciation of the man and the gentleman.

General Parker W. Hardin was born in the county of Adair, State of Kentucky, June 3, 1841. He is the second son of Parker C. Hardin and Miss Carolina Watkins. The names of his parents are both well and favorably known throughout the State and the Union. The lady's ancestors emigrated to Kentucky as early as 1776, and the name of "Hardin" is part and parcel of Kentucky, from border land to border land. The annals of the State teem with recitals of the dash and bravery of the Hardins, and a full quota of the splendor conferred on the State by the brilliance of her sons belongs "by rights" to this noble race of people.

The Hardin family—that is, the most prominent branch of it—settled in Washington county in the year 1786. The legend of the family runs, that after the massacre of St. Bartholomew three brothers named Hardin, being Huguenots, emigrated from France to Canada; but the climate being too severe for them, they left that country and again emigrated, this time to Virginia, at that period a British colony and not a State. At this point two of them settled, and the third continued his journey southward until he reached South Carolina, at which point he also settled.

Martin Hardin, a descendant of one of these three brothers, in the year 1765 moved from Fauquier county, Va., and found his permanent abiding place at "George's Creek," on the Monongahela river. He married and was the father of seven children, three sons and four daughters. They were all born between the years 1740 and 1760, and in 1786 and 1787 they emigrated to Kentucky, with the exception of one sister, Miss Rosanna, who afterward became Mrs. John McMahon. Reaching this State, they settled within a radius of ten miles, near where the town of Springfield, Washington county, Ky., now stands, and stretching away toward Lebanon, Ky., upon their own land; and for more than sixty years they or their descendants occupied it. In 1849 the youngest son, Martin Hardin, died, at the advanced age of ninety-two years. He was the last survivor of that family of brothers and sisters. Another of the emigrants, who was but four years of age at the time of emigration, lived to be over ninety-two. He was honored and beloved by all who knew him. He was the venerable Mark Hardin, of Shelbyville, Ky.

Colonel John Hardin, the second of the above-mentioned sons—and the father of Mark—was killed in 1792, in North-western Ohio, by the Indians. He was proceeding to their towns under a flag of truce to offer them a treaty of peace, sent so to do by General George Washington, then President of the United States. He was held in the highest esteem by General Daniel Morgan. A warm personal friendship existed between them. More than once he was the subject of complimentary reports by superior officers in the army. It is said that he was in almost every engagement fought with the Indians after he settled in Kentucky. He was a man of the kindest and gentlest heart, and his manners at all times dignified and unassuming. His will was inflexible. He was a devout Christian, being a member of the Methodist Church. A town was laid out on the spot where he was so treacherously killed. This was done in 1840, on the State road from Piqua, through Wapakonetta, and was named "Hardin" in his memory. He left three sons and three daughters, several of whom became distinguished or whose descendants were distinguished.

General Martin D. Hardin, one of his sons, was one of Kentucky's great men. He was a man of marked character and brilliant ability. He was in war a brave, vigilant, and efficient officer. He was secretary of State under Governor Isaac Shelby, 1812 to 1816; was appointed by Governor Gabriel Slaughter to fill a vacancy in the United States Senate, serving one session, 1816 and 1817. He died at Frankfort, Ky., October 8, 1823, aged forty-three. Colonel John J. Hardin, an ex-member of Congress from Illinois, 1843 to 1845, was his son. He fell in the battle of Buena Vista, in Mexico, February 23, 1847.

Miss Sallie Hardin, one of Colonel John Hardin's daughters, became the wife of Rev. Barnabas McHenry, and was the ancestor of a distinguished family. Miss Lydia Hardin was the wife of Charles Wickliffe and the mother of Robert Wickliffe, of Lexington, Charles A. Wickliffe, of Bardstown, Maxwell Wickliffe, Nathaniel Wickliffe, and five daughters, all of whom raised families of useful and influential citizens.

Miss Sarah Hardin married her cousin, Ben Hardin, and was the mother of the great lawyer, Ben Hardin (who was born in Westmoreland county, Pa., in the year 1784, and died in Nelson county, Ky., September 24, 1852, at the age of sixty-eight years), of Warren Hardin, Mrs. Rosanna McElroy, and three other daughters, who also reared useful and prominent families.

The descendants of this great family are scattered all over the State, and by marriages and intermarriages they are connected with many of the greatest people in the Commonwealth. The Wickliffes, Helms, McHenrys, Hammonds, Colers, McElroys, Tobins, Barnetts, Chinns, Rays, Ewings, Caldwells, Bufords, Raileys, Fields, Torrences, Yagers, Roberts, all trace back with pardonable pride their splendid lineage to the Huguenot brothers who fled from persecution to Virginia, Pennsylvania, South Carolina, and thence to the wilds of Kentucky. A great people they are! And they and their descendants make their mark on every community in which they settle. A county in this State is named for them, another in Ohio, and a town in Shelby county of that State covers the very spot where General Hardin was murdered while on his peace mission.

Benjamin Hardin, one of the greatest lawyers Kentucky ever produced, was the son of Sarah and Ben Hardin (cousins). He was educated in Springfield, Ky., studied law in Richmond, Ky., with Martin

D. Hardin, in 1804, and with Justice Felix Grundy at Bardstown, Ky., in 1805. In 1806 he married Miss Barbour, of Elizabethtown, Ky. Two years later he moved to Bardstown, which was ever afterward his place of residence until his death. He was an indefatigable practitioner, and amassed a handsome fortune. It is said he was on one side or the other of every seriously-contested case in the State. He possessed a most extraordinary memory, and it was cultivated to a wonderful degree. As a speaker he was famous for his perspicuity and his clear array of facts. His force lay in these. Allied to them was an air of animation which delighted his listeners and commanded attention, even though not always carrying their conviction. He served his county in the House of Representatives in 1810, 1811, 1824, and 1825, and in the Senate from 1828 to 1832. He represented his district in Congress from 1815 to 1817, from 1819 to 1823, and from 1833 to 1837. From September, 1844, to February, 1847, he was secretary of State under Governor Owsley, with whom he had one of the most heated controversies which has ever taken place among the public men of this State. It is said that his speech before the Senate Committee on Executive Affairs in January, 1847, was never excelled for length, power, and keenness. He was one of the convention that formed the present Constitution of Kentucky. This was in 1849 and 1850, and was his last public service. In the summer of 1852 he was crippled by falling from his horse, and in September of that same year he died, aged sixty-eight. In person he was tall and commanding. He had splendid eyes, and a face which beamed with intelligence. In politics he was a Whig. Parker C. Hardin, the father of the subject of this sketch, was in the Senate from Adair from 1840 to 1848, and was acknowledged to be one of the foremost men of his time in point of ability and strict adherence to party and to principle. He was pious and gentle as a woman. And above all public emoluments he desired that his sons should be good men and good citizens.

Parker W. Hardin—he of whom I write—was educated in the schools of Adair county. He studied law with his father, and while still a student he fell a victim to the wiles of Cupid, or—as he himself gallantly and poetically expressed it not long since, when speaking of his wife—he "culled the fairest flower that ever grew on the peaks of the Cumberland!" He married Miss Mary E. Sallee, of Wayne county, Ky., one of the most charming and accomplished ladies in the world, and not a whit less lovely than she is gifted. This was in December, 1864. A year later, 1865, he was admitted to the bar at Columbia, the county-seat of Adair. He immediately began the practice of his profession. He was full of   ability, and was   of pride and ambition among his relatives and friends, and the latter, because of his grace and good breeding and noble heart, were counted by legion. He is the brother of Judge Charles A. Hardin, who married Miss Jenny Magoffin, the daughter of Colonel Ebenezer Magoffin, of Missouri, one of the knightliest spirits ever shrined in human form. With Judge Hardin, some time after his happy marriage with Miss Sallee, General Hardin formed a partnership in the practice of law, in the town of Harrodsburg, Mercer county, Ky., and he immediately took position at the bar in Central Kentucky second to none. The Hardins are like the Marshalls—born lawyers—and to these two families Kentucky owes much of her legal precedence in the learned science which governs her sovereigns. Another brother of General Hardin is Benjamin Lee Hardin, also a lawyer and resident of Harrodsburg, Mercer county, Ky. This gentleman is widely and favorably known throughout Kentucky for his versatility of talent and his genial disposition. He married Miss Sue Cardwell, a kind-hearted, gracious, and estimable lady, daughter of Captain John Cardwell, of the well known Kentucky family of that name, who as soldiers and citizens confer honor on their name and their State.

In the May convention of 1879 Parker W. Hardin was nominated for attorney-general of Kentucky. Nomination is equivalent to election. He served his State nobly in that capacity for four years. Was renominated at the Democratic convention which convened in the city of Louisville in May, 1883, and is now a candidate for the third term, and if elected will bear himself as hitherto with unimpeachable honor and unsullied dignity. He is a man of mark and fine ability. He has represented the State with great credit to himself and to it before the Supreme Court of the United States, and his name was conspicuous in many of the leading criminal cases in the Commonwealth while he practiced at the Mercer bar. In person he is distingue, being tall and well-formed, with a fine, soldierly bearing. His face beams with intellectuality.

The Hardins of the present generation are congenital Kentuckians, possessing all the fervor of oratory and the love of liberty which distinguished the adventurous pioneer who felled the trees and opened up the way for the advancement of civilization in what was then the most Western country of this great republic.

HON. THOMAS F. HARGIS.

The people of Breathitt county may be proud of the fact that their county is named in memory of a governor of Kentucky—John Breathitt—whose success, spirit, and popularity were of that intense character that it has been averred that but for his untimely death (he died at the early age of forty-seven) there was scarcely an honor within the gift of the people but he would have obtained it. They may be proud of their native hills and rich valleys, proud of their coal and iron ore, proud of their advancement and prosperity, but they have need to "plume" themselves upon nothing with more sincerity than the fact that Hon. Thomas F. Hargis was born in their midst; and that amid all his successes and his ever-increasing popularity, he loves to remember that Breathitt is his native county—that with it must forever be associated his tenderest and most endearing recollections of the past.

Thomas F. Hargis is the son of John Hargis, Esq., and his mother's maiden name was Miss Elizabeth Weddington. Her people were of German extraction—excellent, progressive, and endowed with marked

Miss Weddington was American by birth, having been born in Russell county, Va. His father, John Hargis, Esq., came to Kentucky from Washington county, Va., as early as 1823. He was a man of strong character, marked spirit and independence, and took position with the leading men of his day and time. He was a member of the convention which framed the present Constitution of Kentucky, assembled at Frankfort, October 1, 1849. He represented the counties of Breathitt and Morgan. He also represented Breathitt county in the years 1855, 1856, and 1857 in the House of Representatives of the State Legislature. He was a man highly esteemed for his intelligence and integrity, and the ability, zeal, and firmness with which he maintained his principles and adhered to his opinions. His son, Thomas F. Hargis, was born in the quiet hamlet of Jackson (named in honor of Andrew Jackson), situated in Breathitt county. The date of his birth on the family record reads, 24th day of June, 1842. He was reared in his native county, and something of the spirit and strength, capability and resource of it seems to have taken root and flourished in his sturdy, enduring, but affable and sunny disposition.

Breathitt county abounds in picturesque scenery, which would inspire the true artist to behold, and also lend a theme to the poet. The scenery is fine, the waters are pure, and the air is redolent with the perfume of wild flowers growing with profuse luxuriance on those lofty mountain peaks.

Here in his native county he was educated, even then giving promise of future eminence by his remarkable powers of application, and his aspiring mind, which was never satisfied with anything less than his "level best" in his pursuit after knowledge. In that charming time of the year 1861,

> When the willow shoots forth a green feather,
> And the buttercup burns in the grass,

The fires of youthful ardor began to glow with fervid heat in his heart. His dreams early and late were all of war—and only war. The song of the Lurhe among the rocks could not have equaled in harmony the sounds of the ear-piercing fife and the martial music of the drum, calling the sons of the South to arms to battle for God and the right. At least could not have equaled them when regarded from the standpoint of his youthful judgment. So it was that he joined the Fifth Kentucky Infantry, commanded by General John S. Williams, in Western Virginia, in General Humphrey Marshall's Brigade. From the time he "buckled on his armor" to the close of the war he was constantly in the service of the Confederacy. He was promoted to the position of captain of cavalry at the time that he was wounded at

Milford, in the Valley of Virginia, in November, 1864. He was captured and imprisoned at Johnston's Island. He was peculiarly unfortunate in this regard, having been captured four times. But he was equally fortunate about procuring his liberty, for he every time succeeded in escaping or being exchanged. He was brave and daring, and to-day bears several meritorious scars upon his person which he gained by gallant conduct under fire and scourging sword.

But after the long struggle was over, and peace was restored to our suffering country, many of those who had wandered away from old familiar places returned. Among them was Thomas F. Hargis. He applied himself to the study of law, and in April, 1866, he received his license to practice his profession. He entered upon the same in Rowan county, Ky., but in 1868 he removed to Carlisle, Nicholas county, Ky., where a finer opening awaited his energy and his ambition, and where the culmination of his heart's desire was reached, for in the month of June—the glorious time of sunshine and roses—on the 23d day of said month in the following year, 1869, he was married to Miss Lucy Stewart Norvell, of Carlisle, Ky. From this auspicious moment fortune and honor seemed to have clasped hands and united energies in their desire to shower benefits on him.

At an especial election for county judge held in September, 1869, he was elected to fill the position, which he did with such credit to himself and satisfaction to the general public that in August, 1870, he was re-elected to the same position without opposition. In 1871 he was nominated by a Democratic convention, and at the August election, 1871, he was chosen senator from the Thirtieth district, defeating Judge James W. Anderson by four hundred and fifty-nine majority. He served four years in that position, winning many friends in his public career, and endearing himself to his constituents by a manly and conscientious adherence to their interests.

At the convention held for the purpose of nominating a criminal and equity judge of the Fourteenth Judicial district, Mr. Hargis was nominated unanimously, and was elected in March, 1878, over Colonel John L. Hickman (Republican), of Maysville, Ky., by twenty-two hundred and fourteen majority. He filled this position also with great credit to himself until April 24, 1879, when he received the nomination at Owingsville, Ky., as the choice of the Democratic party for the Court of Appeals for the First Appellate district, and on the 12th day of May, 1879, he was elected over the present incumbent, Judge W. H. Holt, of Mount Sterling, Ky., and this by the handsome majority of thirty-five hundred and fifty-five votes. He served on the bench of the Court of Appeals until the 1st day of September, 1884.

At the close of his term Judge Hargis removed to Louisville, Ky., and began the practice of law, having declined to run for re-election to the arduous position he had so creditably filled. His opinions while on the Supreme Bench of Kentucky met with the highest praise among attorneys in and out of the State. He has formed here a partnership with Captain George M. Eastin, than whom lives not on earth a more gallant and gracious gentleman, and the firm name is "Hargis & Eastin," and I venture the prophecy that it will become a power at the bar throughout the Commonwealth, for as practitioners of the law both gentlemen have a profound and thorough knowledge of its principles, and the most approved forms of practice, and as a consequence are bound to hold their eminence in the profession and add new laurels to their fame as clear, logical, and forcible practitioners.

Judge Hargis is candid and honest, bold and fearless, a ready debater, an able lawyer, and exhaustive thinker. His intellect is of a high order. In every relation of life, by firm and inflexible integrity, he has won the approbation of his fellowmen, and the warm and sincere affection of his many personal friends. He is a self-made man, and is one of the finest examples of the ennobling tendency of Republican institutions, and an encouragement to all meritorious and aspiring young men in America.

His marriage has been a peculiarly happy one, he declaring that his wife has indeed been "the star of his destiny," since he dates all his successes in public life from their wedding day. They have five children, four girls and one boy, who is named after our distinguished citizen, Robert Woolley, Esq.

HON. THOMAS H. HAYS.

Thomas H. Hays is the oldest son of William H. Hays, Esq., and his mother's maiden name was Miss Nancy Neil. Their ancestry were among the earliest settlers who came to this their native State—Kentucky. That they were endowed with the noblest attributes to which the human heart can fall heir is evidenced by the character and principles of their son, Thomas H. Hays, whose popularity and manly excellence in every way endear him to associates and friends. Mr. Hays was born in Hardin county, Ky., on the 6th of October, 1837. He matriculated at St. Joseph's College, Bardstown, Ky., which was established by the Legislature of Virginia in 1788, and was formerly known as Bairdstown, having been named after David Baird, Esq., one of the original proprietors of the one hundred acres on which the town was laid off. The county was named in honor of Governor Thomas Nelson, who was a distinguished Virginian, and one of the signers of the Declaration of Independence.

But, as the French say: *Revenons a nos moutons.*

Thomas H. Hays, in 1857, graduated from that noble and historic Catholic institution of learning, St. Joseph's College, after which he immediately began the study of law with Governor John L. Helm and J. W. Hays. In the early part of 1861 he was licensed to practice the legal profession, and entered upon a copartnership with William Wilson, Esq., a lawyer of great eminence and ability in Elizabethtown, Ky.

Before the civil war began Mr. Hays was senior major of the Salt River Batallion of the State militia. Early in 1861 he joined the Southern army, and was commissioned major in the regular service of the Confederate States Army, being promptly assigned to duty with the Sixth Confederate regiment of infantry, commanded then by General Joseph H. Lewis. Major Hays served with his regiment for twelve months, participating in the arduous campaign from Kentucky to Shiloh. He captured the first train of cars in Kentucky after the war began. This was done on the 17th day of September, 1861, at Elizabethtown, Hardin county, Ky.

After the battle of Shiloh, Major Hays was ordered to report to General William Preston, then in command of Vicksburg, Miss., and before the battle of Chickamauga he was ordered to report to General Ben Hardin Helm, who was his brother-in-law, and by General Helm he was assigned to duty as the inspector-general of his brigade. He was with General Helm when he fell at the head of this same splendid brigade on Chickamauga's blood-stained field, covered with martial glory, the grandest exemplar to the future soldiery of our State, as to how a Kentuckian can die for love of country and in defense of his national principles and his rights as a freeborn American citizen.

In 1864 Major Hays was assigned to duty with General Joseph E. Johnston, then stationed at Dalton, Ga. He served with General Johnston as assistant adjutant-general, and filled this position in the general's retreat back to Atlanta, Ga., contesting with the foe for every inch of Southern soil as he retired, and dying, in spirit, a thousand deaths because compelled to retreat. Unexpectedly, upon reaching Atlanta, General Johnston was superseded by General John B. Hood, on the 19th day of July, 1864, who was a soldier of distinguished presence and fine ability, who had by his valor, exhibited on many a hard fought field, won the confidence of the President, Mr. Jefferson Davis. The removal of General Joseph E. Johnston, a splendid officer, a graduate of West Point in 1829, and a superb tactician, created almost a panic of surprise among the soldiers; but the panic did not change the face of the fact that this gallant chieftain was superseded, and that General John B. Hood, who was a Kentuckian and a West Pointer, class of 1853, was duly inducted into the high and responsible position General Johnston had so nobly and honorably filled.

Among officers of rank, and universally among the soldiers of the South, throughout the Confederacy Mr. Davis received general invective for making the change in commanding generals at so inopportune a moment for the life of the Confederacy, and for the fulfillment of General Johnston's plans. He had made such a gallant resistance; he was such a magnificent officer, and the odds had been so overwhelming in the retreat from Dalton to Atlanta! And to be thus thwarted in all his noble plans on the eve of their fulfillment must, indeed, have brimmed the cup of bitterness for General Johnston. But who heard him murmur against the august decree of superior power? Not a man living or dead could testify to his rebellion against "the throne, or the powers that lay behind the throne."

Suffice it to say that the sudden change in commanding generals created such consternation amid the troops that it necessitated a strategic movement on the part of General Hood to restore confidence. He at once took up the line of march to Nashville, Tenn., on September 1, 1864, but the scarcity of commissaries and the condition of the country through which he had to pass caused delay, and thus enabled the enemy to re-enforce General Thomas, who was in command at that point.

In the autumn of 1864, General Hood, after trials and tribulations and foot-sore marches over a country sterile of products, because of the invasion of the enemy, met General Thomas in battle at Franklin, Tenn., on the 30th of November, 1864; and on the 15th and 16th of December following, same year, the battle of Nashville was fought. Never was such heroism exhibited by man as was there displayed by the soldiers of the Confederate army, unless, indeed, it was equaled by Napoleon's soldiers of France, in their weather-beaten marches to Moscow, or their loyalty and despair at Waterloo.

They forgot toilsome advances, exposure, and privation; they remembered only that they were Southern soldiers fighting for a noble cause. With flushed faces and glowing eyes that shone with the feverish dream of moving northward on the enemy, these brave fellows did devoir for God and right; but they failed. "They fought like brave men, long and well—they fell—bleeding at every vein;" but endurance, chivalry, daring, availed them nothing. General Hood sustained irretrievable defeat, losing many of his most trusted and chivalrous officers, among them the immortal Cleburne, of Arkansas. Major Hays was with General Hood as an assistant staff officer, and rendered valuable service to him in his campaign. The war in the West, and south of the Mississippi river, was virtually closed with the battle of Franklin, Tenn.

After the surrender of the Confederacy, Major Hays returned to his native county and entered upon the most honorable and independent of all pursuits known to civilized men—that of a Kentucky farmer.

In August, 1869, however, he was elected to the Legislature from Hardin county, and the history of the Commonwealth will bear me out when I say that the Kentucky Legislature of 1869 was the ablest General Assembly that ever convened at Frankfort. Record cites their honorable names, but they at once placed Kentucky upon a prosperous financial basis.

A sharp contrast this to the Legislature of 1886, which finds riot and confusion in the State borders, and the Treasury minus a dollar with which to pay for the services of her legislators. However, as the Latin phrase goes: "*Tempora mutantur, et nos mutamur in illis.*"

In 1871 Major Hays was made Superintendent of the Pullman Palace Car Company, and he has been chiefly instrumental in obtaining for it advantageous legislation along its almost illimitable lines over the country. In 1881 he was chosen second vice-president, which honorable position he continues to hold with acceptability to the directory of the company. He is one of the projectors of the Versailles & Midway Railroad Company, of which he is the vice-president.

Until now I have ommitted to say that, in 1861, amid the excitements of the civil war, Major Hays was married to Miss Sarah Hardin Helm (now deceased), the daughter of Governor John L. Helm, of Elizabethtown, Ky., also deceased. They had born to them two children, Lucinda Hardin Hays and Nancy Neil Hays.

In 1871 Major Hays was married to Miss Georgia T. Broughton, of Lagrange, Ga., the daughter of Judge Edward Broughton, of that State. They have six daughters, who, on State occasions, make the home place look like a fairy garden.

In 1880 Major Hays was chosen by a Democratic convention the nominee for Congress from this, the Fifth Congressional District, but was defeated by the Hon. Albert S. Willis, who ran as an independent candidate. The nomination came too late to insure thorough organization and success, and as a consequence, Major Hays sustained defeat.

Major Hays is a gentleman of the old school, and it is always a pleasure to the herald to place upon record the nobility and valor of those who add honor and glory to Kentucky as a State and a Commonwealth of free and enlightened people.

HON. JOHN K. HENDRICK.

"In the highways of life, here and there, now and then,
Amid muslin called ladies and buckram called men,
One meets, though the race is hardly called human,
A man that's a man and a woman that's woman."

So wrote the poet, William D. Gallagher, expressing a homely truth with the quaint and rhythmic eloquence which characterized the emanations of Robert Burns' genius.

And they come to my mind to-day full of forceful suggestions in connection with the name of the distinguished gentleman which graces this number of my sketches of those who uphold Kentucky.

Hon. John K. Hendrick, of Livingston county, is the only son of William H. Hendrick, of Logan county, Ky. He was born on the 10th of October, 1849. His mother was Miss Susan Bennett, a sister to Judge Bennett, the logician and scholar, who is now a candidate for the Court of Appeals, from the First Appellate District, to succeed the Hon. Thomas H. Hines, of Warren county, who declines to succeed himself on account of ill health, which latter fact of his melancholy physical condition should be a cause of painful and personal regret to every man in Kentucky who takes pride in his native State, for a grander, braver, truer, more chivalrous soul was never shrined in human form than is that which looks forth from the kind and gentle eyes of Thomas H. Hines.

The parents of Mr. Hendrick were Virginians by birth, but came to Kentucky at an early day, and first settled in Christian county, subsequently removing to the county of Logan, that haven of the brave and chivalrous. "Bluegrass" is the indigenous herbage of the State; in the same ratio it might be said that cavaliers were the indigenous growth of Logan county, for, added to her historic record in the days of the early settlement of the State, during the civil war she gave one thousand soldiers to the Confederate army and over five hundred to the Federal army, from which data one might conclude that, like the men of Roderick Dhu's Scottish clan, who sprang up at a sign, a man for every heather plume, she had cavaliers as thick in her midst as the feathery herbage which tufted her hills and dales. One can not resist the spell of enthusiasm which a knowledge of the record of Logan county casts over the contemplative soul. How it must inspire her sons and daughters with the emulous spirits of honor and goodness! What a glory to claim her as a mother county! From the years 1770 and 1771, when the "Long Hunters" penetrated the wilderness, now comprised partially in her borders, down to the present time of 1886, over a century, Logan county has contributed great men to the nation. Just read her record: Four governors—John Breathitt, James T. Morehead, John J. Crittenden, and Charles S. Morehead; four chief-justices—Ninian Edwards, George M. Bibb, Ephraim M. Ewing, and Elijah Hise. Five times the chief executive chairs of other States have been filled by her sons: Ninian Edwards and John McLean to Illinois, Richard K. Call to Florida, Robert Crittenden to Arkansas, and Fletcher Stockdale to Texas. Besides these, William L. D. Ewing was lieutenant-governor of Illinois. She gave one major-general to the United States army, James Boyle; and one surgeon-general to the same, Dr. D. McReynolds; and one supreme judge of Mississippi, Joseph E. Davis. All were able, accomplished, and efficient; and in addition to those there were many others not less upright, cultured, and principled, who never entered the arena of public life. In this grand county then, the subject of my sketch was educated at Bethel College, during which term of intellectual training he exhibited those characteristics which gave promise that he would some day "make his mark in the world." In 1867 he began the study of law with his uncle, Judge Bennett, and in 1873 he was admitted to the bar in Livingston county, and entered upon the practice of his profession. His energy, his studious attention to business, and his uniform good habits, united to his various exhibitions of the latent brilliance of which he was master, he won the respect and the admiration of the people, and in 1878 he was elected county attorney. In 1882 he was re-elected to the same office, and holds it at the present time. He possesses fine oratorical power; and his analytic mind renders him a foe to be dreaded by those who have given cause for their public arraignment at the bar of justice. He is now a candidate for the position of Commonwealth's attorney, in the First Judicial District, and the First Congressional District also, known in Democratic parlance as the "Gibraltar district, where Democracy runs high and patriotism never dies."

Livingston county was established in 1798, out of a part of Christian county, and named in honor of Robert P. Livingston, the distinguished American statesman, who was born in the city of New York in 1746, studied and practiced law with great success, was a member of the first general Congress, and was one of the committee which prepared the Declaration of Independence; in 1780 was appointed secretary of foreign affairs, and throughout the Revolution signalized himself by his zeal and efficiency in the cause; was for many years chancellor of his native State, and while occupying that position, in the year 1789, on the 30th day of April, he administered the oath of office, as the first President of the United States, to General George Washington, on the balcony in the front of the Federal Hall, in the presence of both branches of the National Legislature and thousands of spectators. In 1801 he was appointed by President Jefferson Minister to France. He was a general favorite at the French capital, and in conjunction with Mr. Monroe conducted the treaty which resulted in the cession of Louisiana to the United States. He died in 1813. The "old time" people of Livingston county were conversant with these historical facts, and did honor to the great man by naming their county for him by way of keeping his memory green in the hearts of his countrymen. By so doing they gave evidence of their appreciation of honor and valor. Their descendants have proven themselves worthy of their progenitors, by doing honor to another brilliant man, who, if not enabled to display the glorious national record of Robert P. Livingston, has proven himself worthy the admiration of his family, his friends, and his State. If success attends merit, if it is the test of merit, then those who cherish hopes of his election to the office to which he aspires will not find them "nipped in the bud by an untimely frost." He would reflect additional luster over "Jackson's Purchase," and crime and lawlessness would hide their uncanny heads before his fearless eyes.

It has been said that nature can not lie; that when she endows one of her children with beauty, it is but the index by which one can read the goodness of the heart; it may be that extraneous circumstances sometimes pervert this loveliness from its original atmosphere of purity and nobility; but when they are powerless to subvert, then truly must the splendor of the soul shine out with the light of the morning star. Mr. Hendrick is a man of fine *personnel*. The stamp of intellectual superiority beams from his dark eyes, and displays itself in calm self-containment of his facial expression. He has a richly-modulated voice, and when he speaks he but enhances that charm of intellectuality which wins him hosts of friends. To a singer, such a voice means gold; to an orator like John K. Hendrick it means ever increasing popularity and power to sway the multitudes.

It is to be hoped he will not fail of his noble ambition. Kentucky needs men of ability in all her positions of trust, and the First Judicial District in electing him next August will be doing itself honor, for John K. Hendrick is a man among many men; unimpeachable in character and incorruptible in mind and heart.

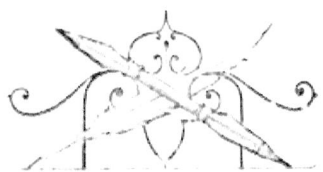

GENERAL FAYETTE HEWITT.

The present Auditor of Kentucky, General Fayette Hewitt, was born in the county of Hardin, State of Kentucky, on the 15th day of October, 1832. He is the son of Robert Hewitt and Elizabeth Chastain. Both father and mother were native Virginians, and both were persons of unusual intelligence and accomplishment. Robert Hewitt, Esq., the father of Fayette Hewitt, was a professor of languages. He was a gentleman of finished education, and for many years taught school in Elizabethtown, Ky. Fayette was carefully educated by him, and was the assistant in the college for ten years. When his father died he succeeded him in the position of principal and head of the family, on whom his mother and younger brothers were compelled to look for support; but fully capacitated as he was to be a preceptor, he had not the inclination to continue in the profession he had so long honored with his acceptance. He changed his location from Elizabethtown to Washington City, and there found employment in the Post-office Department of the United States Government. At the commencement of the civil strife, he resigned his position as early as the 4th of March, 1861, and then proceeded South, where he was retained by the postmaster general to aid in establishing the mail system of the Confederacy.

In November, 1861, he was appointed acting adjutant-general, and was assigned to duty in the Trans-Mississippi Department of the army, where he served efficiently with Generals Holmes and Pike. In March, 1863, he was ordered to report for staff duty to General John C. Breckinridge, then commanding a division in the Army of Tennessee. Later on he was assigned to duty as the acting adjutant-general of the "Orphans' Brigade." This was the Kentucky brigade, which was first commanded by General Breckinridge, subsequently by the peerless Roger Hanson and Ben Hardin Helm, and afterward by General Jo. H. Lewis, now of the Court of Appeals. The title of "Orphans' Brigade" was given it because Kentucky was in the Union, and the soldiers who were enrolled in it had therefore no mother State to furnish them with supplies, to bestow on them the blessed boon and comfort of her sympathy, nor yet to receive them when furloughs broke happily in upon the irksome monotony of camp life. It was a valiant struggle for principle they made—claiming the earth for a bed and the star-broidered canopy of heaven for a covering, and counting life from sunset to sunset, nor looking beyond it.

General Hewitt, after joining the "Orphans' Brigade," remained on duty with it until the termination of the war. He surrendered with it on the 7th day of May, 1865, at Washington, Ga., after which he returned to Elizabethtown, Ky., and assumed temporary charge of a female school. The confinement of such a position was naturally objectionable to a man who had been a soldier for four years, and he soon abandoned it, beginning the practice of law in 1866 as the partner of William Wilson, Esq. In September, 1867, he was appointed quartermaster general of Kentucky by Governor Helm. He retained this position for nine years, under Governors Stevenson and Leslie, and Governor McCreary continued him in office during a portion of his term, General Hewitt having resigned previous to its close. While serving in that capacity, General Hewitt collected from the Federal Government over two millions of dollars of Kentucky's war debt which other accredited agents of the State had endeavored but failed to collect. In 1876, he resigned his position and returned to Elizabethtown in order to recruit his health, which had become delicate, and to rest from the arduous mental labor that had taxed his brain for years.

Not satisfied, however, with so quiet a life, in 1879 he became a candidate for auditor of the State, and received the nomination over

Colonel D. Howard Smith, who had served acceptably as Kentucky's auditor for twelve years. John A. Williamson was the Republican candidate and Henry Potter, Esq., the Greenback candidate for the same position. These gentlemen were all defeated.

In 1883, General Hewitt was re-elected auditor without opposition, save that offered in the person of the Republican candidate, Mr. L. R. Hawthorn, there being no Greenback candidate.

General Hewitt is a bachelor, doubtless owing to the fact that his life has been such a busy one that he has never had time to get married, although he is universally admired by the fair sex, and the gayest ball or the most brilliant coterie would be willingly abandoned by any or all of his acquaintances for the quiet, intellectual pleasure of an evening at home with Fayette Hewitt to read aloud from a favorite author. His elocutionary powers are wonderful; his utterance is peculiarly soft and melodious for a man's voice, and his selections are always admirable. But it is only the chosen who ever hear or see him in his charming moods of sociability. To the outside world he is usually the calm, rather austere gentleman, who is devoted to his studies and fully occupied by the onerous duties of his office.

He is a gentleman of great attainments, and speaks several languages fluently. He is a thorough student, devoted to books and the fine arts. He never has time to idle away as do most men. He is always profitably engaged in some intellectual pursuit. The old revenue laws, which were most imperfect and unequal in their distribution of the burden of taxation, were remedied by the General Assembly of 1885 and 1886 by the passage of the new revenue law through a confidence in the wisdom and experience of the author of the bill, General Fayette Hewitt, than whom the State of Kentucky has never had a more honest, painstaking, and able official. His judgment was clearly manifest to the people in the operations of the new law, to which the only objectionable features urged against it were such as were not written by him, but proposed and adopted as amendments by the Legislature. The new law, on a reduced rate of taxation, will largely increase the revenue by the assessment of a species of property which has hitherto escaped the assessors. The tax-payer owning much personal property can not hereafter evade his just proportion of the government expenses by an absent-minded failure to list or properly value his personal property, under oath, and thereby shift an added burden to real estate which can not be concealed or sent out of the State, as money, stocks, mortgages, and bonds. He must make an honest return or perjure himself, and as there are few Kentuckians who are likely to do that, it might be said that the question of equalizing the taxation between the rich and poor, the farmer, manufacturer, merchant, and professional man, which has always in the past been difficult to adjust, has at last been fully met and demonstrated by the "Hewitt Bill."

General Hewitt is an attractive man. He is of medium height and slender; his eyes are dark as his hair, and his complexion is decidedly brunette. His facial expression denotes decision of character and intellectual development of the highest order. In manner he is quiet and unobtrusive, bearing with him that subtle dignity which is indefinable in words, but which commands the respect of every one who has the honor of his acquaintance, and which endears him to those who know him best.

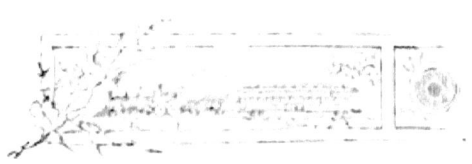

HON. JAMES R. HINDMAN.

In the inspired pages of Holy Writ it has been said that a tree may be judged by its fruit, and the ancient simile of comparing human beings to shrubs and trees is not less frequently applicable in the present day than it was in the past. The name of James R. Hindman revives the thought in my mind to-day, and surely, according to the light that ripe seed planted in rich soil brings forth good fruit, those who personally know the honorable gentleman who is the subject of my present biographical sketch must feel convinced that heaven smiled on the nuptials of Miss Margaret A. Walker and Alexander Hindman, Esq., and that genius and good fortune were the fair lady's handmaidens on the natal day of James R. Hindman, their son, blessing him beneficently with such glorious endowments as gallantry, grace, and goodness. They were Virginians. To say this is like giving a guarantee of respectability and prominence, and when, added to it, we find beauty, intellectuality, and excellence we can scarcely use words of praise sufficiently adequate to express their right to homage and admiration. The high position they held in society, and always maintained, was proof of their deserving qualities.

Their son, James R. Hindman, was born in Adair county on the 4th day of February, 1839. He was educated in the schools of Adair county, then and now considered among the most thorough in the country. To be born in Adair county is to have, as it were, a liberal education, its citizens are so free-hearted, so intelligent, so courageous and enduring—but all Kentuckians know the worth of those fellow-statesmen who live in what is known as the "Green-river country." It goes without saying that they are clever.

Mr. Alexander Hindman was by occupation a farmer, and a very successful one; but because his son James was, as a consequence, reared amid agricultural pursuits, that was no reason the brave heart of a soldier should not beat in his breast. Wrought on by enthusiasm, the youthful heroes of France could fight and die fearlessly for Napoleon—could stand like summer grass and be mowed down upon the battlefield by grapeshot, and cannon-ball, and shining sabers, even as that same grass fell beneath the keen sweep of the sickle—could face such a fate without faltering or flinching. So could the trained armies of Frederick the Great of Prussia meet such deaths and glory in their dying; but the pioneer sons of Kentucky could leave their plowshares and their firesides at the first rumor of war, and wield swords and muskets with the ease of those who are inured to the hardships of camp life, and whose serried ranks in conflict seldom know dismay. Young James R. Hindman was one of these, though born sixty-three years later than the Declaration of Independence. "The Union, indivisible and forever," seemed to be the watch-word of his soul. When the war between the sections began, he joined the Northern army as second lieutenant in Colonel Hobson's regiment, the Thirteenth infantry. He was afterward promoted to the position of captain of Company "H," of the Thirteenth infantry. He served one year as chief of ordnance of the Twenty-third Army Corps, Second division, commanded by Major-General Schofield, and he participated with gallantry and efficiency in the principal battles of the Army of the Cumberland.

In 1865, Mr. Hindman was elected to the Legislature from his native county, and so well pleased were his constituents with his ability and progressive spirit that they returned him in 1867, and still again in 1869. He was ranked among the ablest solons in the State. He studied law in Columbia, Adair county, and in 1870 he received license to practice his profession. He formed at first a partnership with Hon. H. C. Baker, and, subsequently, he formed one with John R. Sampson, the son of the late Justice Sampson, who was a judge of the Court of Appeals.

In 1872, he abandoned his state of single-blessedness and married Miss Ermina Young, on the 24th day of June. Their wedded lives were exceptionally happy. They had two sons, bright, manly youths, of whom any parents, even the most exacting, might be very proud. Their names are Robert and James. They are aged respectively twelve and seven years, and the writer of these lines ventures the prophecy that they will yet assume positions in the politics of the country and the State and national councils second to none of their day and generation. In 1879, he was again the leader of the vanguard in Adair, and, as is usual with one who does all he undertakes to do thoroughly and well, he gave entire satisfaction to his constituents.

In November, 1881, he met with affliction in the death of his estimable wife, but he did not long remain a widower. Two years later he found surcease from sorrow in marriage with Mrs. Fanny M. Raney, of Franklin, Simpson county, Ky. They were married in Dallas, Texas, on December 19, 1883. Mrs. Hindman is a most brilliant and attractive little lady. She is versatile and charming to an unusual degree, and her popularity with her many friends is only excelled by her beauty. She is young, and bids fair to queen it in society for many a bright day, no burden of domesticity shutting the sunlight away from her happy heart. Her husband is very proud of her, a compliment to her superiority which she most graciously reciprocates, for it is patent to the coldest observer that she rates him above all the world, which is a state of sentiment beautiful as it is admirable. His acquaintances all envy his felicity.

Captain Hindman is tall and spare in physique, with a manly bearing, and an intellectual face, which bespeaks the generous soul that abides within his "tenement of clay." He is universally popular. The Blue and the Gray forget party and political lines in their friendships with him. He is modest and unassuming, but it may be safely said he is one of the most prominent and promising of the public men in the State of Kentucky.

In May, 1883, when the State Convention met in Louisville, he was nominated for lieutenant-governor on the ticket with Governor Knott, and is now presiding over the Kentucky Senate.

JUDGE WILLIAM B. HOKE.

To introduce the distinguished gentleman whose name graces this article to the people of the city of Louisville and Jefferson county would scarcely be less infelicitous than to offer an introduction from an old man to his wife, with whom he had for half a century been toiling and struggling up the hill of life. Judge Hoke knows everybody, and everybody knows him, and is proud of it. He is the youngest son of Cornelius Hoke, Esq., a gentleman of German extraction, although born and reared in the county of Jefferson. He possessed both influence and popularity. His mother was Miss Jane Dunbar—a most estimable and Christian lady—whose native county was that of Nelson, and whose ancestors were of Scottish origin.

William B. Hoke was born in Jefferson county, Kentucky, on the 1st day of August, 1838. He graduated from Asbury University,

Indiana in 1857. After this he studied law with ex-Attorney General James Speed and James Beattie, Esq. Subsequently, he entered the Louisville University, graduating with honor from that institution in 1859. He was the valedictorian of his class, and a brilliant one.

Opening an office, he began the practice of his profession, which proved both lucrative and successful, his popularity being instantly assured through his extensive acquaintance and many warm friends, both in and out of the State, who took his success to heart, and left nothing undone to cheer and encourage him in his aspirations. His clientage absorbed his time and attention until 1866, when he became a candidate for the office of county judge, with Judge John Joyes and Andrew Monroe—both lawyers of reputation and marked ability—as his opponents. At the election he was chosen to preside over the county court, and for five consecutive terms he succeeded himself. He will doubtless continue to hold the office as long as it is his choice to do so, for his popularity continues and his friends are as devoted as ever to him and the cause he espouses.

He was a delegate from the Fifth Congressional District to the National Convention which nominated Tilden and Hendricks in 1876. He has had many honors and has worn them with grace, reflecting credit on every position he has filled. In the years 1880 and 1881 he was the Supreme Dictator of the Knights of Honor for the United States. For one term he was Supreme Chief of the Order of Foresters for the United States, and in 1878 declined a re-election to that office. In 1879, he was the Past Grand Chancellor for the Knights of Pythias. To this position also he declined re-election, offered by acclamation. He was recently selected as the representative of Kentucky to the convention of the "Chosen Friends," which was held in New York city, September 1, 1885, from which it will be seen that honors assuring him of the confidence and respect of his fellowmen are still tendered to him.

He has gone through all the degrees of Free Masonry, and has been one of the Board of Trustees of the Masonic Widows' and Orphans' Home from the time of its organization to the present day. This institution is a shining mark made to the credit of Masonry, whose silver light vies with the glory of the stars, for its radiance reaches the shadowed homes of many helpless widows and orphans. Its existence in Kentucky gives luster to her borders, since it is the only home of the kind in the United States. It was established and is maintained strictly by the Masonic brotherhood.

Before he was eligible to fill the position, Judge Hoke twice received the Democratic nomination to the Legislature. His popularity has never seemed to be confined to locality—it is universal—and wheresoever he goes, or has gone, he has increased it by his courteous manners and his fine conversational powers. In presence he is portly and elegant—just such a man as seems born to preside. The brightest and most lovable side of his nature is seen at home, which to him is indeed "the dearest spot of earth." His wife was Miss Wharton English. She is a most estimable and excellent lady, full of intelligence and noble charities, respected by her associates and beloved by her friends. She has added much to the popularity of her husband by her wisdom and goodness. Their home is blessed with bright and attractive children, and is the center of enjoyment to their many friends.

Judge Hoke was re-elected county judge in August, 1886, without opposition.

HON. WILLIAM L. JACKSON, JR.

To one who takes pride in the grandeur of his State as I do, in its varied and beautiful scenery, its lovely women, and its magnificent men, it can but be a source of pleasure to record the worth and excellence of those who have given that State distinction and added honor and brilliance to her escutcheon by the enrollment of their worthy names upon it.

The subject of to-day's sketch—William L. Jackson, Jr.—though younger in years than any of the distinguished gentlemen whose biographies I have written, has availed himself of every opportunity Fate and Fortune have offered him to prove to the people of Kentucky that he will reflect credit upon every position of trust he may ever fill. His mother was Miss Sarah E. Creel, of Virginia, a most excellent and accomplished lady. His father is Judge William L. Jackson, who presides over the Jefferson Circuit Court, and who also claims Virginia as his mother State. He was a candidate for lieutenant-governor of Virginia on the ticket with Henry A. Wise when he made his famous race in 1855 against the Know-Nothing party, and, being the candidate of the Democratic party of Virginia, the eye of the nation was turned upon that State, and the result of the canvass was the election of the entire Democratic ticket. Judge Jackson filled many offices of public trust in Virginia before the erection of the State of Western Virginia. After the war, he removed to Kentucky and began the practice of law in Louisville, in 1865. On the 1st of January, 1866, he was joined in this city by his family, and their adoption of Kentucky as their future home was assured, and from that time their interests became identified with hers.

William L. Jackson, Jr., was born in St. Mary's, Wood county, Va., the 12th day of August, 1854. In 1875, he graduated from the Louisville High School as the valedictorian of his class. He chose the profession of law as the one best adapted to his inclination and ambition, and, after earnest prosecution of his studies, graduated from the University of Law in this city in 1877, and immediately thereafter opened an office, with young Henry Clay, deceased, as a partner. After Mr. Clay was elected Prosecuting Attorney of the City Court of Louisville, they dissolved partnership, and in August, 1881, Mr. Jackson was elected to the Legislature. He has succeeded himself for two consecutive terms. He is recognized as one of the most brilliant and promising of the rising young men of Louisville. As a lawyer, no commendation, written or uttered, can enhance the luster of the noble reputation he has already made for himself, for the reason that he inherits his knowledge of law from his distinguished father. The name of "Jackson" is dear to the American people. It carries with it a national recognition of personal courage and taste for political preferment. No name in the United States is more loved or more honored than this. Andrew Jackson, who was the seventh president of the United States, and who was first inaugurated on March 4, 1829, left an impress upon the annals of this country which will live as long as liberty endures; and coming generations will recall his noble and valorous deeds with that pride which stimulates every American who has love for his country and who glories in American independence. History owes reverence to the names of those who give it luster, and it pays its debts with unstinted measure. It is but justice rendered to those to whom it is due, for they formulated the future of America and gave impetus to the development of her powers; and, no matter how grand and expansive may have been her progress and enlightenment, in the untrodden ages — not one of us will live to welcome — the hearts of those who come after us will throb as lustily as our own to recall the events that marked the eras when men tilled the soil and waged war; when they endured and died in the service of their native land while it was yet a wilderness, glorying in their privations, buoyed on forever with the winged dream, the halcyon hope, of the coming time when the dissemination of knowledge, the whirr of machinery, the building of cities, the linking of States, should mark an opened and prosperous country, recognized and honored by other nations, and inviting the competition of the industries, the arts, and the sciences of the world.

Well may our popular and distinguished legislator take pride in the knowledge that his progenitors have left their names and the memory of their devotion to American Independence graven upon the hearts of the people!

Mr. Jackson is a man of distinguished and attractive *personnel*. He has blonde hair, and eyes of "heaven's own blue." His address is graceful and persuasive, and well calculated to confirm a popularity which is beyond question, and everywhere well sustained.

HON. RICHARD A. JONES

There are but few, if any, gentlemen in Kentucky who are better or more favorably known than he whose name leads this biographical sketch. He is a man of "infinite variety," and his popularity is unbounded. His friends think of him with the gentle regards and respectful delicacy due to the fair sex only. Not that he is at all effeminate, for he is the soul of manliness and honor; but there is about him that refined sensibility, that genial consideration for others which usually belongs to women. Candidly, he is the only man I ever met who, in every relation in life, makes the "Golden Rule" the precept and the moral of his existence. It seems to be the impulse and the habit of his heart and mind to love the world, and to be kind to his fellowmen. The incalculable advantages of the society of such a man in the social circle can scarcely be aggregated in a volume, much less a sketch, brief as this is necessarily compelled to be.

Richard A. Jones is the second son of W. L. Jones and Lucy Dent Fox. William L. Jones was born in Shelby county in 1815.

He was emphatically a gentleman of influence, probity, and diffuse popularity. He was devoted to his business pursuits, and seldom went out of his way to "dabble in politics," or to seek public office, although he did represent the county (Shelby) in the House of Representatives in the General Assembly of Kentucky from 1846 to 1848; but he was a prominent and popular citizen, and counted his friends by the host. In after years he removed to the city of Louisville, Ky., where he died in 1863, lamented by all those who knew him. His widow still survives him, and is a lady of sterling worth and undaunted energy. She has accomplished what one woman in a thousand is able to do. With great honor and credit to herself, she has combated with the difficulties that confronted her in the struggle of life, and she has succeeded. Her native place is Alexandria, Va., but her people moved to Kentucky at an early day, settling in the county of Nelson. And thus it was that Kentucky became her adopted State. She is certainly a credit to it and to herself.

Richard A. Jones, her son, was born in Shelby county, Ky., on the 18th day of December, 1846. Perhaps more sunshine and gladness hallowed his youth than falls to the lot of most men, and thus renders explainable the sunny-heartedness, the charming propulsions of enthusiasm which to this day are so evident in his nature and disposition. When his parents came to Louisville to reside young Jones attended the high school of the city, from which he graduated in 1861. This school fostered the intellects of more than one of our prominent and rising young men, among whom may be particularly mentioned as residing in this city the names of A. G. Caruth, A. S. Willis, and W. L. Jackson, Jr. There are many more whose hearts turn to the same Alma Mater, who have settled in different parts of the State, or who have gone to seek their fortunes in the far wilds, or the prosperous cities and hamlets of the West or South.

Mr. Jones studied law with Hamilton Pope, Esq., and in 1866 he graduated from the Louisville University of Law, after which he duly entered upon the practice of his profession in this city.

In the Greely campaign of 1872 Mr. Jones was chosen, in the Democratic Convention, elector from the Fifth Congressional District, in which position he did valiant service to his party and won for himself an undying record for eloquent oratory. In 1873 he was elected to the Legislature. In August, 1882, he was re-elected, and again was he re-elected in August, 1885. He is recognized as a ready debater and a man of elegant finish. He is more universally popular than any man in the State. Such is my own warm personal feeling for him that my heart swells with the impulse to supersede the name of

"State" by the word "nation," for indeed "none know him but to love him." Mr. Jones has twice canvassed the State for attorney-general, and has lost the nomination in two State conventions by small majorities, but these were supplemented by overwhelming regrets on the part of his friends and well-wishers. Regrets, however, bring no emoluments of office.

In 1885 Mr. Jones wrote a book, entitled, "Sand-bagged; a Tale of Any City," which is now completed and ready for publication. A rich literary treat is in store for those who enjoy romance, wit, and humor. As a writer Mr. Jones is recognized by the press of the State for his pithy, pertinent sayings, he having on divers occasions accepted the editorial chairs of the gentlemen of the quill while they paid visits to "French Lick," or some other health-giving resort whose springs spout something else beside chalybeate water. The representative men of Kentucky all know Colonel Jones, and universally speak of him as a princely gentleman, who bears no ill will to any living thing. In manner he is as gentle as the most *suave* lady who ever queened it in aristocratic drawing-rooms. He is unmarried, and rapidly approaching the line of confirmed bachelorhood. Once over the border of this state of semi-existence, the fair sex never send a flag of truce, and manifest no interest in a man's future salvation. Mr. Jones' many friends hope that in this regard a word to the wise may prove a sufficiency.

HON. LAFAYETTE JOSEPH.

Gallatin county was the thirty-third county erected in the State of Kentucky. It was taken from the counties of Franklin and Shelby in 1798, and named in honor of Albert Gallatin, who was born at Geneva, Switzerland, on the 29th of January, 1761. In his infancy he was left an orphan; but through the beneficent thoughtfulness and generous protection of one of his mother's female relatives, he was enabled to receive a thorough education, and graduated at the University of Geneva in 1779. His family were wealthy and prominent, being composed of people of the highest respectability. Knowing full well that consent would be withheld, if sought, when only nineteen years of age, young Albert, in company with a youthful comrade, left home to seek glory and fortune, and more than all, liberty of thought and speech, in the infant republic of America. Dr. Franklin was then in Paris, and to him young Gallatin bore the recommendation of a friend. He came to America, arriving in Boston in July, 1780, and not long thereafter he proceeded to Maine, and purchasing land in that State, he resided there until the close of the year 1781. While there he served as a volunteer under Colonel John Allen, and made advances from his private purse for the support of the garrison. In the spring of 1782 he was appointed instructor in the French language at Harvard University. He occupied this position about a year. In 1783 he went to Virginia to attend to the claims of a European house for advances made to that State. Here it was he became acquainted with the great orator and patriot, Patrick Henry, and by him he was treated with marked kindness and respect. It was under the advice of Governor Henry that young Gallatin sought his fortune in the new and wild country then just opening on the Ohio. He purchased a large tract of land in Fayette county, Pa., December, 1785, and there he made his residence. His talent was pre-eminent and brilliant for public life, and soon becoming generally known, in 1789 he was elected to a seat in the convention to amend the Constitution of Pennsylvania. In 1793 he was elected to the United States Senate, but lost his seat on the ground that he had not been nine years a legally naturalized citizen of the United States. Soon after this he married the daughter of Commodore Nicholson. In 1794 he was elected to Congress. While in Congress, where he continued three terms, he was distinguished as a leader of the Democratic party. In 1801 Mr Jefferson appointed him secretary of the treasury, which post he filled with pre-eminent ability for several years. In 1813 he was made one of the commissioners to negotiate the treaty of Ghent, and was afterward associated with Messrs. Clay and Adams, at London, in negotiating the treaty with Great Britain. He continued in Europe as ambassador at Paris until 1823, when he returned to America.

In honor, then, of this brilliant and distinguished man, the county of Gallatin was named. In 1819 some of its territory was taken in forming Owen county; in 1836 another portion was appropriated in forming Trimble, and in 1838 the entire western portion was cut off and called Carroll county. Gallatin county is situated in the northern part of the State. Its surface is generally hilly, but it is well timbered with poplar, walnut, ash, beech, oak, hickory, and sugar-trees. The soil is generally productive, especially the river and creek bottoms. Much attention is given to stock-raising, because of the luxuriant growth of grass and clover. And the facilities of reaching the markets of Cincinnati and Louisville by the Ohio river on one border, and the Short Line railroad through the other, have developed gardening and the culture of small fruits. It was to this county, so full of natural resources and beauty, that Isaac Joseph, Esq., came in the year 1837. He located in Napoleon, a town of the aforesaid county, and became at once a citizen of recognized probity and ability, and readily won the respect and esteem of his associates, and the years only added to his widespread popularity. His wife's maiden name was Miss Caroline Lieberman, and with her husband she divided the laurels of respect and popularity, for she was eminently a lady of noble character and fine sense.

Lafayette Joseph, Esq., the subject of my sketch, was a native of Gallatin county, being the second son of Isaac Joseph and Caroline Lieberman. He was born on the 4th day of May, 1842, and was educated in the public schools of Louisville. He also matriculated at Asbury University, Indiana, which is now known as the DePauw University, and from that institution of learning he graduated in the class of 1865. Afterward he entered the law office of L. N. Dembitz, of this city, as a student of law. The community in which he lives—Louisville, Ky.—know well who Mr. Dembitz is, and what his legal acumen is generally acknowledged to be. At present he is the able assistant city attorney. He is generally recognized as one of the most scholarly men at the bar.

In 1865 Mr. Joseph matriculated at the law department of the University of Louisville, and from that old and reputable institution he graduated in 1866, after which he formed a partnership in the law with his distinguished preceptor, L. N. Dembitz, who is conceded to be not only a lawyer of great prominence, but the best mathematician in Louisville.

In 1869 Mr. Joseph was elected by the school board of the city of Louisville as its attorney, in which position he served with great credit until 1872. In August, 1872, he was elected prosecuting attorney of the Louisville city court, in which position he served the people for two years. In 1879 he was elected to the board of common council of the city of Louisville, and was chosen as the president of that body. He occupied that position for five consecutive terms, and it has often been declared that he was the most finished parliamentarian who ever occupied the chair. Mr. Joseph served through the administrations of both Mayors Baxter and Jacobs, and he is yet a member of the board of councilmen.

In 1882 he formed a law partnership with Humphrey Marshall, who is a son of the late General Humphrey Marshall, the greatest intellect, the grandest soul, the truest heart that was ever shrined in human form. And being gone, no man will look upon his like again. The firm name reads "Joseph & Marshall." They have a fine, lucrative commercial practice in this city, being the attorneys of some of the largest wholesale houses on Main street. They are also the attorneys of the Golden King Mining Company, and the Snider Land &

Stock Company, and also of the Kentucky, Kansas, and Texas Land & Cattle Company, which owns large bodies of land in those States. They are likewise the attorneys of the Ohio Valley Cement Company, which is furnishing the cement necessary for the erection of the capitol building at Austin, Texas. In addition to those mentioned, they are attorneys for other large and flourishing corporations. Mr. Marshall possesses the massive frame, and much of the massive intellect of his distinguished father. He is the descendant of a race of lawyers, almost all of whom have left the impress of their genius and judgment upon the jurisprudence of the country, and Mr. Marshall bids fair to emulate the brilliant examples set before him. Mr. Joseph is one of the best known men in Kentucky. He is a finished gentleman, a man of profound acumen, being one of the best judges and readers of human nature it has ever been my good fortune to meet. He is a clear and forcible speaker, and whoever confronts him in argument, whether before legislative committees or at the bar, will find a lion in his path. Those who heard his arguments last winter in behalf of the Louisville Gas Company, before the committees of the General Assembly of Kentucky, will bear me out in my assertion, for here he was confronted by the best legal minds in the State, and they conceded his power and brilliant ability.

In the city of Cincinnati, Ohio, on the 23d day of December, 1873, Mr. Joseph was married to Miss Julia Heinsheirmer, a lady of great beauty and many accomplishments. Her family is one of the finest in Cincinnati in point of wealth and social prominence, and Mr. Joseph certainly " drew a prize in life's lottery " in winning her affection and her consent to share his fortunes, good or ill, in this world.

Mr. Joseph is well and favorably known to all the representative men of his native State. He is universally popular, and everywhere regarded as a man of high literary attainments and sterling worth. He is yet in the prime of life, and a brilliant future is before him. For charity, liberality, and popularity, he is noted wherever he is known. He is positively without stint in his friendships. Those who care for him at all love him sincerely. He has a most affectionate and gentle nature. His hand is never closed when an appeal is made for or by the needy, and his sympathy is as boundless as the roll of the seas.

HON. J. D. KEHOE.

The subject of this sketch, John Dexter Kehoe, was born on the 24th day of March, 1854, in Lewis county, Ky., and very early in his boyhood his widowed mother removed with her family of boys to Maysville. Born in honorable poverty, his fight for existence with the big world commenced when he was eight years old. Beginning at twelve years of age, in a printing office in Maysville, the work of his life, he began at the same time a systematic and rigid course of self-instruction, in the face of difficulties that might appall the stoutest heart. Having worked with merited success in several Maysville offices until 1873, he then went to Cincinnati, where he remained two years under the instruction of the celebrated Harpel, and other masters of the "art preservative of all arts." Returning to Maysville he worked as foreman in the *Excelsior* office, and in 1876 established his own printing works, which he still maintains under the management of a younger brother.

He has been an active worker in politics since he was nineteen years old, and has again and again been honored by his constituents with places of profit and honor. In 1878 he was city clerk of Maysville, and has always been an active worker in all enterprises looking to the upbuilding of his adopted city. In 1879 he was the Democratic nominee for a seat in the Legislature from the county of Mason, and in a contest of great heat and asperity was defeated by Hon. Robert Cochran, one of the wealthiest citizens of Mason, by a majority of only two votes. He was again nominated in 1881 by his party, and elected by a handsome majority. In the Legislature of 1881 and 1882, he was a prominent, though unsuccessful, candidate for public printer. In 1883 he was re-nominated by his party, after a close and exciting contest with Hon. A. P. Gooding, and in the August election of the same year he defeated A. A. Wadsworth, Esq., by a large majority. Speaking of his political experience, the Vanceburg *Kentuckian* said:

"Although there were evidently grounds for a contest, Mr. Kehoe refused to resort to this mode of obtaining office, but again announced himself a candidate in 1881, and was triumphantly elected. During his term of office he proved himself to be a man of more than ordinary intelligence and ability, and labored hard and unceasingly as a representative of the people's interests, making himself familiar with the business of the Legislature and the departments, and is consequently capable of accomplishing more by his experience of one term than any new member whom the people could elect. In his campaigns, it is said that Mr. Kehoe did not spend a cent outside of legitimate campaign expenses, even refusing money which was tendered him. This, of itself, is sufficient argument in favor of his re-election, and proves beyond question the noble qualities of the man who can hold his strength and win a race in the face of fierce and determined moneyed opposition. As a printer Mr. Kehoe has no superior in the United States, and his elegant office is sought by all business men who desire the best work that can be accomplished with type."

Since 1884, while he has continued to hold his residence in Maysville, he has been prominently identified with *The Capital*, and the office of Public Printer and Binder, at Frankfort.

Mr. Kehoe is eminently a man of the people. Frank, open, and courteous in manner, there is little about him to indicate the self-made man, but his friends understand perfectly his tendencies and sympathies are with the men of brawn. With the laboring classes of his own section he is the recognized leader, and he is more—he is their idol. Among the young politicians of the State, there is not one who possesses more elements of strength than does Mr. Kehoe, and the history of Kentucky politics for the next twenty years can not be written with his name left out.

In 1884, Mr. Kehoe made what came near being a winning fight for the Democratic nomination for Congress in the Ninth district. He needed only the fraction of a vote to secure the nomination in the district convention, and, while failing himself to receive the honor, he was able to dictate the nominee of the convention. He was again a candidate in 1886, Judge Wall, of Mason, and himself holding a primary in that county to decide the question of their candidacy. Refusing to spend money in the primary, he was defeated, and gave to his successful antagonist a cordial and earnest support in the ensuing canvass between Messrs. Wall and Thomas.

The sentiments of Mr. Kehoe's friends can not be better expressed than in the language of the gentleman who nominated him for Public Printer in 1881. Referring to the need of such men in public life, he said:

"For twenty years Kentucky has been kneeling with idolatrous devotion at the shrine of her dead heroes. Forgetting the work, she has deified the workmen. Other States and other peoples have passed us on the highway of progress, as tourists in Italy tell us they sometimes pass a devout pilgrim counting upon bended knees his beads before a wayside cross. With a veneration for the heroes and a respect for the worshipers that will not be misunderstood, there are yet those among us who insist that the energy and enterprise, the brain and muscle, that have pushed ahead of us, those who started behind us a hundred years ago, will also send the warm blood of a new and vigorous life pulsing through the veins of our body politic and place the grand *new Commonwealth* of Kentucky, where we have fondly but vainly imagined the *grand old* Commonwealth stood—a star of the first magnitude in the constellation of States. The pluck and energy, the brain power and the heart power of this young son of the new Commonwealth would shine with resplendent luster among your jewels if you would make them yours. The tender of his services, if accepted by you, will mark an era in your history, will be a trumpet-tongued declaration of your sympathy with the struggling young brain and muscle of our State that can not prove more agreeable to him than inspiring to thousands he represents."

As a member of the Legislature, Mr. Kehoe was generously complimented by the State papers. As a sample, we give the following from the Lexington *Daily Press:*

"Among the prominent and leading members of the Legislature who is surely and steadily making himself felt all over the State is the Hon. J. D. Kehoe, of Mason. We express not our own but rather the judgment of his fellow-members and of the prominent men of the

State who, gathered to Frankfort by every cause, have had occasion to note his standing and course. There is not in the Legislature a gentleman of clearer or more level head; not one expresses himself more forcibly and in language more chaste, and no one is listened to with more respectful attention, for it is recognized that he never arises simply to be heard, but always to state and urge a substantial proposition in a forcible and original style. Mr. Kehoe disdains all clap-trap, and is what might be called a practical legislator, seeking to inaugurate such legislation as will advance the public interest; in short, he is one of the most valuable men in the service of the State."

Mr. Kehoe is of Irish descent, and has five brothers and two sisters, all living, his brothers being well known as prosperous business men in the State. His mother still resides at Maysville.

JUDGE WILLIAM LINDSAY.

The State of Virginia is the oldest of the permanent settlements made by the English, and the oldest of the thirteen States that confederated at the Revolution. The story is familiar to all; how it was settled by a party of English, led by the celebrated Captain John Smith, in 1607, and had in its earliest career great difficulties to contend with in the varying forms of famine, disease, and hostilities of the natives, often incited to depredations by worthless settlers; how in the autumn of 1816 the most serious rebellion broke out because Berkeley refused to commission Bacon to lead the whites against the savages who had invaded their settlements, slaughtering, burning, and pillaging, as it was their custom to do; how, in defiance of the governor, the people arose, with Bacon at their head, and cried revolt; how Bacon was declared a rebel; how, as a consequence, civil war began, in which conflict Jamestown was burnt, and the total defeat of the governor was prevented only by the unexpected death of Bacon; how many of Bacon's party were put to death; how a new charter was granted to Virginia, but depriving her of some of her privileges as a punishment for her rebellion, which charter was soon afterward annulled by Charles II. because of the discontent of the people. Then, in 1752, Washington, quite a young man at the time, was sent by Governor Dinwiddie as an envoy to the French commander at Fort Du Quesne (Pittsburg), and two years after, at the head of four hundred men he defeated the French party at the Great Meadows, but was obliged to capitulate shortly afterward to nearly a quadruple force. In 1775, Washington served as a colonel in Braddock's army, and saved it from utter ruin. In the conduct of the war, and in the events leading thereto, Virginia took an active part, and to the army and the nation she gave that noble and illustrious chief, whose wisdom and firmness not only conducted us through the perils of the seven years' war, but also contributed so much toward establishing our government on a firm basis. Besides Washington, Virginia has given many eminent statesmen and soldiers to our country. There was Jefferson, Madison, Monroe, the two Lees, Patrick Henry, Chief-Justice Marshall, Henry Clay, and a number of others for the early days of her settlement, and in later years many more who were not less brave, illustrious, and gifted. On her soil occurred several notable events of the Revolution, the most prominent among them being the surrender at Yorktown, October, 1781, which virtually put an end to the war. And in the late civil strife scarce a road within her borders but has been fought over by her sons against opposing forces, and again and again has her brown breast been deluged with the blood of her children, and the blood of the valiant children of her sister States of the South, shed in defense of what they esteemed to be their rights. Virginia is a wonderful land. Rich in minerals (and some of the precious metals), such as gold, copper, iron, lead, coal, salt, plumbago, gypsum, porcelain, clay, fine granite, slate, marble, etc. Then her objects of interest are many and remarkable, the best known to the outside world being her medicinal springs. But above and beyond all, commencing at the north, is the far-famed passage of the Potomac through the Blue Ridge at Harper's Ferry, so eulogized by Jefferson. Then there are caves, and the Chimneys in Augusta county, and the celebrated Natural Bridge in Rockbridge county, the Peaks of Otter in Bedford, and the White Top Mountain in Grayson, the Natural Tunnel in Scott county, through which a stream passes under an arch of seventy feet in elevation, and twice that thickness of superincumbent earth, and many more natural curiosities too numerous to mention in this restricted space. The day will come, as it ought to come, when Americans will care less about traveling in Europe and viewing the "wonders" of the Old World, while they neglect the beautiful around them lying,

"Offering up its low, perpetual hymn."

And when that auspicious period shall arrive, Virginia can scarcely fail to attract extensive travel within her borders among wealthy pleasure-seekers and valetudinarians. She has no Niagara, but her springs are situated among the mountains, abounding in the most picturesque scenery imaginable. One needs to care less about the Pyramids, and the Sphinx, and the Cheops, and the blue of Egyptic skies; less about the ruins around Rome, and the Parthenon at Athens, until they visit the caves, the springs, the mountains, the water-falls, and the natural bridges of Virginia. "Know thyself," runs the ancient Persian maxim, and it might be aptly added, "And know thy country next."

The great natural "lions" of Virginia are the "Hawk's Nest," nine miles from White Sulphur Springs, on New river, where there is a perpendicular cliff of one thousand feet above the river, declared by Miss Martineau to have produced on her mind a greater effect than did Niagara and the world-renowned Natural Bridge, over Cedar creek, in Rockbridge county, formed probably either by the action of water during the long course of ages on the subjacent rock, or by some convulsion of the earth. The fissure is about ninety feet wide; the height of the underside of the arch two hundred, and of the upperside two hundred and forty feet above the water. High up, on this rock, carved by his own hand, the loftier name of Washington stands engraved. Rockbridge county is situated in the central part of Virginia. The soil is highly productive. The capital is Lexington, a handsome post village. It is situated in a valley surrounded by the most beautiful mountain scenery. Washington College was founded at this place in 1798, and endowed by General Washington. It has a library running away up into the thousands. The Virginia Military Institute was established here also by the Legislature of Virginia, in 1838 and 1839. Many brilliant men of the past and the present have received their training here; and dear to the heart of every Southron is the thought that in this hallowed place, called Lexington, our gallant Stonewall Jackson sleeps his last long sleep, from which he will never awaken, until the Trump of Doom shall sound, and the reveille call him forth to the light of Eternal Morning. But that which allies the interest of Kentuckians most closely with Rockbridge county is the knowledge that the late chief-justice of Kentucky, Judge William Lindsay, was born within its borders, on September 4, 1835, and that he was also educated there. Judge Lindsay is descended from Scotch ancestry. In 1854 he moved to Hickman county, Ky.; in 1858 he qualified for and practiced law at Clinton, the county-seat of Hickman. He volunteered and served bravely through the war in the Confederate army, as captain and as staff officer. In 1865, when the rebellion was ended, he was paroled with many others as a prisoner of war, at Columbus, Miss. His heart led him to the home of his adoption, and after so long an absence he resumed the practice of law at Clinton. In 1867 he was elected senator in the General Assembly of Kentucky; and in 1870 he was elected judge on the appellate bench of Kentucky, at the early age of thirty-five. Beyond his attainment of judicial honors, he has remained a private citizen, pursuing the even tenor of his way, building up for himself a large and lucrative practice. He is often spoken of in admiring and respectful terms as a probable and most worthy aspirant for gubernatorial honors, or the United States senatorship. But from him on these subjects the public hears nothing. He seems satisfied with the distinction already conferred on him, and emulous only of increasing success in his splendid profession. As a lawyer and a jurist he has very few equals. He is able, firm, and incorruptible. His clear, comprehensive, and profound appreciation of legal rights and responsibilities is admirable and eloquent of his noble character and fine analytic mind. He is possessed of a commanding presence and an unusually intelligent and expressive face. His manner is to all alike, earnest and kind; his conversation is frequently brilliant and sparkling, but always characterized by that rare good sense which is his strongest point.

He is happily married, and possesses one of the most delightful and elegant homes in the State of Kentucky. He entertains with the same broad munificence that he displays about everything. Nature made him on a grand scale, and his contact with the world has never dwindled his capabilities to suit the "common herd." He is a man of mark. He is a source of delight to his many friends, from a social point of view, and the object of their ambitious dreams of a future life of public usefulness. He deserves success, and he has won it by the might of his genius.

HON. EMMET GARVIN LOGAN.

The Logans were almost co-equal with Daniel Boone, the McAfees, the McCouns, the Taylors, and Bullitts, in coming to Kentucky at an early day (1775), while it was yet a wilderness, and establishing a fort in what is now known as Lincoln county. They were not guided in their wanderings by emblazoned trees, showing them the path through the wild and gloomy forests, where the wolf and the bear, the fleet-footed deer and the buffalo, roamed at will.

They depended alone on their individual, personal prowess, and their knowledge of the use of firearms. And urgent need had they for them; for the ensuing year (1776) was the most memorable one in the early history of Kentucky, because it was one of peculiar peril. The woods surrounded with savages, who were excited to desperation by the white settlements that were being made in their hunting-grounds. There was no species of outrage possible to be committed against the whites that they left undone in order to destroy them. They stimulated themselves with the cruelest ingenuity to overwhelm and exterminate them. Chief among the pioneers stood the grand

and noble form of Benjamin Logan. He seemed to tower above his fellow men, to dominate them by his bravery, his good sense, and his lofty principles. He was one of the boldest, as he was one of the earliest, pioneers, and those who penetrated the Western wilds at the time that he did looked to him for guidance and encouragement, and they never looked in vain. The high and manly qualities of courage, sagacity, and fortitude that he possessed eminently fitted him to be a leader. He was one of nature's noblemen, and needed no titles to make him great.

It was in varying degrees with all who bore the name in Kentucky. They were fearless and daring; they penetrated the wilderness, and by the aid of their compeers drove the wily red man from his chosen hunting-ground. They felled the forest, builded forts, aided in opening up the country and making for us the inheritance we now enjoy.

To read the present statistics of Kentucky, and then revert to those early days, makes the thoughtful student of human nature sigh, that those who endured so much for the advancement of civilization and the aggrandizement of posterity should be so soon forgotten.

Their names ought to be household words. The youths who gather about our hearthstones, who are our embryo statesmen and rulers, should be regaled with stories of Western adventure, peril, and enterprise, as a part of their education; and family traditions, involving the endurance and daring of Kentucky pioneers, should be cherished with the family Bible. Their young hearts ought to swell with admiration, pride, and reverence for those who dared so much and accomplished so much for them.

What matters it that they should burn with youthful ardor when reading of the famous Athenians, and the heroic actions of the Romans, if they remain in ignorance, or panoplied with indifference toward their splendid ancestors, whose exploits were a thousand times more brilliant, and whose great and honorable deeds have in the main gone unrecorded for the want of historians eloquent to do them justice?

Now and then we meet with a youth of the present generation who cares for Kentucky history, but only now and then. Better would it be to bring home to the hearts of our school-boys their hereditary right to the qualities of endurance, abnegation, courage, and fortitude, by putting into their hands the histories of Collins and Smith, and bidding them read, profit, and emulate their ancestors, than it is to buy for them text-books about Rome and Greece, and histories of ancient feuds and   fought on the other side of the world.

From 1775 to the present time in 1886, the Logans have been a great clan, and not least among them is Emmet Garvin Logan, whose distinguished name graces my biographical sketch of to-day. His father was Benjamin Harrison Logan, of Shelby county, Ky., a gentleman who was full of ability and spirit, and whose pride in the development and advancement of his native State was the ruling principle of his life. His wife was Miss Martha Williamson, of Montgomery county, Tenn., a lady of noblest qualities of head and heart, and above all others worthiest to be the mother of the brilliant and promising son whose genius and ability have shed such luster upon journalism in Kentucky.

This son, Emmet Garvin Logan, was born in Shelby county, Ky., on the 9th day of October, 1848. During his early years he was educated under the late James W. Dodd, but at a more advanced age he matriculated at the Washington and Lee University, in Virginia, from which institution he graduated with distinction in the month of June, 1871.

While at college Mr. Logan became especially distinguished on account of his wonderful fluency as a speaker. It was perhaps at the middle of his first session that he was chosen as one of the society orators. At the literary joust he covered himself with glory. His subject was an oration on Lord Byron, and it is said that he electrified his large and critical audience by his eloquence, his delivery, and his presence. Like the "Great Unknown," he awoke one morning to find himself famous. He took it coolly, as he takes everything. He became the boast and pride of the many Kentuckians who were also matriculated at the university, and whenever he appeared in the charmed circles of society he was the "idol" and the "lion," for his personal good looks are only rivaled by his genius and his grace of manner. Perhaps no man in Kentucky has been so richly endowed in these qualities of fascination as Mr. Emmet G. Logan. His face is very handsome, his physique graceful and elegant, and his height unusually commanding.

When Mr. Logan returned to Kentucky he made his first venture into the strange realm of journalism. He started a weekly paper which he called the *Courant*. He edited it with exceeding ability. He attracted universal attention to its brilliant columns. Prophecies were made on all sides that his future would be distinguished and useful. The enterprise, however, was not a successful one, from a financial point of view, owing perhaps to the location in which he made his venture. Not Shelby county, any more than any other county, but Kentucky does not seem to be prolific in any locality of successful literary enterprises. The publication of the *Courant* was abandoned; but it had established Mr. Logan as a brilliant and versatile writer. He readily obtained a position on the *Courier-Journal*. He became editor of the Kentucky and Southern news column, and under his management it became a decided feature of the paper. For several years he remained on the editorial corps of the *Courier-Journal*. Governor Underwood, however, started the *Intelligencer* at Bowling Green, and Mr. Logan's services were engaged for its columns, in conjunction with the Hon. E. Polk Johnston, than whom there is not a more popular and brilliant man in Kentucky. To praise Polk Johnston to Kentuckians is like "carrying coals to Newcastle."

The *Courier-Journal* proprietors soon found that the loss of Emmet Garvin Logan's talents to its columns was too sensibly felt for them not to endeavor to regain him for their corps. He was offered the position of managing editor if he would return. He did so, and he filled the position with great credit to himself and to the entire satisfaction of the readers and proprietors of that great and influential organ. He was especially famous for his terse, pungent, pointed paragraphs, and his contributions were recognized instantly whenever they appeared. He contributed many leading editorials that were frequently attributed to Mr. Watterson.

In October, 1882, Governor Underwood again essayed the venture of a newspaper enterprise. This time it was in Ohio, under the caption of the Cincinnati *News*. He prevailed on Mr. Logan to accept the managing editorship, making the pecuniary inducement a question of such brilliant force that it was not to be ignored by any business man, no matter how careless he was, usually, in business matters.

He again allied his fortunes with those of Governor Underwood. He assumed the management of the *News*, and under his control it took a prominent place in Ohio politics, and was acknowledged to be the principal factor in the election of Governor Hoadly, in that usually Republican State.

This position of managing editor Mr. Logan held for two years, after which period of time he returned to Louisville, where, in May, 1884, with his old friend and co-laborer, Colonel E. Polk Johnston, he launched on the sea of journalism that natty, popular, successful little craft, the Louisville *Evening Times*. He has made the paper a power in all classes of society. It finds its way everywhere, and is everywhere regarded as a cheerful, sunshiny friend. Its wit sparkles and overflows like froth on champagne. Its paragraphs are an ever recurring delight. Rumor has it that Mr. Logan intends to abandon journalism and confine himself to rural pursuits. For the sake of the public generally, and himself particularly, we hope this is not true. Such lights as the mind of Emmet Garvin Logan should not be "hid under a bushel." He belongs to the world of letters, and he should not abandon the fields of fame for the tillage of less productive soil.

Mr. Logan, on the 30th day of November, 1881, was married to Miss Lena Covington, daughter of Dr. Albert Covington, a prominent physician of Warren county. She is a lady of rare refinement and finished attainments. Few ladies in the State equal her in beauty and culture. Two children have blessed their union: Wells Covington Logan, a bright, handsome boy, and Emmet Garvin Logan, another boy, of only a few weeks advent into this weary old world of ours, but by his sprightliness and beauty even now giving promise of being an ornament to society in the future years that lie untrodden before him—a source of pride to his native State, and the object of love and admiration to his friends and his relations.

HON. JAMES B. McCREARY.

The present member of Congress from the Eighth Congressional District, Hon. James B. McCreary, was born in the county of Madison, in the State of Kentucky, on the 8th day of July, 1838. His father, Dr. E. R. McCreary, was descended from a fine old Virginia family, which prided itself upon its ancestral lines. The maiden name of his mother was Sabrina D. Bennett.

Her ancestors enrolled themselves among those whose noble and heroic deeds gave luster to the renown of Virginia, while yet a colony, but at an early day in the history of Kentucky they removed to the new country from the State of Virginia. Mr. McCreary's grandfather, on the paternal side, was a soldier from Kentucky in the war of 1812; and Dr. Charles McCreary, with whom the father of this sketch studied medicine, was a member of the Kentucky Legislature from Ohio county as early as 1809.

In 1857, James B. McCreary graduated from Centre College, Danville, Ky. He was then about eighteen years of age. He immediately thereafter entered upon the study of the law, graduating from the

University of Tennessee in 1859, being a valedictorian of his class which numbered forty-seven members.

Returning to Richmond, Ky., he established himself in a law-office and began to practice his profession, inspired by the resolution to build for himself not only a clientage, whose emoluments would enhance his always more than generous exchequer, but to take honorable position among those who had distinguished themselves at the bar and upon the bench.

The technicalities, intricacies, complications, and perplexities of the law never daunted his youthful ardor and his vigorous intellectuality. Unlike George Rouncewell, who was reared amid the historic grandeurs of the House of Dedlock, he did "take kindly to the craft;" but early in 1862 he was chosen major of the Eleventh Kentucky Confederate cavalry, which was commanded by Colonel Chenault, who joined General John H. Morgan. It would be futile for me to attempt to detail to the reader the brilliant service it rendered to the Confederacy, since history abounds with records of the gallant deeds of Morgan and his men. Colonel Chenault was killed at the head of his regiment at Green River Bridge on the 4th of July, 1863, and Major McCreary was promoted to the rank of lieutenant-colonel, which position he held to the close of the war, in 1865.

He served in the West during the early part of the war, and later on in Virginia under General John C. Breckinridge. His record was that of a gallant and courageous officer.

When he returned to his native county, having realized the glories of war and its attendant hardships, he again entered upon the practice of his profession, finding his enthusiasm for it undaunted, and his purpose as earnest as of yore. On the 12th of June, 1867, he was married to Miss Katie Hughes, the daughter of Thomas Hughes, Esq., a wealthy farmer of Fayette county, Ky. Miss Hughes was celebrated for her beauty, her refinement, and her intelligence.

In 1868, Colonel McCreary was chosen a delegate from his Congressional district to the National Convention in New York, which nominated Seymour and Blair, and in 1869 he was elected to the Kentucky Legislature. He was re-elected and without opposition in 1871, and was chosen Speaker of the House of Representatives. In 1873, he was again elected without opposition, and again made Speaker of the House. During the entire four years that he served in that position no appeal was ever taken from his ruling.

Kentucky has not a more accomplished parliamentarian and diplomatist than the Hon. James B. McCreary. Indeed, it is generally conceded that he is the peer of Kentucky's distinguished John G.

Carlisle, who is Speaker of the United States Congress. He is possessed of fluent speech, a rich, resonant voice, and captivating address, which appeal directly to the hearts, not only of his constituents, but his associates, and make them his friends.

In August, 1875, he was elected governor of Kentucky, defeating two distinguished soldiers and statesmen for the nomination—General John S. Williams, of Mt. Sterling, and Colonel J. Stoddard Johnston, of Frankfort. Judge John M. Harlan was the Republican nominee, and he was defeated by a large majority at the August election in 1875. Colonel McCreary made Kentucky a most admirable executive, and his administration stands out in bold relief for future generations to contemplate with deep respect for the mild and wise excellence it portrays. In 1884, ex-Governor McCreary entered the canvass for Congress in the Eighth Congressional District against the Hon. Milton J. Durham, now First Controller of the Treasury of the United States, and who had thrice represented the district in the Congress of the United States, and the Hon. Phil. B. Thompson, Jr., who had represented it three terms, and who is acknowledged to be one of the ablest lawyers in the State.

After an active canvass Governor McCreary received the nomination in primary election by thirty-two hundred and sixty-nine majority over the Hon. Milton J. Durham, and three thousand majority over the Hon. Phil B. Thompson, Jr. He also defeated James Sebastian, the Republican nominee, at the election in November, 1884, by a majority of twenty-one hundred and forty-six, the largest Democratic majority ever received in the district.

Governor McCreary is a gentleman of accomplishment and erudition. He possesses wealth, and, what is better than gold, noble principles and a good heart. He is not only a successful lawyer and a popular politician, but he is a farmer who produces both corn and cotton, and "keeps his fences in repair" politically and in point of fact, having a farm in Madison county and a plantation in the State of Alabama.

HON. THOMAS E. MOSS.

On the 14th day of March, 1840, the town of Greensburg, and the county of Green, in the State of Kentucky, although at the time unconscious of the added leaf in their wreath of laurel, certainly had the recording angel to smile upon their peaceful boundaries when he took note in the Doomsday Book of the arrival of another soul destined to add luster to a world his presence adorned, and so the name stood upon the register of Time and Eternity, "Thomas E. Moss." How well-known he is to-day, socially and politically, all men in and out of the State who take pride and interest in representative Kentuckians can testify. Mr. Moss is the son of T. S. T. and Judith C. Moss. His father removed to Kentucky at an early day from the State of North Carolina. His mother was a Miss Bullock, of Mercer county, Ky. The ancestors of both father and mother were of Virginia origin. Miss Bullock's relations are mentioned in Kentucky history as among the most dauntless and intelligent of those brave, high spirits that penetrated a wilderness, opened paths for the advancement of civilization, and left as an immortal heritage for their descendants a glorious and expansive State. It was also a brother of hers who was the commonwealth's attorney for that judicial district of which Mercer county formed a part, and who prosecuted Judge Wilkinson in the celebrated trial which in court annals bears his name.

Thomas E. Moss was educated at Columbia, Adair county, Ky. He graduated from the University of Law in Louisville, Ky., and received his diploma as the sign-manual of his ability to fight the battle of life, and "law" himself through any difficulties that might beset his onward march to distinction at the bar. At the first tocsin of war, however, thoughts of the bench and the bar vanished from young Moss' mind. His Southern blood mounted to fever heat. His dreams were of the battlefield—of glory, of liberty.

Early in 1861 he joined the Confederate army, Company "A," Twentieth Kentucky infantry. This company was commanded by Captain J. W. Moss, his elder brother, who had served as captain of Company "A," Second Kentucky regiment, in the Mexican war. This gallant officer was killed at Jonesboro, Ga., as colonel of the Second Kentucky regiment of infantry in the "Orphan Brigade," at the time that Sherman made his fateful march to the sea. After the battle of Fort Donelson the subject of this sketch was promoted, for gallant conduct on the field, to the position of adjutant of the regiment, and in that capacity he did service until the battle of Jackson, Miss., was fought. He was wounded in nearly every fight in which his regiment was engaged. Unfortunately, for his comfort, at least, his wounds would heal and he would return to his regiment just in time to take his position and get wounded again in their next engagement. He probably has more scars to attest his gallantry and daring than any other soldier who was a member of that regiment. After the battle of Jackson, Miss., which was fought in 1863, he was promoted to the rank of major, which position he held until the close of the war.

When Peace unfurled her snowy wings, and the roll of the drum and the shriek of the ear-piercing fife no longer were heard, and the thunder of the cannon no more reverberated among the hills, Major Moss returned to Paducah, Ky., and resuming his old-time occupation, he entered upon the practice of law. But whether it be true that some men seek office, and some offices seek men, certain it is that the musty tomes of legal lore seemed destined not to fetter Major Moss within the narrow limits of an office, for in the year 1869 he was elected to the Legislature of Kentucky. He was conceded the position of an important factor in State affairs, and so fully did the people recognize his ability and acumen, that in 1875 he was elected attorney-general of Kentucky. In this capacity he served the State for four years.

His term of office was conspicuous from the fact that he rendered important service to the State, meeting the talent of Kentucky and Ohio in intellectual debate, and rendering thereby still more secure his position as a man of prominence and brilliancy.

In 1871 he was married to Miss Margaret A. Bright, a lady of beauty and many accomplishments. She was the daughter of Jesse D. Bright, the illustrious gentleman who served in Indiana as senator in Congress for eighteen years, a portion of that time presiding as president of the Senate. He was finally forced to resign his seat in that body on account of his extreme partisanship for the South, which meant his deep devotion and sympathy with the Southern cause.

In August, 1885, Major Moss was again elected to the Legislature, and is at present serving his term in the lower house. As usual, he is upon the judiciary committee, as well as upon revenue and taxation.

Major Moss has the honor also of being a brother-in-law of the Hon. Thomas Poor, who is now one of the affable clerks of the Court of Appeals, and as popular as any man in Kentucky. Three children have blessed the union of Miss Bright and the gallant Major Moss. They are handsome and interesting, and give promise of one day being ornaments to the State of their nativity.

In *personnel*, Major Moss is of captivating presence, medium height, and rather rotund in form. He has dark hair, and very brilliant dark eyes. His head is exceptionally fine, being large and splendidly developed. Dark beard covers the lower portion of his expressive face. His manners are suave, as befits a successful politician, but conveying at the same time an impression of his daring as a soldier and his substantiality as a good citizen.

Major Moss was the leader in getting up the fight on the "Maple Leaf," near Cape Henry light-house, which resulted in the capturing of the vessel and enabling the Confederates on board to escape. This act was considered by both the Union and Confederate authorities to have been one of the most daring acts of the war. At that time Major Moss was suffering from a wound he had received in battle before he was captured.

HON. W. C. OWENS.

It is a noble custom to perpetuate the names of great men who reflect credit on their country by naming the counties and towns of the different States in their honor. It is not only bestowing well-merited compliments on those who are or who were well worthy to receive them, but it is a salient means by which posterity will be led to keep their memories green as long as liberty and independence endure.

Especially is this true in regard to Kentuckians, who, of all people in the world, are wedded to tradition and history. They, one and all, claim personal interest in the distinction of our great men—living and dead—and they are freer from envy in acknowledging merit and ability than men will be found to be in any other part of the universe.

My mind is led into this channel of thought by the name of the gentleman which graces the sketch which I am to write to-day.

I know not if W. C. Owens be a direct lineal descendant to the Colonel Abraham Owen for whom Owen county is named, but it is my belief that where the nomenclature of families is homogeneous the ties of consanguinity are also homologous, and generation after generation the strength, the grandeur, the power of a noble race in one or another of the descendants exemplifies itself, as in this instance—the bravery and dash exhibited by Abraham Owen, when as a lieutenant in Captain Lemon's company he took gallant part in St. Clair's defeat on November 4, 1791—when in the expedition, led by Colonel Hardin to White river, he aided in routing the Indians in their hunting camps, and when as captain of the first militia company raised in Shelby county he endeared himself to his companions by his goodness and bravery and general nobility of conduct—never forgetting the same course, when as major and colonel of a dashing regiment he did fine service for his country in General Wilkinson's campaign, and when in time of peace he was elected to the Legislature by the largest vote ever polled in the county of Shelby, and in 1791 was chosen a member of the convention which framed the Constitution of Kentucky—proving that in peace and war as well he had a strong hold on the affections of the people—serving them also in the Senate of the body politic of the State, when in 1811 he was the first to join Governor Harrison at Vincennes for the purpose of resisting the Indian bands led by Tecumseh and his brother, the Prophet, when he was chosen by General Harrison to be one of his aides-de-camp, and at the memorable battle of Tippecanoe fell at the side of his gallant chief fighting for his country, deeply regretted by the army and his hosts of friends in Kentucky—when in the following December, the Legislature of Kentucky went into mourning for the loss of Colonels Daviess and Owen, and others who had fallen at Tippecanoe, and in 1819 and 1820 Colonel Owen's memory was perpetuated by a county bearing his name—so in the present generation does the same spirit of bravery and gallantry exemplify itself in the splendid power of W. C. Owens, who has taken so prominent a position in the consideration of statesmen since 1877. And if Colonel Abraham Owen in war and council was brave, independent, and fearless, and mild and gentlemanly as a citizen, so in the case of W. C. Owens has the brave, independent, and fearless character displayed itself, for he knows the right, and knowing dares maintain it, no matter how heavy the odds he is called on to face.

No ease or civil distinction could have a charm for him unless won at the point of his own individual merit as a citizen and his ability as a parliamentarian. So is it that we can draw the lines of contrast and similarity between an elegant diplomatist of to-day, and a chivalrous patriot who made war against the North-western savages with a band of soldiers whose deeds of heroism at Tippecanoe in future years will vie in the estimation of posterity with those who fought and fell at Thermopylæ.

W. C. Owens was born in Scott county, Ky., October 17, 1849. He was the son of Charles Owens, Esq., and his mother's maiden name was Miss Eliza Tucker. His parents were both congenital Kentuckians, and more honored and respected names than those of "Owen" and "Tucker" are not to be found in the annals of the State. They were good citizens and brave soldiers and daring pioneers. With love of God and country burning like inextinguishable flames in their hearts, they were true under any and all circumstances to the best principles and the highest resolve. Hon. W. C. Owens attended college for several years at Millersburg, Bourbon county, Ky., situated on the Hinkston creek, forty-eight miles east of Frankfort, and surrounded by a rich farming community, being one of the principal places in Bourbon county, Ky., its high school being especially thriving and meritorious. Here our young student applied himself to his studies with the noblest results. Later on he attended college at Lexington, Ky., finally studying law and graduating at Columbia College, New York, in 1872.

When he returned home the citizens of Scott county delighted to do honor to his brilliant ability and promise of future eminence, and he was therefore elected county attorney of Scott county, Ky., in 1874, and he filled the position with great credit to himself, and satisfaction to the public.

Poeta nascitur, non fit, it has been aptly said; and if this be true in regard to those who aspire to bestride the winged steed, Pegasus, and so to reach the apex of Mount Helicon, how equally true is it when applied to politicians. There are men who are born to dominate others, and whether they choose church or State, art or science, on which to lavish the splendor of their genius and the might of their transcendent abilities as votive offerings, they are *powers* in the land and make themselves *felt* when obstacles beset them, for if they may not surmount the one and avoid the other, then like the wrath of the hurricane, or with the merciless rapidity of the lightning, they sweep away or destroy all that lies in their path to glory. As much as nature trembles at the wrath of the elements, men bow to the sway of the master mind.

In 1877 Hon. W. C. Owens was elected to the Legislature from Scott county, and he has represented it continuously since, this being his fifth term in the service of his constituents. And during the sessions of 1881 and 1882 he was elected speaker of the house. It will be remembered that during that session was run the famous race between General John S. Williams, the hero of Cerro Gordo, and Hon. J. C. S. Blackburn, for the position of senator in the United

States Congress. Mr. Owens at that time proved himself a potent factor in public affairs, and a matchless parliamentarian, and the memory of his influence and his magnetic presence will never fade from the recollection of any man who witnessed his efforts on that occasion. He was also elector for the Seventh Congressional District on the Hancock ticket in 1880, in which position he fairly covered himself with glory because of his splendid oratory. Last winter in the Legislature he commanded the attention and the admiration of the State at large, and his adherents were more than ever steadfast and enthusiastic in their regard for him. He is spoken of for the position of our next governor of Kentucky, with warm and cordial praise of his abilities and his marvelous magnetism, which enable him to command admiration even from opposing political factions. In his *personnel* he is simply superb, being one of the handsomest men one could see in many days' journey around the world. He is tall, exceedingly graceful, well-formed—a perfect model of manly beauty. His eyes are proud, cold, blue as bits of a June day sky, and shining with the fires of immortality—they are, indeed, the "windows of the soul." His features are classic; his expression exalted and full of noble resolve. Nature was in a smiling mood when she opened his eyes to the light, and no one who knows of his claims to personal good looks, and his proud abilities as a scholar, a politician, and a gentleman, can doubt that when she gave him her benediction she said: "He is every inch a man and a gentleman."

He is young yet—in the very bloom and beauty of his manhood. He is brimful of genius and ability. He is bound to succeed in all he undertakes, and those who claim powers of vaticination declare that in him they see "the coming man." Let Kentuckians look to it that the stranger within our gates offers not the meed of praise it is their devoir and right to bestow upon the ambitious, the worthy, and the aspiring.

JUDGE M. H. OWSLEY.

Cumberland county, in Kentucky, is the thirty-second county in the order of the formation of the State. It is, properly speaking, the offspring of Green county, having been erected as a separate county by an act of the Legislature from the county of Green in 1798. It derives its title from the Cumberland river, which intersects it from border to border. Its scenery is wild and romantic; its air is salubrious and health-giving and pure as the breath as the lily o' the valley. To journey through it, the most indifferent traveler could not restrain bursts of enthusiasm, for it is patent to the eye that Nature was in her most amiable mood when she fashioned it, and her smiles are mirrored in its river and tributaries, and the freshness of her beauty is still reflected from hill and plain. Burksville is the county-seat, and, if not claiming an overwhelming population, it repairs its deficiency in that respect by the cleverness of its citizens, and especially by being the birthplace of a scholar, a jurist, and a gentleman—Judge M. H. Owsley. It was in the town of Burksville that he was born, on the 10th of December, 1834. He was the youngest of nine children. His father was Doctor Joel Owsley, who was born in the county of Lincoln, State of Kentucky, in 1790. His uncle was Governor William Owsley, who was the fourteenth governor of Kentucky, and who was born in Virginia in 1782. Doctor Joel Owsley, the father of Judge M. H. Owsley, was a gentleman of the "old school," and possessed of magnificent attainments. In his early manhood he was married to Miss Mary Ann Lewis, whose ancestors were Virginians, and subsequently numbered among the pioneers of Kentucky. She was also the niece of the celebrated Colonel Whitley, who was born August 4, 1749, in Augusta county, Va., and who, like the illustrious and brilliant Joseph Hamilton Daviess, tendered his life as a patriotic sacrifice to his country. Colonel Daviess fell at Tippecanoe on the 7th day of November, 1811. He was one of Kentucky's most gifted sons—that is, Kentucky claims him, for, although born in Bedford county, Va., on March 4, 1774, Kentucky was the home of his early adoption. He was the first lawyer to appear in the Supreme Court of the United States hailing from the land west of the Alleghenies and his case was the celebrated one of Wilson vs. Mason. He married the youngest sister of Chief-Justice John Marshall.

In 1806 he was attorney-general of Kentucky, at which time Aaron Burr had a preliminary trial for treason. It was in this trial that Daviess measured lances with the "Great Commoner," Henry Clay, and distinguished himself as a patriot and an orator. Two years subsequent to the melancholy death of Colonel Daviess, Colonel Whitley fell in the battle of the Thames, fought on the 5th day of October, 1813. Although one of signal triumph, the victory had a shadow on its brightness in the loss of the gallant Whitley.

Judge Owsley's paternal ancestry were of English origin, and came over to the colonies on account of what they esteemed to be "religious oppression," claiming, as all freemen should, the right to worship God according to the dictates of an honest conscience. They removed to Kentucky while it was yet a Territory, and they were among the brave and intellectual spirits who opened up its civilization, for it was then almost a trackless forest.

M. H. Owsley graduated from Centre College, Danville, Ky., in 1854, and from the University of Law, in Louisville, in 1856. He entered upon the practice of his profession in Burksville, continuing it until 1861, when he joined Colonel Wolford's First Kentucky Federal regiment of cavalry, with the rank of captain.

Subsequently, he was elected major of the Fifth Kentucky Federal cavalry, commanded by Colonel Haggard. In August, 1862, he was elected commonwealth's attorney of the Eighth Judicial District, and re-elected to the same office in 1868. In 1874 he was elected judge of that circuit, which had so long and so ably been presided over by Fontaine T. Fox, Sr., and re-elected in 1880. At the close of his present term, in 1886, he will have worn the official harness for twenty-four years, and should he offer himself for re-election, I question whether there is a man in the district (which extends from Garrard to Cumberland) who could beat him, such is the hold he has upon the hearts of the people in that section of the country. He was a candidate for governor in 1883, but was defeated before the State convention by the nomination of Hon. J. Proctor Knott, as was General Buckner and also Hon. T. L. Jones, of Newport, Ky.

In 1865 Judge Owsley was married to Miss Ellen Letcher, the daughter of Dr. Joseph P. Letcher, of Jessamine county, Ky., a physician of popularity and prominence. She is a remarkably handsome lady, intellectually brilliant, and possessing the most charming vivacity of manner, she adorns society wherever she appears. Mrs. Grainger, the widow of General Gordon Grainger, is an elder sister of Mrs. Owsley, and Governor R. P. Letcher was her great-uncle. Their social status is the highest in the State.

Judge Owsley himself is "every inch the gentleman," both in appearance and address. He is easy and graceful, and most captivating in his conversational powers, which are absolutely unrivaled. He is warm hearted and generous to that degree that it amounts almost to a fault.

Although defeated in his gubernatorial aspirations, I venture the prediction that Buckner and Owsley would make a "winning team" for the next candidacy for that office. They would sweep the State with the force of a typhoon. The very brooks in the mountain passes would sing their praises, and the stars of Heaven would brighten in their vigils to insure their election. Let that be the next gubernatorial ticket, "Buckner and Owsley."

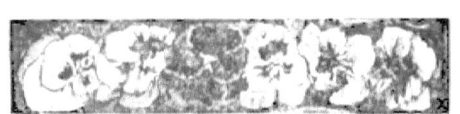

HON. P. BOOKER REED.

In Frankfort, Ky., that natural mosaic of sylvan beauty set among the gloomy and rugged hills, P. Booker Reed was born on the 7th day of October, 1842. His father, William D. Reed, was the secretary of State under Governor Owsley's administration, and he was the Democratic elector for the State at large in the year 1855—that momentous time of Know-Nothingism which marked its era by the blood that dyed the streets of Baltimore, by the indelible stain set upon the political escutcheon of Louisville, and by the sorrowful memories that cluster in many cities of the Union, until that time united in interest and prosperity. Mr. Reed's mother was Miss M. Jane Sharp, the daughter of Colonel Solomon P. Sharp, the progenitor of the New Court party, and the victim of the assassin Beauchamp at the capital of the State in 1825. Colonel Sharp was a lawyer of great versatility and power, and at the time of his sudden and cruel taking off was probably one of the most prominent men in the State, and certainly one among the many who left his impress upon the time in which he lived.

In 1860 P. Booker Reed was placed at Centre College, but in 1861, when war was proclaimed throughout the country, he, in company with many other young and patriotic Kentuckians, followed Morgan into the Confederate army. Afterward he joined the Ninth Kentucky regiment, commanded by Colonel Thomas H. Hunt, in the brigade of General John C. Breckinridge, and during the entire period involved in the battle of sections for the maintenance of liberty and principle, Mr. Reed served his country in the capacity of a private soldier, refusing promotion and desiring only to do his duty faithfully and well. The soldiers on both sides in the struggle know in what battles that grand old brigade participated, know how it covered itself again and again with glory, and what history it made for Kentucky. Once, during the war, I had the pleasure of seeing it pass in review at Dalton, Ga., after General Bragg had been dislodged from Mission Ridge, and its tread was every inch that of the soldier. I speak of it as one man, because the command moved as such, and the cheers that went up making the welkin ring thrilled and filled my heart with joy that I, too, was a Kentuckian; that my principles, aspirations, and desires were synonymous with theirs, and that I could, as it were, through community of interest, claim a soldier's kinship with them. When the war terminated Mr. Reed returned to Kentucky. After the lapse of a year he enrolled himself as a student in the University of Louisiana, situated in New Orleans, from which institution he graduated with the highest honors in 1870. Subsequently, he went to Wurzburg, Germany, completing his education to the finest finish possible to impart in any college. After this he made a tour through Europe, visiting historic places and viewing famous scenes, becoming conversant with people and acquainted with manners and modes, going, not only in the beaten tracks followed by idlers and seekers after pleasures and novelties, but traversing highways and by-ways in a seriously contemplative mood, where he could study art and nature, and see, for himself, the success and the opulence that followed the advancement of civilization and enlightenment into uncultivated and benighted lands of the serf and the minion. Returning to Louisville in 1872, Mr. Reed was appointed resident graduate of the city hospital, but he resigned his position on account, as he thought, of the mismanagement of its affairs.

In 1873 Mr. Reed entered the race for tax receiver, but owing to the fact that Mr. Baxter was at the head of municipal affairs, he withdrew from the canvass. In 1880 Mr. Reed became the manager of the race between Chancellor I. H. Edwards and Judge Alexander P. Humphrey. When Mr. Edwards was elected Mr. Reed was appointed Receiver of the Chancery Court, and filled this office in the most acceptable manner for four years. He is a superb leader in a political campaign, and has placed the victor's crown on more than one head that would have bowed beneath the cloud of defeat but for his cool judgment and intrepid daring, displayed in perfecting organization.

When he was elected to the mayoralty of the city—carrying every ward and precinct against his opponent, Wheeler McGee—entering upon his duties in January, 1885, he found the financial arm of the municipality suffering from a compound fracture—left in this condition by his predecessor, and innumerable sinecures feeding upon the taxpayers without rendering any service to the city. He at once inaugurated a system of reform which necessitated the dismissal of many of them. This course of action upon his part brought down on his head the storm of their indignation. The primal and only motive of the mayor was, and is, to make the revenue of the city meet the current expenses without involving the city more deeply in debt merely to gratify those who pay no taxes, and who seem to care little or nothing for the future destiny of the city. I would suggest to Mr. Reed's enemies not to go into any "rhapsodies" over his business, but to await results, and after he has failed there will be time enough to comment upon his downfall. Mr. Reed is the mayor of the city not only in name, but in point of fact, and such will continue to be while he fills the office. Whatever he does at all, he does well. He is a thorough-going man and a highly-polished gentleman, and at the expiration of his term of office I confidently predict that the city will ring with his praises, and where we now see evidences of neglect and decay, his magnetic will and skillful hands will produce prosperity and improvement. That system and caution and good sense, which characterize Mayor Reed's management of his private affairs, will evolve all that is to the city's interest out of its affairs. He injects success into whatever he undertakes. He is a man of marked fidelity and independence of speech and action.

Mr. Reed, on both sides of his house, is descended from the finest and noblest families in the Commonwealth, and the strong characteristics he displays are as much his by inheritance from a race of people who helped to make Kentucky a State and who also made her history, as they are the natural outcome of a strong and pure-blooded physique, and a vigorous and highly-cultured intellect. He has been twice wedded, his first wife living but a brief period after their union, and his last marriage having but recently taken place.

In appearance, he is tall and well built, of muscular but supple frame. He has light hair and blue eyes, a strongly-marked face, indicative in feature and expression of great intellectuality and resolution.

He is genial and affectionate in his disposition, without ever unbending from the dignity of the man and the gentleman to friend or foe.

From his earliest years—save when he endured the hardships of war—he has been accustomed to every luxury and refinement belonging to wealth and position, and their influence upon his character is subtly apparent in manner and speech, to that degree that no contact with the world renders him less the object of admiration and respect in his domestic circle.

HON. JOHN S. RHEA.

To the reading public it would seem that great men are indigenous to certain localities in Kentucky as certain plants are indigenous to the soil. I have hitherto mentioned the fact that Logan county was exceptionally endowed with gifted sons, not as a matter of personal opinion, but of State and national record, and I repeat the assertion to-day with additional emphasis, since it becomes my pleasant and distinguished privilege to add to my biographical sketches so popular and brilliant name as that of John S. Rhea, of Russellville, Ky.

Mr. Rhea was born in the county of Logan on the 9th day of March, 1854. He was partially educated in his native county, but he completed his collegiate course at Washington and Lee University, Virginia.

He read law under his father in Russellville, Ky., and was admitted to the bar in 1873. Immediately thereafter, he was elected county attorney of Logan county, and so universal was the satisfaction he afforded in his fulfillment of official duties that at the expiration of his term he was re-elected for four more years.

At the State Convention in 1884, Mr. Rhea was chosen elector for the Third Congressional District, and his personal activity and eloquent oratory combined had the most telling effect upon the people. He attained the largest Democratic majority of any elector in the State He received more votes than the Hon. John E. Halsell, the present member of Congress from that district.

The subject of this sketch is the son of Hon. Albert G. Rhea, whose ancestors were M........... ......and w..... place of residence for generations was in that State. .... people of superior culture and magnificent courage. Th........... position was the best. There was none higher. Albert G. Rhea represented the historic county of Logan in both branches of the General Assembly of Kentucky. He was also elected circuit judge of that judicial district, and the fact was generally conceded that he was a lawyer of profound attainments. The bar of the State of Kentucky was prompt to admit his superiority and erudition.

Mr. John S. Rhea's mother was Miss Jane S. Stockdale, of Pennsylvania. Her lineage was distinguished as she was herself personally refined. She was closely related to Hon. Elijah Hise, deceased. This gentleman was a profound logician and a brilliant statesman. Kentucky was proud of him. His unexpected "taking off" was bewailed as a bereavement to the Commonwealth. It cast a gloom not only over the people of his own State, but the sorrow became universal through those who had been associated with him in Washington when he served as a member of the Congress of the United States. His great intellect planted the seed of respect in the minds of those who sat under the sound of his rich and mellifluous voice, when from the depths of his soul he pleaded for the maintenance of the constitution and the enforcement of the laws as they were bequeathed to us by our forefathers, sanctified by their blood and tears, the most inestimable treasures, the loftiest gifts ever transmitted by valor and virtue to posterity for the preservation of future generations since the world began; and when he died it was found that the seed of respect had sprung into honors in the hearts of his countrymen, and, ripening, had fallen on the record of his death in the form of a nation's regret.

Elijah Hise had no peer for love of country. The memory of him goes on like the murmuring sea. While life lasts it will endure. His name is mentioned by those who had the honor of personal acquaintance with him with almost the intonation given to the voice of adoration. To a great extent John S. Rhea possesses many of his noblest qualities—his fine legal mind, his earnest and impassioned eloquence, his dignified and impressive address, and his unwavering adherence to the principles he conceives to be right. Although a young man, he has made himself felt as a power by the legal fraternity in the section in which he lives and where he practices his profession.

In presence, he is very attractive, and his voice alone, though his handsome face should not be seen, would instantly rivet attention. In physique, he is slight, but of commanding excellence in dignity and style—one man among many—and the charm in his manner is exceeded only by his remarkable mental qualifications. It is with himself to decide to what sublime heights of fame he will climb. Like the poet's clarion-voiced youth, who bore the banner with the strange device, "Excelsior," those who know John S. Rhea know he will be satisfied with nothing but the brightest triumphs. They anticipate them for him, and they expect them of him.

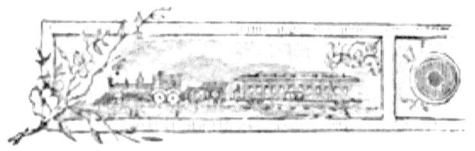

HON. HENRY HAMILTON SKILES.

In the United States it is the breach rather than the observance where property descends through generations from father to son. In the State of Kentucky this is especially true. The people as a people are warm-hearted, impulsive, and generous. They live well and keep "open house" the year around for their friends. They never count the costs. While it lasts all are expected to enjoy it. And, as a consequence, when the demands of "the butcher, the baker, and the candle-stick maker" are made, estates often dwindle to meet the legal requirements in the case. Only now and then do we see able management and discretion go hand in hand, and the law of inheritance remains as forcible through generations as that of unavoidable entailment.

A special case in point is "Rich Pond Grove," the homestead of Henry Hamilton Skiles, the place of his birth, and descended to him through his father, William H. Skiles. It is situated in Warren county, Ky., and is as well known to the denizens of Warren as the county-seat.

Warren county is a splendid country to live in. The people are intelligent, progressive, and aspiring. The lay of the land is undulating, the soil fertile and productive, the water especially fine and health-giving. The exports are prolific and of that character of production for which Kentucky is famous—tobacco, wheat, corn, and pork.

The county was named in honor of General Joseph Warren, M. D., a physician of note, a patriot, an orator, a politician, and a soldier. The Bunker Hill monument occupies the site where he fell—the first general on the American side of the struggle to lose his life for liberty. He was one of the grandest officers of the Revolution, second to none but the immortal Washington. And from his grave, as it were, have sprung the immortelles of genius that must forever bloom imperishably in the hearts of the American people, even as the stars glow in undimmed splendor at the zenith; for such orators as Webster, Everett, and the Abbotts have woven the immortelles of memory into fadeless wreaths of eloquence that can not die while the Republic endures. The pride of name has resolved itself into the hearts of the people of Warren and has aided in making it one of the noblest counties in the State. It has ever been the chosen home of the Underwood, the McElroy, and the Skiles families, than which there are none more honorable, gifted, and distinguished in America.

William H. Skiles, the father of the subject of this biographical sketch, was born in Goochland county, Va., in 1799. He was the son of William Skiles, a native of Virginia. The Skiles family originally came from Copenhagen, Denmark. That was some two hundred years ago. They divided into two settlements—one part in Pennsylvania and one in Virginia.

William H. Skiles was brought to Kentucky when quite a child. His education was received in Kentucky and Virginia. He acquired by inheritance, supplemented by personal industry, a fine farm of splendid land in Warren county, on which he lived, and by which he accumulated a large fortune. He was a man of unflagging industry, of superb mental attainments, of remarkable originality and distinctive character. His acumen, when weighing human nature in the balance, was instantaneous and unerring; his infinite variety of jest and repartee and his conversational powers were unsurpassed. It was the attic salt of superior intellectuality which to this day fills the neighborhood in which he lived with observations and witticism that have outlived their author.

The mother of Henry H. Skiles was Miss Lucy A. Underwood, a daughter of John Underwood and a sister of Judge Joseph R. and

Hon. Warner L. Underwood. The lady was as famous for her grace, beauty, and elegance as her brothers were distinguished for their ability and dignity of character.

Judge Joseph R. Underwood represented his county in the Legislature for twelve years. He was Speaker of the House; served eight years in the United States Congress; served six years in the United States Senate; and for seven years he was judge of the Appellate Court of Kentucky. Hon. Warner L. Underwood was a member of the United States Congress for four years, and for several other years he was American Consul to Scotland.

John Underwood, the father of Mrs. Skiles, was a native of Goochland county, Va., and for many years he was a member of the Virginia Legislature. To be this nowadays has grown to be an empty honor. But then such public positions were awarded by the sovereign people only as a recognition due to ability and superior merit.

The father of John Underwood was Thomas A. Underwood, a native of Hanover county, Va.— a man of prominence in the Revolutionary war, a colonel in Washington's army, and for many years a member of the House of Burgesses. He was the son of William Thomas Underwood, who came to Virginia from England in 1680. He settled near Richmond and amassed quite a fortune. He was ever a man of prominence in his adopted State.

Henry Hamilton Skiles in a rare degree has inherited those qualities that marked the distinctive individuality of his ancestry on both sides of his house.

From his father he inherited sterling manhood, clear perceptive faculties, quick wit, a keen sense of the ridiculous (which makes him one of the most entertaining and companionable of men), and a splendid physique.

From his mother came a high type of intellectuality, a love of the beautiful, the true, the good; a rich vein of poesy, and an easy and graceful fluency of speech.

Mr. Skiles received his early education in the country schools in the neighborhood of his father's residence.

But this procedure of mental attainment did not satisfy his aspiring mind, remarkable even at that early age. The monotony incident to life on a farm palled on his soul, and, finding no marked opposition at home to his desire to change the course of his destiny, while yet a youth he left its sacred precincts, and going to Bowling Green he obtained a place to write in the County and Circuit Court clerk's office. Here he continued his labors for two years. Full of ambition, glowing with the aspiring ardor of youth, he felt that somewhere in the world there was a niche that he was created to fill. Desiring to perfect his education, he left the clerk's office and was sent to Hopkinsville, Ky., where for several terms he prosecuted his studies with conscientious vigor, acquiring a first-class English education.

In 1855 he matriculated at Harvard University, Cambridge, Mass., took the entire law course, and graduated with high honor in 1856.

After his return from Harvard he began the practice of his profession in Bowling Green, associated with Captain W. W. Western, one of the most talented young men in Kentucky.

About that time the Kansas fever of emigration seized on the hearts of the people everywhere, and young Skiles, with a keen foresight that would have done credit to an older and more worldly head, took a trip to Kansas City, in which place he invested a few hundred dollars, which proved a veritable gold find, for that investment now constitutes a good part of his fortune.

After this he was often in the West. He was full of speculative talent which amounted almost to genius with him. He failed in nothing he undertook. He had many thrilling experiences with Indians and border ruffians, and when he returned to his native heather he was none the worse off for his extended knowledge of his fellowmen.

In 1860 he combined with the practice of his profession the occupation of an editor. In that year he purchased the *Gazette*, and until the destruction of his printing office by fire in 1862, he conducted his literary venture with ability and brilliance. The fire was accidental, having been caused by the Federal soldiers occupying the office as a shelter from the biting cold on the night after the Confederates had evacuated Bowling Green.

During the war, Mr. Skiles was a "Union man," *i. e.*, he was opposed to secession, because in its adoption he could see only woe and disaster for the South and the interests of the entire Union. He opposed, however, every Republican encroachment on constitutional rights with equal fervor. He was, as he is to-day, at all times, a consistent, true, conscientious Democrat—an honor to himself and his party.

In 1863, he was elected county attorney. He served a term of four years. As a prosecutor, he was able, fearless, and independent. A rare combination of characteristics in the turbulent condition of affairs incident to civil war.

In 1866, he revived and again edited the *Gazette*. It was during this time in his career that George D. Prentice became his close friend. It is a subject of pride on the part of Mr. Skiles to recur to this gentle friendship, whose memory survives the opening and closing of a grave. His fidelity to the great man's memory is but one of his many attractive qualities, and his reminiscences, in which Mr. Prentice was associated, are not the least enjoyable of his pleasant conversations.

Mr. Skiles was dilettanteish in light literature. His verses are, many of them, stamped with the unmistakable genius of the true poet. Many gems from the storehouse of his fancy are still to be seen in the exchanges. His prose is at once vigorous and ornate. But through all his literary work runs visibly the fine silver line of poesy. His poems are usually the creations of impulse, as the following attests—it having been inspired by the sight of a pretty girl at vespers. It is called:

THE BEAUTIFUL AT PRAYER.

I saw a sinless maid bow down
  At God's unsullied shrine,
Her pure, pale cheek, her hair's gold crown,
  Her air devout and half divine
    Embodied her as Prayer.

She seemed a wandering spirit come
  From off her Pleiad flight
And bringing from her heavenly home
  The soft, supernal light
    Of glory that is there!

What matter could it be to me
  That she was clad in Fashion's guise?
Had my soul not in reverie
  Beheld the angel in her eyes?
    The aureola 'round her brow?

Her parted lips exhaled a sigh
  Sweet as the rose's breath
When, thrilling 'neath the sun's glad eye,
  She bursts from her green silk sheath
    And the flowers before her bow.

She seemed not to have felt the taint
  Or touch of earthly care,
But, silent as a sweet-browed saint,
  Continued kneeling there,
    Absorbed in holy thought.

And yet an arrow had been sent—
  A swift, unerring dart!
And the cruel barb its power had spent
  In piercing her young heart,
    And Grief the blood had caught.

This I knew by the mourning garb,
    That wrapt her fairness 'round,
And crepey vail with jet-black barb
    To hold its dusk folds down
        From her sorrow-shaded face.

Black-robed, I saw her bosom swell
    As though with feeling blent,
While from the sacred altar fell
    The promise: "If ye but repent
        Ye shall receive all grace."

I looked upon the maiden there,
    So pure and undefiled,
Resigning to her Saviour's care
    And guidance like a child
        Her whole heart's bitter grief.

And longed to rouse me from the dreams
    In which I walked apart,
Aspiring still to nobler themes—
    To purer faith—a steadfast heart
        And holier belief.

The prayer was hushed. Soft on the air
    The mellow music pealed;
The altar lights, and the flowers fair
    New brilliance seemed to yield,
        And censer fires burned low.

And yet I lingered with a prayer
    Unprayed within my heart,
To that fair maiden kneeling there.
    Her fragrant lips apart—
        I lingered, loth to go.

Blest being of a purer light,
    I longed to breathe to you
A wish—a hope—a soul's respite
    That when God thou didst woo
        Thou wouldst remember me.

And if, albeit from afar,
    The hour were known to soul of mine,
I'd turn, as pilgrim to his star,
    And blend my prayer with thine
        In pure felicity.

In August, 1869, Mr. Skiles was elected by a large majority a member of the House of Representatives. In this capacity he served his constituents for two sessions.

Subsequently, until 1879, he was engaged in the management of his rapidly-accumulating business, for which he gradually abandoned the practice of his profession, devoting himself almost entirely to his Western investments and speculations.

In 1879, he was elected from the Eleventh district to the Senate, in which body politic he served with distinction to himself and satisfaction to his constituents for a term of four years.

A re-election was tendered him, but the press of private affairs forbade his continuance in public life.

As an illustration of his ready wit, quick perception, and fertility of resource the following incident is not inappropriate:

When Robert J. Walker was appointed governor of Kansas, and was already on his voyage up the Missouri river, he was expected to stop for awhile at Wyandotte, at which point the people proposed to meet him with a welcoming address to Kansas.

Mr. Skiles was at the wharf also for the purpose of meeting him, although he, too, was a stranger to almost every one.

Finally the steamer appeared and was greeted with wild enthusiastic huzzahs. The wharf-boat was crowded with people. But just before the steamboat landed there came a sweeping gust of wind, and the rain fell in torrents. This unexpected "damper" placed by the elements on the welcome made many serious faces in the crowd. When the boat landed it was but a moment until it was off again steaming along its destined course.

The editor of the Wyandotte paper (who knew Mr. Skiles personally) was expected to deliver the address on the occasion. He had already prepared it; indeed, it was "set up" for publication. As the steamboat pushed off he was in despair, for the governor had not arrived. Happening to be near Mr. Skiles, he asked him in a subdued voice what he was to do, briefly explaining his dilemma.

Fertile in resource, Mr. Skiles appreciated the situation, and said in an entre-nous voice that Walker was a stranger to the crowd, and so was he, and if it would be any favor to the editor that he would personate the governor—that he was confident in the rain and the confusion it was not known if Walker had or had not arrived, and there was no danger of detection. It was a bold proposition, but it seemed a capital one to the editor. They warmly shook hands. After which cordial procedure the newspaper man delivered his welcoming address in the most approved style to the acting-governor of Kansas. At the proper moment Skiles, with an impromptu eloquence, responded, thanking him for the kindly reception, and promising to do all he could for the advancement and development of the infant State.

The scheme proved a success. The governor was introduced to a few persons. He soon, however, escaped from the crowd and disappeared on the next boat. The next day everything was in the paper —speeches and all—and everybody was happy.

To this day Mr. Skiles, to many of the older citizens of Wyandotte, is "Governor."

The incident is characteristic of the man. He is full of dash and humor. His life has been an eventful one.

He is still a bachelor.

HON. JAMES W. TATE.

To those who are well acquainted with the topography of Kentucky, "The Forks of Elkhorn" is synonymous with splendid scenery. The surface of that part of the country is finely diversified, undulating, and hilly; in many places the cliffs rear themselves to almost precipitous heights. The people who inhabit this portion of the State are endowed with the open-hearted, open-handed characteristics for which the grand old Commonwealth has been so long famous. And chief among the chosen stands James W. Tate, her well-beloved representative, and her trusted and honored treasurer. Mr. Tate's birthplace was near the "Forks of Elkhorn." He was an only son, and was consequently idolized by his parents. He was born in Franklin county, Ky., on January 2, 1831. His father was Colonel Thomas L. Tate, a gentleman well known throughout Kentucky for his probity and sterling worth. Colonel Tate was a native of Kentucky, but was descended from a Virginia family of Scotch-Irish extraction; and the faithful adherence to principle and conviction which usually marks the character of a true Scot, allied to the suavity and open-heartedness of a genuine son of Erin's Emerald Isle, was well defined in his character, and they still glow and sparkle in undimmed luster in the mind and manner of his son. Colonel Tate's father was a soldier in the Revolutionary war, and did conspicuous service with the Virginia Continentals. The pride and dignity of this honored family naturally concentrated in James W. Tate, and from his birth, as it were, much was expected of him. He was educated in Franklin and Woodford counties, his teachers being such accomplished and popular instructors as John Lewis, Esq., and Dr. L. W. Seely. In 1848, he completed his scholastic course, and during that same year he received an appointment in the post-office at Frankfort, Ky., under B. F. Johnson, Esq., who was at that time postmaster at the capital. The position young Tate held developed in him business habits of method, accuracy, and promptness, to that degree that he became quite celebrated. His urbane manner, which would do credit to a courtier, won for him many admirers and friends, and "Dick Tate" then was the same "Dick Tate" of to-day, who counted his adherents by the score, and who, never forgetting a kindness done him, never lost an opportunity to reciprocate it. In 1854, under Lazarus W. Powell, one of the most excellent and efficient Chief Magistrates who have ever stood at the helm of public affairs, Mr. Tate received the appointment of Assistant Secretary of State, and in this capacity he served throughout Governor Powell's term.

Mr. Tate is eminently a Democrat—an ultra Democrat of the most pronounced Jeffersonian and Jacksonian principles; therefore, when, in 1855, the Know-Nothing party gained public ascendency in this State, James W. Tate, declaring that public life had lost its charms for him, retired, with the regrets of his friends following him to civil walks, and became engaged in mercantile pursuits in the city of Frankfort. In this venture, as in everything else he undertook to accomplish, he was highly successful, for system and application are the fundamental and essential principles of success, and as I have hitherto said, Mr. Tate, in a wonderful degree, possessed ability in both directions.

In 1859, however, he was again appointed Assistant Secretary of State under Governor Beriah Magoffin, and after the resignation of Governor Magoffin (for purely political reasons that are as well-known to Kentuckians as the name of their State), Mr. Tate, at the request of both parties, continued to serve through the term of Governor James Robinson.

The zest of public service was no longer attractive to him, it seemed, for in 1863, despite the protests of his admiring friends and well-wishers, he returned to the more quiet pursuit of commerce. He did not because of this abandon his influence as a politician, for he was all the while an active member of the Democratic State Central Committee. He was always a great adherent of Breckinridge, and he belonged to his "wing" of the party.

Two years later—in 1865—he was elected, as the only Democrat, assistant clerk of the House of Representatives. His popularity increased with every public office that he filled.

On the 22d day of February, 1867, the greatest crowd that ever assembled in Frankfort was at the convention which nominated John L. Helm for the position of Chief Magistrate of the Commonwealth. In this same convention James Barrett, Esq., of the German Security Bank, our own well-known and highly-respected citizen, put Mr. Tate's name in nomination for State Treasurer.

From that time it has proved to be a biennial office with him, for he has been nominated for it and successively re-elected every two years since, and that, too, by the most overwhelming majority of votes.

When he concludes his present term he will have served the State of Kentucky in one capacity for twenty years, always presenting the same unblemished record for probity and principle for her indorsement, which has ever been enthusiastically given. It is a question whether any other man in the United States has ever been honored by such frequent election to the office of treasurer of public moneys as Mr. Tate has been. His majorities have been greater than those of all other candidates, no matter to what office they aspired. In his last election it exceeded the count of sixty-seven thousand.

His public popularity does not surpass the warm personal regard in which he is held by every one who has the honor of his acquaintance. They are all his friends, who would esteem it a privilege to make a sacrifice to prove their affection for him.

The secret of this ardent esteem may be traced to the fact that, beyond most men, he adheres staunchly to principle in all his dealings with his fellowmen. He is energetic, accurate, and perfectly sincere; he is generous, unselfish, and amiable. In his boyhood he was taught that honesty was the best policy, and he grew up in that belief. He was trained to the conviction that the "golden rule" will guide a man to the Holy Land, and bear him across seas without wings. He goes straight to the heart of every human being who knows him, because his charity is universal, and deference to the feelings and wishes of others makes him at all times a pleasant associate and as genial as the sunshine. In presence, he is of medium size, with engaging manners and a fine, expressive countenance. In 1856, he was married to Miss Lucy J. Hawkins, the daughter of W. W. Hawkins, Esq., of Woodford county, Ky., a most excellent and accomplished lady.

They have one child living, a daughter, Mona. She is now grown, and is acknowledged to be one of the loveliest and most accomplished young girls who ever graced the capital with their brilliance and beauty.

HON. WILLIAM PRESTON TAULBEE.

Morgan county was formed in 1822, the seventy-third in order of formation, out of the counties of Floyd and Bath, and named in honor of General Daniel Morgan, who was a distinguished officer of the war of the Revolution. He was with the army at Braddock's defeat He commanded a company in Dunmore's expedition against the Indians. He commanded a detachment consisting of three rifle companies under Arnold at Quebec, and led the forlorn hope in the assault. Here he was taken prisoner. On his exchange he received the appointment of colonel in the Continental army. He was at the head of his riflemen in the victorious battle of Saratoga. For his gallantry in this action the Legislature of Virginia passed a resolution presenting him with a horse, pistols, and a sword. He lived in the hearts of his countrymen, and naming a county in Kentucky in memory of him was to do high honor to his name. Morgan county, in number of square miles, is the seventh largest county in the State. In 1846 its territory, although part of Johnson county, was taken from it in 1843, and was fully six times as large as that of some other counties in Kentucky;

but parts of each of five counties have since been taken from it: Rowan in 1856, Magoffin and Wolfe in 1860, and Menifee and Elliott in 1868. In 1871, fifteen counties were assessed upon more acres of land, but it is probable that an actual survey would show Morgan to be, as stated, the seventh largest county in Kentucky. It is in the central eastern portion of the State. The Licking river runs entirely through it. The face of the country is hilly, but it is interspersed with fertile valleys. The soil is based on freestone, with red clay foundation. Iron ore, the finest of cannel coal, other bituminous coals, alum, and copperas, with mineral and oil springs, abound. Corn, cattle, and hogs are the leading productions.

But Morgan county can boast a still finer production than any recorded in her past annals; and that is, that the Hon. William Preston Taulbee was born within her borders, on October 22, 1851. His father served ably in the General Assembly of the State, and has ever been a man conspicuous among his fellowmen as being plain, practical, but fervid, honest, and earnest, and in all things worthy of public honor and private trust. The idea has often been advanced that the mental attrition generated in cities makes the growing youth of our country brilliant and intellectual, while their less fortunate rustic brothers, although thanking heaven for free air and good health, are led to ascribe to the inaccessibility of the "maddening crowd" their heavy manners, and their slow, methodical thoughts and modes of expression. Whatever verity appertains to this theory in other localities it is certainly not true when applied to Kentucky. As a general rule, our least brilliant and efficient men are those who have been reared in cities. When they rise out of the ordinary level of every day struggles to gain the "almighty dollar," it is usually to figure in rings and cliques, and to manipulate city politics. If they have the luck which comes with leisure and fortune, they go to Europe. They pine to ascend the sublime altitudes of the famed Alps, etc., forgetful of the natural beauties of our native land. Still it is admitted that when we need vim, spirit, dash, we look for our leading men in cities. But when we need heroes and statesmen to represent us at home and abroad —when we require profoundness of thought, unselfish nobility of action, grandeur of purpose, and splendor of oratory, we instinctively turn to the country, where men have time to think, and where their motives spring as fresh and pure from their hearts as the crystal gurgling from the mountain rocks, and we are seldom disappointed in our quest.

Hon. William Preston Taulbee is a living exemplar of my theory. He grew from youth to manhood among the hills of Morgan, where nature is forever panoplied in the royal richness of her brilliant robings, varying in their hues from the vermeil tintings of the blushing spring, to the stainless ermine of winter snow. He became acquainted with her in the solitudes of her changeless hills. The richness and beauty, the warmth and gentleness she possessed passed with magnetic current into his soul and expanded it to meet the advancing issues of a brilliant and useful public career. He worked upon the home farm and attended country schools until grown. If restive of the quiet duties of his daily existence, and emulous of greater opportunities to prepare for his entrance upon the arena of public life, I know not; but certain it is that he availed himself of the chances to acquire knowledge with a magnificent appreciation of its advantages, when, like the king's son, he should claim his own, at the hands of the world, whose winding paths through various cities his young feet were fated one day to tread as he advanced toward the throne of public appreciation at the capital of the nation. Love even came to him as to one of the chosen of earth, and, in 1871, his marriage with Miss Lou Emma Oney set the seal of peace and happiness upon his soul. After his marriage he taught school, and this he did well, as he has done all things; and it was not until 1877 that the school-room doors closed on him, and he found himself face to face with a holiday. After this he began to study theology. His earnest, fervid nature urged him on in another path—the path of religion. He entered the Methodist ministry; but with all his love of the grave and gentle pursuit of a theologian, the world awaiting for him afar off sounded a tocsin in the distance, and with his eyes fixed on heaven's heights the ringing clarion voice of Fame called to him in the veiled distances of the future, and he paused to listen to her summons; and finally, to obey them. In 1878, and again in 1882, Mr. Taulbee was elected clerk of the County Court. That he fulfilled the duties of the office creditably and acceptably goes without saying.

Mr. Taulbee studied law, and he obtained license to practice his profession. This was in 1881. He built up a fine clientage. With his splendid intellectuality, and his remarkable magnetism, he was doing more for himself. He was making a reputation for ability, and evincing on all occasions a public spirit of advancement which endeared him to the hearts of those frank, free, generous, and independent people of Eastern Kentucky, who appreciate merit and know how to reward it, and who, pledging themselves to a man, uphold him.

I am perfectly familiar with Eastern Kentucky, and I speak "by the book," as one might say, for I have ridden over nearly every mountain ridge, and rested in the low, green valleys, and forded the streams that girdle the hills like silver ribbons. It is the most romantic portion of country in the State. I traversed it during the war, and I joyously avail myself of this opportunity to "put it to record" that I never met more cordial and hearty hospitality than I enjoyed in Eastern Kentucky— no matter in what part of the United States Fate or Fortune led my wandering feet. And in the course of time that section of the State—with its untold hidden wealth centered in ores, and minerals, and coal, and lumber, and great water-power, all alike placed there by the same Infinite Hand that traced the divine laws upon the tablets of stone, while the thunders roared and the lightning girdled the mysterious heights of Mount Sinai—in the course of time that section will become, through future development of the State, the wealthiest portion of it. The capitalists of the country have already begun to project railroads there, and when the Swiss and Germans shall wreathe those rugged mountain peaks with the graceful tendrils and velvety leaves and purple and juicy globules of the grape, then indeed will Prosperity smile, and Misfortune forget to frown.

Small need is there for wonderment that William Preston Taulbee has "made his mark" among his fellowmen, and that he has written it boldly and legibly on the scroll of Fame that all eyes may read it. In 1884 he was nominated for Congress by the Democratic convention and he was elected a member of the Forty-ninth Congress from the Tenth Kentucky District, and on the second of November, 1886, he was re-elected to the Fiftieth Congress. With the people of Eastern Kentucky he is a very great favorite, and the confidence and esteem in which he is held are as limitless as they are sincere.

Mr. Taulbee is a brilliant speaker, and rarely fails to carry his audience with him. In presence he is tall and well-formed. His movements are at once lithe and dignified. His face is one of high intellectuality, his mouth betraying eloquence by its very formation. Mr. Taulbee is yet young, and the world is gathering honors to lay upon his shield. His residence at present is in Magoffin county, at the town of Salyersville, but no matter where he goes, be it North, South, East, or West, he will still bear with him the confidence and the love of those who know him best, and the respect and admiration of the general world who only see in him the idol of the mountaineers who have sent him to Washington to "fight their battles," and represent them in national council, as in the days of old the men of Greece and Rome stirred the hearts of their listening countrymen with burning eloquence and valorous deeds.

JUDGE REGINALD HEBER THOMPSON.

For one who takes pride in the soldiers, the statesmen, and the representative citizens of his native State or county, it can be but a pleasing task to attract the attention of the public to those who deserve its respect and command its admiration. Whether the subjects of my sketches be Kentuckians by birth or merely by adoption, because they are the recognized representatives of that State, I take pleasure in citing them as examples of worth and ability to those who emulate them in the present, or may do so in the untrodden years of the future.

Chief among the chosen stands Reginald Heber Thompson. He was born in Kanawha county, W. Va., on October 31, 1836. He is the second son of Robert Augustine Thompson, Esq., who was also a Virginian, born in the county of Culpeper, Va., in 1805, and who was a member of Congress from the Culpeper district from the year 1848 to 1852. Indeed, somewhat singular to relate, his father before him was a member of Congress from that same district during the administration of Mr. Thomas Jefferson, who was the author of the Declaration of Independence, as well as the third President of the United States.

Robert Augustine Thompson was also appointed by Mr. Pierce in 1853 to settle Spanish land grants in California. His wife was Miss Mary Slaughter, the daughter of Captain Philip Slaughter, who commanded the minute men in the Revolutionary war from Culpeper county, Va. Dear old Culpeper! Sacred is every rood of land within thy borders, for it was on thy brown breast the woes and passions of thy children were hushed and hidden after the battle of Manassas!

Reginald Heber Thompson was educated at the University of Virginia, and in 1858 he went to California, and there practiced law until the outbreak of the civil strife between contending sections. In July, 1861, he returned to Kentucky, and thence to Arkansas, where he was elected first lieutenant of infantry, and attached to the Seventh Kentucky regiment, commanded by Colonel Charles A. Wickliffe. After the battle of Shiloh he was transferred to the Thirteenth Arkansas regiment, commanded by Colonel J. C. Tappan. This regiment, being consolidated with General Claiborne's old regiment, was attached to Claiborne's division. In 1862, Reginald H. Thompson was promoted to the position of captain of his company. Again in 1863 he was made major of a regiment of cavalry, and again in 1864 he was made lieutenant-colonel, and held that rank to the close of the war. He was with General Kirby Smith on his march to Kentucky in 1862, and participated in the battle of Richmond, and was also in the fight at Perryville, October 8, 1862. Always gallant, efficient, and fearless, he was equally popular with superiors and subordinates; and, even in times of peace, to recur to his war record must be a source of infinite pride and pleasure to him, for he was a participant in all the important battles and skirmishes of the Western army, and in every one gathered new laurels and fadeless bays for his wreath of glory and renown. What an array of names and what memories do they evoke! Shiloh, Murfreesboro, Chickamauga, Richmond, Perryville! And, to-day, the sun shines bravely, and the sounds of civil traffic and occupation hum in our ears, as if the past had never been aught but a troubled dream.

On June 7, 1866, Colonel Thompson was married to Miss Lily Thompson, of Jefferson county, a lady of many accomplishments, and who was the daughter of William L. Thompson, Esq., a gentleman at that time possessed of a fine fortune, and who had always been prominent among the early settlers of Jefferson county as a citizen of probity, energy, and progressive ideas.

In 1865 and 1866 Colonel Thompson, having laid aside the sword, took up what in   is esteemed the mightier weapon—

the pen. He became a member of the editorial staff of the Detroit *Free Press;* but in 1867 he returned to Arkansas and formed there a partnership in the practice of law with Hon. J. C. S. Blackburn. They settled down to their legal duties in the town of Napoleon, in Desha county, Ark. Each one pined for the free airs and familiar scenes of Kentucky, and in September, 1869. Colonel Thompson came to Kentucky and entered upon the practice of law in Louisville, where he remained engaged with his clientage until December 25, 1882, when he was appointed judge of the City Court of Louisville by Governor L. P. Blackburn, and was re-elected to the same position in 1883, and again in August, 1886. He is a Mason and an Odd Fellow, and has taken high degrees in both societies.

As judge of the City Court he has made himself most acceptable to the people of Louisville. He has shown impartiality, and meted even justice to that class of citizens who would be defenseless without the protection of a man of noble principles and unshaken courage as Judge Thompson always shows himself to be. His duties are onerous and manifold. He has not only the control of judicial matters coming before him for adjudication, but he has the pardoning power from the Work House, and his indorsement goes far with the superintendent of the House of Refuge in obtaining the release of boys sent there on account of their vicious habits and ruinous associations, and restoring them improved and orderly from the effect of example and moral training. Many beautiful girls in their tender years would be led astray were it not for the timely interference of the city judge, who throws the strong arm of the law about them and shields them from danger and evil ways when the affectionate appeals of their parents have fallen unheeded, like seed sown upon sterile soil.

Judge Thompson is not a man of large stature, but great dignity of manner. His features are strongly marked, his face one of great intellectual vigor. In speech he is gentle and impressive. His voice is exceedingly mellow and pleasant to the ear, and he can be approached at all times by those in distress. His heart is kindly, his charity great and unbounded as his popularity both as a gentleman and a judge.

THE THOMPSON BROTHERS.

One of the best known residences in Central Kentucky was the fine old brick mansion belonging to the Thompsons of Harrodsburg, and occupied by them until in recent years it was destroyed by fire. It was famous because of the courtly and generous hospitality extended to all who stood within their gates. The doors were ever open to welcome the coming or speed the parting guest, for the friends of the Thompsons were legion. Philip B. Thompson, Sr., is a lawyer of distinction, and a man of unsurpassed courage and independence. In the Mexican war he commanded a company with brilliance and gallantry, reflecting great credit on himself; and in the late war he was a member of the provisional government of the State of Kentucky. He has been Commonwealth's attorney and is now a member of the Legislature. His acquaintance throughout the State is extensive, and co-equal with his influence, which was—and is to-day—a power in the community in which he resides. His wife is a most excellent lady, handsome, accomplished, and sincerely admired and beloved by those who know how to esteem the pure and lofty nobility of true womanliness. Her maiden name was Miss Margaret Montgomery. And it may be safely said that on no more lofty brow than her own could the crown of maturity descend, or the halo of silver hair rest like a benison. It was not at all surprising, therefore, that their hospitality was generous, and the general appreciation of it diffuse. They had, to bless their union, three splendid children; all were sons—Daviess Thompson, Philip B. Thompson, and John B. Thompson, the last two being twins. They were bright and promising as the human heart could desire, Philip, especially, being confessedly the "apple of his mother's eye," because of his gentle and loving disposition. The twins were born in Harrodsburg, Mercer county, Ky., on the 15th day of October, 1845. They were educated in the academy of Harrodsburg, and had matriculated at the Kentucky University when the civil war began in 1861. At the ages of sixteen years they enlisted in the Confederate army. Indeed, all three of the youthful scions of this distinguished family at an early day identified themselves with General John H. Morgan's squadron, and in his command they served through the entire war, participating in all the battles and raids made by that peerless cavalryman, notwithstanding the fact that they were mere youths. They never at any time shrank from the arduous duties of the faithful soldier. And throughout that long, dark, internecine struggle—during whose fierce continuance so many chivalrous spirits, in defense of Southern rights, deserted their tenements of clay and winged their way to realms beyond the stars—throughout it all, these young and gallant soldiers were spared the breath of life, and allowed, through the dispensation of Divine Providence, to return to their native heather, to greet the old familiar faces, and to be welcomed home again by the friends of their youth. Peace being restored, upon reaching home these brilliant and dashing young patriots took choice of their future professions. Daviess, a singularly handsome and gifted young man, began the study of medicine, graduating with honor, and receiving congratulations on all sides from admiring friends and relations.

Phil and John entered upon the study of law with their father, Philip B. Thompson, Sr., who is recognized throughout Kentucky as one of the best criminal lawyers within her borders. They could not have received finer training than they did at his painstaking hands, for his pride was centered in his sons, and his loftiest ambition was for their advancement in the professions they had chosen.

Upon receiving their licenses to practice law, Philip B. Thompson, Jr., was chosen city attorney of Harrodsburg by the trustees of that town. He filled the position with credit to himself and to the entire satisfaction of the trustees. While occupying this position, he was appointed by Judge George W. Kavanaugh, of the Seventh Judicial District of Kentucky, Commonwealth's attorney *pro tem*. In this capacity he served with marked ability until 1871, when he was elected to fill the unexpired term of the Hon. J. W. Schooling, of Lebanon, Ky., resigned on account of sickness. In August, 1874, he was elected for the full term of six years. He entered upon his duties and served to the general satisfaction of the people. It was universally acknowledged that he was one of the most effective and able prosecutors who ever filled the position in that district. In 1878 he was nominated for Congress at the Stanford convention, over the Hon. Milton J. Durham, after a heated contest, by the small majority of one-tenth of a vote, and at the November election he defeated the Hon. George Denny, Sr. (Republican), by a handsome majority.

In 1880 he was re-elected to Congress, and again in 1882. In every contest, both for nomination and at the elections, he had formidable opposition, and had it not been for personal controversies, he would to-day be a member of Congress from the Eighth Congressional District. He is now practicing law in Washington, D. C.

JOHN B. THOMPSON

Although a young man, Philip B. Thompson, Jr., is admitted to be one of the ablest lawyers as well as one of the safest politicians in Kentucky. In presence, although of slight stature, he has great dignity of manner, allied with much grace and urbanity. His face is intellectual in its cast, with fine expressive eyes. In his friendships he is as true as steel.

His twin brother, John B. Thompson, was named after his uncle, the famous John B. Thompson, who departed this life in 1873, and who was one of the few rare spirits who, living, was universally beloved, and who, dying, left not an enemy behind him. He filled in his lifetime many offices—from county attorney to United States senator—and he filled them all with most brilliant ability. His wedded life was a glimpse of idyllic peace and happiness. It occurred late in life. He married Mrs. Mary Bowman, one of the most elegant, accomplished, and gifted women in the Union, and their association was a felicitous presentment of a well-ordered household and intellectual companionship, based on genuine affection.

Young John B. Thompson possesses many of the admirable qualities of both head and heart that distinguished his splendid ancestor. He is especially a fluent and winning speaker. His address is captivating and magnetic. He scores his friends everywhere. He has not figured so conspicuously as his brother Philip in politics, but as a lawyer he has gained a brilliant reputation, and as county attorney he has won encomiums enough to satisfy the most ambitious heart. He has, however, turned the "cold shoulder" to politics, and is engaged strictly in commercial pursuits. He is handling large sums of money with great success.

John B. Thompson, in *personnel* and manner, is his brother's counterpart—friends often declaring that they can not distinguish them.

Mr. Thompson married Miss Mattie Anderson, the daughter of the distinguished divine. She is one of the most attractive women in the State, brilliant and versatile to an unusual degree, highly accomplished, and personally very handsome. She is a woman to "mark and remember." She is a fine singer, a splendid pianist, and yet, above all other accomplishments, running like a gold thread through the darker fabric of existence, is her charming domesticity, she being even more attractive in the home circle than when she shines supreme in society.

Mrs. Maria Daviess, the author of the able and interesting work on Mercer county and its early settlers, is an aunt of the Thompson brothers. She was a Miss Thompson before she married Major William Daviess, nephew of the celebrated Joseph Hamilton Daviess.

COLONEL STERLING B. TONEY.

I know not if there be few or many who are in harmony with me in the idea that a halo of romance surrounds certain Southern States which can never be dispelled by modern innovations or the varying tides of mutability; but certain it is that in the depths of my heart it is a sweet fancy which I cherish along with memories of the past that " were not born to die."

South Carolina!

Who, to hear the name even of this noble State, but may instantly see arise, like the misty figures in the Fata Morgana, the sad faces of the Huguenot exiles driven from France by the revocation of the Edict of Nantes? And, with the thought of Nantes, comes the train of royalty—the powdered heads, the ruffs, the velvet doublets, the buckled shoes, the silken hose, the perfumed knots of gay ribbons, the light hearted and merry following of the French court, the royal wedding between Anne of Brittany and Louis XII., when the proud possession of Bretagne became the property of the crown of France; the long line of names that loom up like columns of Fame adown the corridors of Time: Henry IV., Louis XIV., Fouche, Bougner, the mathematician—all these visions come at the sound of a word. We can go back and back through the hallowed realms of the past, and remember how South Carolina was settled in 1670 by the English; how a constitution for the colony was formed by the celebrated John Locke on the plan of Plato's Model Republic, but failed; how South Carolina remained a proprietary government until 1717, when it become a royal colony. In 1690, however, the Huguenots settled the State, and subsequently their presence was supplemented by the arrival of a number of Swiss, Irish, and Germans. In the Spanish contests in Florida, South Carolina, with Georgia, under Oglethorpe, did noble engagements. She suffered much from Indian depredations in the early days of her settlement, the Yemasees being especially aggressive; but in 1715 they were effectually expelled. This gallant colony took an active part in exciting the other colonies to revolt and in aiding and upholding their rebellion.

They furnished six thousand troops to the Federal forces, and many a bloody struggle in those dark days took place within her limits—at Fort Moultrie, Charleston, Monk's Corner, Camden, King's Mountain, Eutaw Springs, and Cowpens, with varying success, now the British, and now the Carolinians, having the advantage. The greater part of the years 1780 and 1781 the enemy occupied the State. In the affairs of the National Government, Carolina has ever taken an active part, and in the national councils she has ever been ably represented, having furnished to the country some of the most distinguished statesmen of which America can boast. In the assertion and vindication of the rights of the sovereign States, she has always led the other States as opposed to the powers of the Federal Government. Among her most distinguished statesmen have been Lowndes, Pinckney, Hayne, Legare, Poinsett, and Calhoun. Of her bravery, her decision, her pride, her strength, her martyrdom in the late civic strife, who shall place his pen in rest to do her justice, however fervent his homage? I confess I am not the one who dares lift the veil from the face of the Isis who guards the unknown from the known. The dead past has buried its dead. The *resurgam* is not for the biographer to evoke. In the swift sweep of time's tide it would be no more noticed than the soft piping of a bird at twilight, when the wild waves of ocean are chanting their fugues to the shore. Suffice it that South Carolina is a fitting altar-stone for the people of the South, on which they may offer the balm of tears and prayers in memory of heroism, valor, and fidelity, the immortal record of those who died to serve their native land.

A native of this grandest of all magnificent Commonwealths was Washington Toney, Esq., a citizen of Edgefield, S. C. He was a finished gentleman of the old school, a hero of ante-bellum days, replete with elegance and erudition, an honor to his country, the pride of his family, and a credit to himself. He was celebrated through the South for his hospitality, which bordered on magnificence, and his superb intellect, which rendered him the peer of any man, no matter how brilliant his parts, in all the United States. He married Miss Sarah Bass, of Columbus, Ga. General Alpheus Baker (an attorney at the bar of this city, whose fame as an orator and whose ability in his profession need no heralding from me, for the luminous glow of his genius pales not "with ineffectual fire" before the splendid intelligence of any of his compeers at the bar of this State or any other in the Union)—General Alpheus Baker, speaking of the noble wife of Washington Toney, Esq., said she might aptly have been called the mother of the Southern Confederacy, for she toiled for the soldiers of the Southern army— she wove, she spun, early and late, for them. The Toneys were a grand Southern family. Life, fortune, time, personal service, self-sacrifice, all were their generous offerings on the shrine of Southern liberty. Mrs. Toney adored the South; she would have died to save it, with a song of triumph on her lips which would have rivaled that of Miriam the Prophetess when the children of Israel were saved, and the chariots and hosts of Pharaoh were swallowed up in the Red sea. Hallowed be her name and the memory of her in every Southern heart and every Southern home!

The second son of this amiable and excellent husband and wife was Sterling B. Toney. He was born in Russell county, Ala., on May 24, 1849. His youth was exceptionally happy. He was educated in his earlier studies at the University of Alabama, and at a later day he was matriculated at the University of Virginia, graduating from that institution of learning in 1872 as a B. L. He studied law in Eufaula, Ala., with a jurist of great ability, and entered upon the practice of his honorable profession in that handsome town; but he afterward removed to New York City. While a resident there he met his fate in the person of Miss Mattie Burge, the daughter of R. Burge, Esq., a well-known tobacconist of this city (now deceased). This was in 1876. Subsequent to his marriage, Mr. Toney came to the city of Louisville, Ky., choosing it as a place of permanent residence, and here in that same year (1876) he entered upon the practice of law. He is studious and accurate in his profession, and an orator of elegant diction, and was admitted, on motion of Samuel F. Phillips, Solicitor General, to the bar of the Supreme Court of the United States, March

27, 1886. He is an earnest and enthusiastic worker and always in the van in the assertion of his rights and the maintenance of his principles and opinions. He took an active interest in the Greeley campaign when hardly more than a boy. In the Tilden campaign he was also an earnest laborer for the cause he esteemed to be right; and in the Hancock campaign he raised a club by his indefatigable industry and perseverance, he, himself, canvassing Indiana. He never lost faith or heart in the eventual triumph of the Democratic party. In this last campaign he made fifteen speeches upon the invitation of the State Committee of Indiana. He has been engaged in many important lawsuits in and out of the State, acquitting himself always with great and commendable credit. He recently appeared as counsel for a New York company in a very important case, involving great mining interests, growing out of the invasion of Maximilian into Mexico and his usurpation of the Mexican Government. The title of the claim is that of "The La Abra Silver Mining Company against Mexico." Mr. Toney made his argument before the Committee of Foreign Affairs, House of Representatives, Forty-ninth Congress, which elicited much gracious comment on his ability, and it has been pronounced an admirable effort, which has been seldom excelled for pungent, terse acumen, and thorough knowledge of national amenities and individual rights of corporations. His fee in this one case is ten thousand dollars.

Mr. Sterling Toney is very popular with his friends, and in a recent race for the position of judge of the Louisville Law and Equity Court he received nineteen thousand votes.

He is not better known politically and at the bar than his charming wife is known socially. She is a lady of the finest judgment, the kindest heart, and noblest charities. She is a queen in society, and her influence for the development of the purity and refinement of society and the culture of the mind is very marked and elevating with all who have the honor and pleasure of her acquaintance or her friendship. Their marriage has been exceptionally happy. Two children, have blessed their union—R. Burge Toney, a son, and Miss Emma Louise, a charming daughter, of whom the proudest parents might well be fond.

HON. HENRY WATTERSON.

There are now and then individuals who are so resplendent with genius and magnetism that their names are watchwords to the world.

Kentucky possesses such names! So does Virginia; so does South Carolina; so does Massachusetts. Indeed, each State in the Union can boast of its shining lights—heroes, statesmen, divines, orators, and artists! But where is there an American-born citizen who does not take pride in perpetuating the names of Webster, Everett, Winthrop, Sumner, Clay, Calhoun, Marshall, Madison, Monroe, Henry, Pinckney, Rutledge, Breckinridge, and hosts of others want of space forbids me to mention? How do the sounding honors of courts and thrones bear contrast with them? What are the transient glories of earth in comparison with their immortal renown? The possessors of these names were intellectual giants. Their minds were of an order of intelligence that seems to have almost completely passed away. They were socially and personally prominent, and politically and in a civic sense they were pre-eminently masters of their day and time. It was not at all strange, therefore, that they shrined themselves in the hearts of their countrymen, and left Fame to "guard with solemn round" their resting-places among the dead, while posterity cherished their memories in unison with their love of God. We have living and to-day but few brilliant exemplars of their eloquence and strength. The race of intellectual Titans bids fair to become extinct. In Kentucky, especially, we have Blackburn and McKenzie and Breckinridge, and one or two others, versatile but less prominent, who have won national reputations for eloquent oratory.

But there has lived a man in our midst for a number of years who can not be excelled in any school. He shines like a planet among stars. His genius, the profoundness of his logic, the depth of his philosophy, the versatility of his talent, the soundness of his principles, positively can not be surpassed.

That man is the Hon. Henry Watterson.

He has been the object of more general interest, personal regard, and genuine admiration than perhaps any man who has ever made Kentucky the home of his adoption.

It has been said that Nature repeats herself. If this be true, then the exception makes the rule, and Henry Watterson is the exception; for he has not his superior, and, in point of brilliance, address, policy, and magnetism, it is an open question if he has his peer in the United States.

He is the son and only child of Hon. Harvey M. Watterson, who was born in Bedford county, Tenn., in the year 1811. His mother's maiden name was Miss Tabitha Black. She, also, was a Tennessean. Her birth-place was in Williamson county, Tenn. She was born on the 21st of June, 1812.

Mr. Watterson, Sr., was a member of Congress from Tennessee, and his residence was in Washington City at the time of the birth of his gifted son, which event bears date of February 16, 1840.

Of Henry Watterson, it could scarcely be said that he at any time attended public schools or colleges, having been principally educated by private tutors. His parents were very proud of him. His precocity was remarkable, and it elicited anxiety as well as admiration in their hearts, through fear that his brain would outgrow the strengthful power of his body to sustain it.

Because of this circumstance, his education was conducted with singular care in the privacy of the domestic circle. The advantage of such tuition is always evident in after years. The intellectual development of the recipient of the attention is more brilliant and well-defined because the course is more thorough than can possibly be acquired in the classes of public institutions of learning. It was thus that the germ of genius in his soul was fostered with the tenderest care.

The passion for literature which he possessed and soon evinced defined its existence at an early age. He began to write for the Washington *States* (a paper edited in Washington City) when he was about fifteen years old. From that time on he became a constant contributor to papers and periodicals.

The first newspaper of which he became the editor was the Chattanooga *Rebel*, in the early part of 1862. Subsequently, he moved to Montgomery, Ala., where he continued his newspaper labors, this time assuming editorial care of the Montgomery *Mail*.

Those were stormy days, and the publication of any sort of literary matter was a hazardous undertaking, because labor was so uncertain. Active service was required on the part of all men able to shoulder a musket, and steady printers were a "scarce commodity." When the war was ended by the surrender of the Confederate States, Mr. Watterson proceeded to Memphis, Tenn. But, at that time, the outlook for newspaper enterprise was anything but cheerful. As a consequence, he continued his travels to Cincinnati, Ohio, where he became one of the editors of the Cincinnati *Evening Times*, the duty devolving on him to act as critic of theatrical matters. But Henry Watterson had not yet found the niche Fame meant for him to fill. His restless spirit led him to Nashville, Tenn. There he revived the old (yet ever dear) Nashville *Banner*, which, in other days, had been one of the leading and most influential journals of that State. Before the war it was a Whig organ; but Henry Watterson revived it as a Democratic paper of such purity of principle, of such soundness of doctrine, and such spirit and perspicuity that it at once sprang into popularity, and on every hand won praise and admiration. Mr. Watterson continued to edit it until the spring of 1868, when he received a letter from George D. Prentice, Esq., inviting him to come to Louisville, Ky., and saying that he would sell to him his interest in the Louisville *Journal*. Mr. Watterson acceded to the proposition. He came, he purchased Mr. Prentice's interest in the *Journal*, and by so doing he planted his foot securely upon the step leading to the throne of public popularity. Mr. Haldeman was at that time publishing the Louisville *Courier*. In the latter part of 1868 the *Courier* and Louisville *Journal* were consolidated, and the old Louisville *Democrat* was also purchased from Mr. Harney, and merged into the *Courier-Journal* Company, Mr. Watterson becoming the editor, a position which he has held from that time to the present. He has ever taken a deep interest in the success of the Democratic party and what should be its policy in those questions involving the national weal. Frequently he has taken the stump, North and South, in the respective States, needing his influence and argument, for he is not only a splendid writer, but he is an orator of great finish and power, and the new adherents to the party principles of Democracy won by his eloquence were like the clans of Roderick Dhu—there was a man for every heather plume.

In 1876, when the National Democratic Convention was held at St. Louis, Mo., Mr. Watterson was chosen by its delegates as the speaker of the convention, with Mr. McClernard, of Illinois, as its secretary. In November, 1876, he was elected to Congress to fill the unexpired term of Hon. Edward Parsons, deceased, and served to March 4, 1877.

It was during that memorable winter that the abnormal electoral commission was formed by Congress, and the result was the establishment of Rutherford B. Hayes as President of the United States, notwithstanding the fact that Mr. Samuel J. Tilden had received a majority of the electoral vote of the States and a large majority of the popular vote.

Mr. Watterson was a delegate from the State at large from Kentucky in the years 1880 and 1884 to the Democratic National Conventions.

In December, 1865, Mr. Watterson was married to Miss Rebecca Ewing, the daughter of an eminent lawyer of Nashville, Tenn. She is a lady of great refinement and beauty. Their marriage has been an exceptionably happy one. They have five children—three boys and two girls.

Mr. Watterson has made three trips to Europe, never forgetting while there to regale the readers of the *Courier-Journal* with a charming narration of the people of the Old World whom he meets, and the wonderful scenes that his appreciative eyes behold. At the present time he is traveling in Europe with his family, and as usual, his letters are sought for and read with great avidity by his admirers, who may be found in every State in the Union.

He is a man of remarkable personal magnetism. I say remarkable because his manner is gentle, quiet, almost cold; but the tones of his musical voice, the suavity and dignity of his address, the pertinent good sense of his conversation, never fail of the fair fruition, of winning friends and adherents to his cause, to his opinions, to his party, to himself. When the time shall come for Henry Watterson to go hence to the undiscovered country, where lie the pleasant fields of eternity, those who live after him will tell to the rising generation that they " will never look upon his like again."

"May he live long and prosper!" is the fervent wish of every friend he cherishes, and every American citizen who has the success of the Democratic party at heart.

HON. ALBERT S. WILLIS.

No man in the city of Louisville is as familiarly known as the distinguished subject of this sketch. Rich and poor speak of him as though he were a member of their immediate families. Nowadays the phrase "Have you seen Albert Willis?" has almost resolved itself into an aphorism, implying as it does (especially among office-seekers) a conviction that he not only holds the key to success, but that in him lie the secret of power and the knowledge of all that is worth knowing. When this term closes, he will have served his constituents for ten years, with zeal, ability, and good faith, in the Congress of the United States. He entered that body March 4, 1877, subsequent to the reconstruction acts, which cost the country nearly as much as did our civil war. Mr. Willis participated particularly in the debates upon the resumption of silver currency, that being a question which greatly agitated the minds of the people, the efficacy of the move upon the financial interests of the country involving grave doubts, and being the subject of much excited discussion. John Sherman, finally fixing his grasp upon the mooted dollar as firmly as the Goddess of Liberty is stamped thereon, formulated the majorities in its favor, and so far settled the remonetization of silver. The Chinese question and the school prorate of the unlimited moneys in the Treasury among the respective States have both been subjects of earnest debate since Mr. Willis has been in Congress, and so manifest has been his influence in Washington that no doubt there are many of his constituents who regard him as the central power in that august body politic. They speak of the large appropriations which, through his vigilance, he has received for his district, and of the pension applications that had slept in the dusty departments for years, until they were resuscitated by his magic hand and placed properly upon the rolls. No effort is too laborious for him to make in behalf of his constituency, and indeed for years his life has been one of arduous endeavor to serve well the people of his district, a duty which I may as well add he has faultlessly accomplished.

He is very quiet and unostentatious in his manner and address, yet singularly magnetic. The blind, the halt, and the maimed alike want to talk with him—and sometimes even family matters are brought to him for discussion as though a word from him could restrain the wayward, comfort the invalid, and banish despair from the hearts of the unhappy. If ever a man verified the idyl of "the shining mark" to the rising generation, Albert S. Willis is that person. He is no less admired than he is beloved as an intelligent, moral, and conscientious gentleman. Higher praise than this could not be uttered, and its truth renders it the more harmonious to the ear, for it is the voice of the people that speaks it of him. When in Washington he neglects no duty involved in his position, and even to respond to his manifold correspondence is an onerous task; yet the humblest and poorest of his constituents command his prompt and respectful attention equally with the rich and the influential.

Albert S. Willis is the son of Doctor Shelby Willis, who was a native Kentuckian and a near relative of Isaac Shelby (for whom he was named), who was the first governor of Kentucky.

Mr. Willis' mother was a Miss Harriet Button, the daughter of Captain Button, of Oldham county, Ky. After the death of Doctor Willis she married Mr. Clemmons, a lawyer of this city. The subject of this sketch was born in Shelby county on the 22d day of January, 1841. He is a congenital Kentuckian. No wonder he possesses so many estimable attributes. In 1860 he graduated from the High School in the city of Louisville. He immediately adopted the law as his profession, and after reading a thorough course with his stepfather and present law partner, Mr. Clemmons, he entered the senior class at the University of Law in Louisville, and graduated from that institution, delivering the valedictory of his class in 1865. He then entered upon the practice of his profession with Mr. Clemmons, and with him enjoyed a fair and profitable clientage until 1870, when Mr. Willis entered a hurdle race with nine contestants for the office of county attorney. A convention was held and one by one his opponents were dropped until he was declared the nominee. In 1874 he was re-elected without opposition. In 1876, after an active and somewhat acrimonious canvass, he was nominated for Congress, defeating Doctor Lawrence Smith, the distinguished chemist and scientist, who was possessed of great wealth, allied to wide influence, and also defeating the Hon. Robert Mallory, of Oldham county, who had formerly been in Congress, representing a part of the Congressional district. The Republicans nominated the Hon. Walter Evans (the ex-Commissioner of Internal Revenue), who was gracefully defeated in November, 1876, at the polls, by the election of Mr. Willis with a complimentary majority. Before Mr. Willis had served his first term in Congress, the Hon. John Watts Kearney announced himself as a candidate for his place. He was known to be immensely rich, and the "bummers" commenced without delay to herald his fine parts and peculiar adaptability for the position. Calls were inserted in the newspapers signed with innumerable names, and maps with artistic lines of Kentucky and a portion of Tennessee were published at great expense and delivered over the district, with fans of variegated patterns and designs as bizarre and brilliant as if they had been manufactured in Japan, and the name of John Watts Kearney for Congress was on every one of them. As the time for the election drew near and the organization was formed for the contest, money, to buy the floating votes of the city, was planted like gourd seed about the cabin of the old-time Guinea negro. The campaign song rang upon the air to the tune of "My Old Kentucky Home," where it says:

> "We will sing no more by de glimmer ob de moon
> On de bench by de little cabin door."

Money was so plentiful every other bummer seemed to expect to move into a palace that mirrored its marble walls in a placid lake, or at the least into a "brown-stone front," as soon as the election was over. At this juncture of affairs, Colonel Blanton Duncan fired a soap bubble into mid-air by way of announcing himself as a candidate for Congress. His speeches and peculiar appliances for conducting his novel and brilliant campaign received his undivided and individual attention, winding up by petitioning the United States district judge of

Kentucky to appoint United States supervisors to prevent the wholesale purchase of suffrage at the polls. A picture of Colonel Duncan and his "lay-out" (as it is called in modern parlance) conducting that famous campaign would fill a page in *Josh Billings' Almanac* worthy a first class chromo-lithograph.

Colonel Horace Scott was the Republican nominee. But despite money and appliances and party power, Mr. Willis was elected by a handsome majority. His third race was made against Judge William B. Hoke, who withdrew, and a portion of the Democratic party nominated Major Thomas H. Hays, in whom all the attributes of the gentleman center in one grand and refined gem of a man. Colonel Thomas E. Burns was the Republican nominee. Mr. Willis, however, was again re-elected. For his fourth term Colonel Silas F. Miller was the Republican candidate—always with the same result, in the favor of Willis. His fifth (and present) term the Hon. A. E. Willson, with confidence in his election, was pitted by the Republicans against him, and, as a consequence, the fate of all his political predecessors became his at the election in November, 1884; but in 1886, in a similar aspiration, Mr. Willis was himself defeated by Hon. Asher G. Caruth in the primary election, which took place on October 9th.

Mr. Willis was an assistant Democratic elector for the State at large in what was called the "Greeley race," and by his arguments in many of the towns in the State he made for himself the reputation of being familiar with national politics long before he became a member of Congress. Mr. Willis has strong adherents among the fair sex who invariably espouse his interests when he is a candidate, and while the cold, chilly winds of November whistle without, they manage to "make Rome howl" around the hearthstone, and the promise to vote for Willis is much more efficacious in restoring peace than the tempting anticipation of a sealskin sack, with a vote for the opposing candidates. Mr. Willis married the daughter of Mr. W. H. Dulaney, of Louisville, Ky., one of our wealthiest and staunchest citizens. He is of medium height and spare build. His eyes are gray; so is his hair. His manner is gentle, his voice persuasive. In brief, he is "never afraid to talk out in church" in regard to national, State, and municipal affairs. He is a bona fide Democrat and advocates its doctrines with seriousness and effect. Mr. Caruth, in defeating him in this district, has won a victory worthy of record, for among his constituents Mr. Willis seemed to have gained a right to the title of "Willis, the invincible."

HON. LEANDER COBB WOOLFOLK.

When one considers everything in connection with the history of Kentucky—from her earliest settlement to the present time—the savage warfare within her borders—the many disadvantages under which she labored before becoming identified as a State, with rights and privileges of her own, and the power to repel infringements and oppressions on whatever hand they might be presented—the splendid people who voluntarily cast their lot with her, to rise or fall, as she might do, in the union of brave spirits, who had crossed the ocean in order to maintain principles and opinions in the matters of liberty, free speech, and religion—when one considers all these things, I say, it seems a natural sequence—arguing from cause to effect—that such noble endeavors and heroic courage should still be apparent in the speech and action of descendants, even to the third and fourth generation, of the grand people who settled Kentucky over a century ago. It seems natural that in their proud natures and aspiring minds they should still exhibit something of the primal strength and ennobling genius of those ancestors who not only left them land and renown as rich inheritance, but made Kentucky a star among States—a splendid Commonwealth which has stood for lo! these many years, like Minerva among the gods! In the midst of wars and the calmness of peace alike able to defend her honor and to uphold her principles in the face of the civilized world.

From border to border, it is the same old story—the best blood of Virginia, of North and of South Carolina, of Maryland, of Georgia, and of Florida, have mingled with each other in the veins of the present inhabitants of Kentucky. It is not strange, therefore, that the chronicler finds themes for his praise and admiration in the lives of those who represent us, abroad and at home, who everywhere clothe themselves with the mantle of honor, and who bear the palm of public respect in their stainless hands.

Kentucky gentlemen as a rule are unpretentious and unostentatious. They know well who they are, and to what they are entitled; and if not willingly ceded to them, they know how to wring that respect from the general world which is their due.

Oftener is it true than otherwise that we find men of the most brilliant parts indifferent to their greatness and nobility, and as modest in asserting one or the other as wayside violets are shy about seeking the sunlight, when they grow beside the blatant buttercup and the flaunting scarlet of the cardinal flower. Indeed, such gentlemen take greater pleasure in pressing their friends forward to receive the meed of public praise and emolument than they do in being themselves heralded as worthy to wear the crown of general favor, and to guard the throne of the people with the grace and courage of cavaliers.

Such a man is the Hon. Leander Cobb Woolfolk, the subject of my present sketch. He is the fifth son of Thomas J. Woolfolk and Adeline Caldwell, both of whom belonged to the best families in the whole country, Miss Caldwell being a native of Woodford county, Ky., she having been born in that county in 1813, and a descendant of the family of John C. Calhoun.

Mr. Thomas J. Woolfolk was born in Orange county, Va., in 1799, but when he was only a year old his father moved with his family to Kentucky—emigrated to the new and wonderful land about which so many stories were afloat—resolved to share the fate of good or evil fortune with the valiant pioneers. This was in 1800.

They settled in that part of the State which was afterward erected into the county of Oldham in 1823, being named in honor of Colonel William Oldham, of Revolutionary fame, who continued in active service until the spring of 1779, when he resigned and emigrated to the Falls of the Ohio, now Louisville; but he commanded a regiment of Kentucky militia in the memorable battle of St. Clair's defeat, November 4, 1791, where he fell—killed by the Indians.

The face of the country along the Ohio river and Eighteen-mile creek, and in the upper part of the county adjoining Trimble, is hilly and broken; the remainder of the county is gently undulating, and generally good, arable land, based on limestone. The principal products and exports are wheat, hemp, tobacco, hogs, and cattle, and in this rich portion of the State—rich in natural adaptability of soil and resource—the Woolfolks cast their life lines, and from that time to the present day they have been people of influence and power and position in the community in which they lived. Many of them—for the Virginia family was a large and prosperous one—moved into other counties, as did also some of the sons of Thomas J. Woolfolk, after they arrived at man's estate; but Oldham has ever been regarded as the "vine and fig tree" of the clan. Whatever places of public trust they have been called upon to fill they have done so honorably and well, and in the councils of the State their voices have at all times rung out with no "uncertain sound;" and the principles they advocated and the opinions they entertained have ever been marked by noble earnestness, purity, and honest endeavor to sustain the right. Joseph B. Woolfolk, who represented Meade county in the lower house of the General Assembly from 1865 to 1867, and S. H. Woolfolk, who filled the same position for the people of Hopkins county from 1871 to 1873, were men of spirit and brilliance; and record gives a not less prominent position to Hon. George Woolfolk, of Shelby county, who was a member of the House of Representatives in the State Legislature from 1822 to 1828. Thomas Woolfolk, who represented Owen county in 1829 to 1831, was also a man of mark and acknowledged ability.

Thomas J. Woolfolk, of Oldham, was always the staunch friend of General Humphrey Marshall. He supported him in every aspiration for public office, and was his chosen and "bosom friend," *as a Whig*. They frequently took counsel together in matters of public interest, and General Marshall's faith in his sound judgment and good sense was often a subject of comment among their mutual friends. What Woolfolk said or thought always had its weight with General Marshall, and he seldom demurred from the strength and wisdom of his friend's opinions.

Leander Cobb Woolfolk was born in Oldham county, Ky., May 27, 1843. He graduated at the Washington and Jefferson College in Pennsylvania in 1866, carrying off one of the honors of his class. In 1868 he attended the University of Law in Louisville, Ky., and in 1870 he entered upon the practice of his profession in the same city. He was recognized as a man of great promise and brilliant ability from the inception of his appearance before the courts as a practitioner. In 1878 he was elected county attorney of Jefferson county. In 1882 he was re-elected without opposition to the same prominent position. In 1886 he was again re-elected without Democratic opposition, but he defeated the Republican candidate for the office by the handsome majority of fourteen thousand votes.

In 1877 Mr. Woolfolk won the hand of Miss Fanny H. Owen in marriage, which was a signal admission of his eloquence and power of fascination, for Miss Owen was herself very popular in society and a lady of very brilliant accomplishments and much personal beauty. They have one child, a bright and charming little girl—Mattie Lea Woolfolk—who is the pride and delight of her parents, and who gives promise of one day being an ornament to society and a blessing to the hearts that now cherish her in her youth.

COLONEL BENNETT H. YOUNG.

Colonel Bennett H. Young is the third son of Robert Young, Esq. His mother's maiden name was Miss Josephine Henderson. Both father and mother are congenital Kentuckians, and the names of their ancestors are among the most honorable and prominent of which the annals of the State can boast. They were all devout Presbyterians.

The subject of this sketch was born in Jessamine county, Ky., on the 25th day of May, 1843. The earlier part of his education was acquired at Bethel Academy, in Nicholasville, Jessamine county, Ky. In 1861, however, he matriculated at Centre College, Danville, Ky.; and in 1862, affected by the spirit of the times and the ardor of the age, with which the surroundings of his hallowed home were no less affected than our entire country, Bennett H. Young found it no difficult duty, as his youthful mind then dictated, to drift into the army of the Confederacy, enlisting in Company "B," commanded by Captain William Lewis, of Fayette county, Ky., under Colonel Leroy S. Clarke, of the Eighth Kentucky Regiment, Morgan's Cavalry.

When General Morgan was captured at Columbiana, Saline county, Ohio, in August, 1863, Bennett H. Young was with him, and was still with him when he was taken to Columbus, Ohio, and there imprisoned.

From now on, until after and for quite a period succeeding the close of this most unfortunate civil struggle, it was Colonel Young's lot to play a more or less conspicuously prominent part.

After a brief confinement in Camp Chase, he was removed to Camp Douglas, Chicago, from where he escaped in January, 1864, going to Canada, where he arrived too late to pass down the St. Lawrence before the close of navigation, and fearing to pass through Kentucky in face of the protests of his friends, where military executions were rife, he at once matriculated in the University of Toronto, remaining until April and passing a highly creditable examination. He was placed in command of a number of escaped Confederate prisoners, and took passage on the first boat going down the river in April, and sailed for the West Indies, in order to catch a blockade runner for either Charleston or Wilmington.

The blockader went in under fire. Several of the crew were killed, and the sailors were so demoralized as to give up all obedience to commands. The cool head and fearless courage of the young Confederate soldier were in this moment of peril exceedingly valuable. With almost reckless exposure, he promptly took the post from which a seaman had the moment before been killed, assisted the officers in giving proper signals, and thus saved the vessel from capture or destruction. The gallant stranger was at once offered a most tempting and lucrative appointment in the blockade-runner service, but declined it.

Appointed to a first lieutenancy in the Confederate service, he was sent to Canada, and subsequently engaged in many daring and hazardous enterprises, the last of which was the St. Albans raid.

Subsequent to this, the life of Lieutenant Young was one of remarkable and thrilling experience. Details have been erstwhile related. They concerned a career in which courage, coolness, danger, hardihood, and resolution played equal parts, where youthhood never forgot itself; but now, in the mature judgment of manhood, not even this modest man's bright boys and girls ever hear on his part any allusion to the gallant deeds of the past recorded history given in a cause in which he then believed, and they therefore need now find no more than a passing mention here.

His disabilities having been removed by the later amnesty proclamation in 1868, he returned from Europe, where he had studied several years at the Irish and Scotch universities, taking first honor in the law course and third distinction in the literary department of the Queen's University. His letters and magazine articles while abroad served in large part to meet his expenses, and were widely read and copied.

He commenced practicing law in Louisville in 1868, and soon built up a large and lucrative practice. He was much of his professional life associated with St. John Boyle, the firm being Young & Boyle. Both members of the partnership became interested in railways, a connection which has been of vital importance to Louisville.

With Mr. Boyle, he first constructed the Louisville, New Albany & St. Louis Air Line railroad, a very difficult operation at the time, the success of which assured a fair prestige. A more serious and important scheme followed, no less than a plan to buy and revive and reconstruct an almost dead line—the Louisville, New Albany & Chicago railroad. Realizing the resources of the rich territory terminated and touched otherwise by this line, Colonel Young conceived the idea, in concert with R. S. Veech, Esq., of securing control of the Louisville, New Albany & Chicago road. Colonel Young designed the entire plan, and with the usual felicitous result, for it was successful and highly contributory to Louisville and her commercial interests. In 1883, Colonel Young became its president, and so remained until the early part of 1884. During his management it was successful beyond all anticipation; but his "peculiar" views about operating trains on Sunday caused some dissatisfaction, when he retired, with his usual vim and independence adhering to his own opinions, he being emphatically one of those men who, knowing he is right, yields neither to the blandishments of friends nor the opposition of foes.

In October, 1885, he undertook the construction of the great cantilever bridge from Louisville, Ky., to New Albany, Ind. After being beset by many difficulties (owing to the amount of capital involved pro and con), the stupendous work was completed on the 15th day of .... The cost involved was probably a million and a half of dollars, and it is past question the foremost structure of its kind in the .... Of this corporation Colonel Young is president at the present time.

He claims for his "monument" the Bellewood Seminary and the Kentucky Normal School, at Anchorage, Ky., of which he is now regent, and which is at this time the leading school of its kind in the Southern Presbyterian church. His friends know him to be generous and whole-souled; in point of fact, as a prince is supposed to be, and he made almost the .... endowment out of his own private purse.

He has always been the moving spirit of the Polytechnic Society, and to him it owes its present distinguished position. It constitutes the remainder of the old public library. The sheriff had secured this property (the old public library) and was about to sell it for debt. Colonel Young promptly went on a bond for a large sum of money, and by his own noble action, in connection with Dr. D. S. Reynolds, persuaded Dr. Robinson and other gentlemen to join him, and, together, they stood for forty thousand dollars. They placed the society on a firm basis, paid off its debts, formulated a series of public lectures to be given by scientific men, and enlarged its collection of valuable books. Now it has an income sufficient to support it and to maintain its art gallery, its lectures, and its free library. So much for having a genuine, noble-spirited, large-brained, kind-hearted man at the front of an affair involving public weal, and which will redound with the greatest good to the largest number. Such a man is Bennett H. Young. And sure am I that the citizens of Louisville will bear me out in the assertion, for he has done her incalculable benefits. He is is in all respects a model gentleman, and possesses not only the regard of the community in which he resides, but the respect and confidence of the leading railroad magnates of the United States and of Europe, which is the handsomest guarantee of ability in the world, for they have among them not only the most successful but some of the most able and cultured of which the Western continent can boast

The highest ambition in Colonel Young's life is said to be to have a happy home and to lend a helping hand to aid the moral and the material welfare of the citizens of his native State. To do this he spends time, energy, fortune. No one will deny that he is the most tirelessly energetic, enthusiastic, and progressively public-spirited man Kentucky now has, or, for matter of that, ever had. He is a most remarkable and usefully-necessary combination, having the ability of a Carlisle, the acumen and strong business judgment of a James Guthrie, led on by the dash of a Sheridan and tempered with the inherited pure Christian spirit of what man has most to thank God for—noble parents.

The enterprises now engaging Colonel Young's attention involve the development of Eastern Kentucky, a region richer than Pennsylvania or Alabama, and the construction of the Louisville Southern railroad. The last line is the hardest fought enterprise of his life, but it is now beyond the injury of its opponents, and its completion gives to Louisville for a comparatively nominal cost all the benefits of a competitive grand trunk line to the South, a territory of which hitherto a single line virtually controlled the transportation rates.

No public enterprise of later years has failed to receive his help and assistance. Unselfish, charitable, modest, and yet a man of aggression and conviction, he commands the respect and confidence of the entire State. Colonel Young is a tremendous power in any contest, a ready fighter, an able organizer, quick to think and act, full of resource and tact, with a bulldog courage that never recognizes defeat, his services are always in demand. One of the shrewdest politicians of a bordering State, who knew him well, said: "Young in a State like mine, in a hard contest, would be worth ten thousand votes." The life and work of such a man in a community yield immense returns. One single enterprise has removed from the commerce of Louisville a tax of over two hundred thousand dollars per annum, and the construction of the Louisville Southern will add millions to the wealth and trade of that city. Doctor E. D. Standiford estimated that the building of the Southern would increase the taxable values of Louisville twenty per cent.

Colonel Young has never offered for any political office. He could have almost any position he would seek, but he prefers to devote himself exclusively to the material development of his city and State, and in this Louisville and Kentucky are greatly gainers. He is a fluent and forcible speaker. Take him in a "rough-and-tumble" fight before the masses and he has few equals and no superior in Kentucky. He has a rare combination of force, logic, and fun, and he never fails to catch, hold, and convince the crowd. A distinguished judge once said of him: "He is the most terrific man on the last speech I ever heard."

In 1866, Colonel Young was married to Miss Mattie R., the eldest daughter of Rev. Stuart Robinson, D. D., the distinguished Presbyterian divine. They have quite a family of children, and their home is noted for its culture, refinement, and hospitality.

MISCELLANEOUS

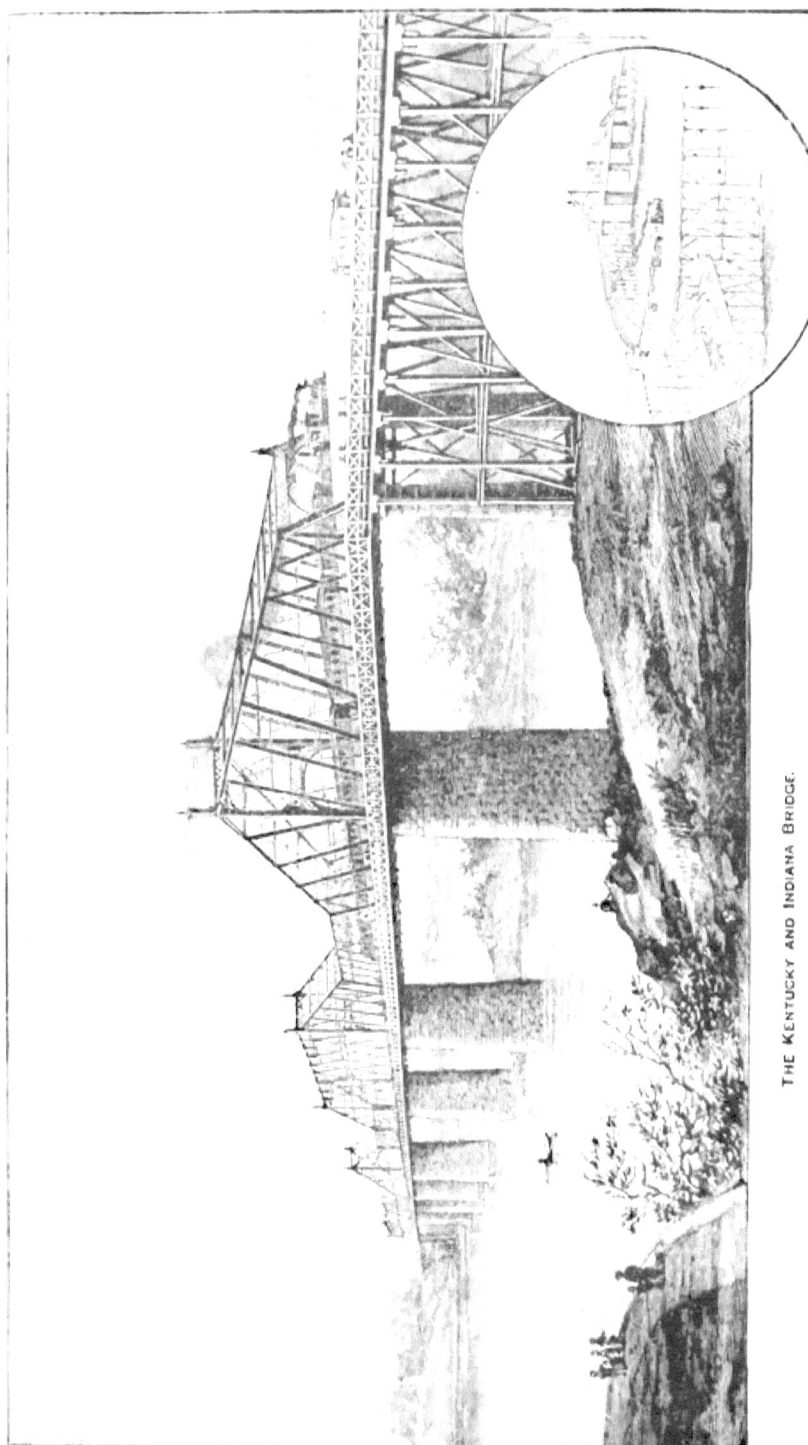

THE KENTUCKY AND INDIANA BRIDGE.

A VIEW OF LOUISVILLE AS A CITY AND A HOME.

COURIER-JOURNAL BUILDING.

Even to the habitual writer for the press, sometimes, the idea of communicating thought to the populace is one which requires more than ordinary reflection, for the reason that it is not everybody who can successfully cater to the public taste and awaken interest in the production. Language is a vehicle which conveys ideas, and thought must necessarily be the germ of the product which becomes the freight of the conveyance. For this reason, when one takes up a pen for the purpose of writing an article which will please, one often lays it down again with the sober conviction that it is a Herculean task.

This is my mood to-day. And, however generous my intention toward my readers, however enthusiastic my feelings over my chosen subject, so much is to be said that I feel myself to be but scantily supplied with eloquence commensurate with the occasion.

Louisville is considered, by tourists and cosmopolitans, as an overgrown village, which can boast of but few of the facilities that other cities claim. Yet, as a place of residence, none can compare with it, for the reason that it is quiet beyond many of the smaller hamlets throughout the State. And yet, Louisville is the home of every nationality, and they are permitted, under our liberal system of government, to worship the great God of the universe according to the dictates of their own consciences, and to delve out an existence by the sweat of their faces, as required by His Holy Word.

One can sit in his office here, and, in the course of the day, hear the tongues of the Saxon, Teuton, Gaul, the liquid melody of the Italian, the sibilant music of the Spaniard, the brogue of the Celt, the harsh mingling of consonants peculiar to the Russian, and the breezy chatter of the Scot, all jumbled together like the tongues that wagged during the erection of the Tower of Babel.

Louisville has charms that fascinate all who become acquainted with her people. Her society may be likened to that which blessed Athens in the days of Demosthenes and attracted Cicero from the city of Rome, when the genius of its men and women shone out upon the world like the sun smiling amid the angry storm clouds.

This is the city, of all cities, where the races clasp hands as friends, and are always ready to put down wrong wherever it lifts its hydra head. Our religious sects are the most tolerant and kindly-disposed toward each other. Our commercial men are emulous of success, but the carping jealousies, sometimes found amid that class of citizens, is never noticed among them. Our legal fraternity boasts some of the most brilliant men in Kentucky. Our public edifices are fine. The Cathedral is noticeably grand, when compared with the churches of the New World. The Court-House is perfect in its various compartments. It is a study to visit our Post-Office, and see the thorough system inaugurated in every department. Our hotels are par excellence. Our places of amusement are popular throughout the State as well as the city, being well built and well conducted. Our police is vigilant, our city fathers careful of our interests and the progress of the city in all that is advantageous and ennobling in its development. The public schools are all that we could desire, and the dissemination of learning among all classes of our citizens, through their instrumentality, is highly gratifying to the public at large, and to every private citizen who takes pride in his city and his State. Our art studios are very fine. Our libraries are social institutions, and reflect credit on the city. We have eight lines of railway; two iron bridges spanning the Ohio, connecting Louisville with two Indiana cities; and an Opera Festival and Exposition. Our "measure" seems full.

New Orleans may boast a gayer population, New York a "faster" one, Chicago a wickeder one. Baltimore may bear the palm for epicureanism and St. Louis for progression, but we bear the palm (and we intend to bear it) for the refinement of our people, for their intelligence, and the lofty cast of our society, as well as the open-handed charity and hospitality of its opulent members and the gentle spirit of fraternity which rules them. Our press is popular, and conducted with that lofty spirit of principle and patriotism which deserves the most generous recognition from the State and country at large.

Search the wide world over, we know of no city where we would prefer to live, and none where we would prefer to die, above or beyond the City of the Falls. Its pleasures are the purest, its emoluments are the noblest, and the peace to be found, at the last, in our beautiful sanctuary of the dead, would, no doubt, be sweeter here than we could hope to find elsewhere.

A EULOGIUM

Pronounced in the House of Representatives in 1873 on the Resolution to Remove the Remains of General John Adair to the Frankfort Cemetery for Re-interment.*

John Adair was born in Chester county, S. C., in the year 1758. His childhood had its full quota of smiles and tears—its freedom from care and consequent happiness—as does the childhood of nearly all who live, let their days be passed under the golden roofs of kings' palaces, or with the tent of the vagrant gypsy above them.

And his manhood had its triumphs and its failures, its disappointments and successes, as do the lives of all men who live in the world, and of it form a part. But that the triumphs were more numerous than the failures, and the successes more frequent than the disappointments, the brilliant record of his political and public career bears ample testimony.

In all positions, military or civil, he discharged his duties faithfully and well. Born amid the thrilling incidents of the Revolution, and his character formed amid those stirring events, when the tocsin of war was sounded, when the ear-piercing fife and the roll of the thundering drum called on patriots for decisive action, he was in the vanguard, whether it was to do battle with treacherous Indians, or route the scarlet coats of the Britishers under Jackson at New Orleans, or under Shelby amid the Canadian wilds!

And again, we see in the annals of our Commonwealth, where he served as a United States Senator from 1805 to 1806. In the years 1831 and 1833 inclusive, he was a representative in the Twenty-second Congress, and last, and highest of all, he was elected governor of Kentucky in 1820. And yet, after the hardships and trials, after the glory and grandeur, the pomp and the circumstance, the closing of the record reads pathetically enough: "He died at Harrodsburg, Ky., on the 19th day of May, 1840, and was buried three miles east of said town."

"And was buried!"   *   *   *   *   *

---

* The resolution was adopted, and a magnificent monument now marks his last resting-place in the cemetery at Frankfort, Ky., the epitaph it contains having been written by the author.

This was the last item to be added to the long list of a good, brave life's deeds! This was the "finis" to the record of one of Kentucky's most chivalrous and distinguished sons!

The book was closed and clasped. *   *   *

Is it strange that strugglers up the steep heights of honor and renown should pause and—thinking of it all—give one heartfelt sigh to his memory?

Is it not simply a just deed to lay this immortelle upon his grave? Was he not an eminent statesman? Was he not a distinguished soldier? Was he not a gentleman of patrician blood, who filled many honorable stations in the public service? And does not that public, indeed, owe to him the reverence of an "In Memoriam?"

It seems like presumption in me to even attempt to pass an encomium upon him! His life was a shining light to his country a quarter of a century ago, and his record survives the dust of time and forgetfulness, and is yet a beacon star to the loyal ambitions among men, let them hail from what State or section they may—North, South, East, or West!

And, therefore, be it known, I come not to do honor to the ashes of dead Cæsar to-day, but justice!

During a former term of the Legislature a fund was voted by the State to be appropriated to the re-interment of Kentucky's deceased governors in the cemetery of the capital.

With but few exceptions this has been done, and these were left by request of the surviving relatives who found a nameless comfort in the nearness of the "loved and lost."

This exemption, however, is not noted in the case of Governor Adair, for his estate has passed from the scions of his house into the guardianship of strangers. And yet the old hero sleeps undisturbed in his narrow home while the blue, jewel-lighted skies arch above him and God keeps his niche in heaven.

Why is this?

Why has John Adair been left to sleep the sleep of the "undistinguished many" when marble stelæ and shining shafts lift themselves above the nameless and unknown?

Why is he not also conveyed to that "eternal camping-ground" where silent tents are spread

"And glory guards with solemn round
The bivouac of the dead?"

It is true that his has been a quiet sleep, and old Mercer is proud to hold him in her heart, but Kentuckians should remember to do special honor to the memory of one who so honored the Commonwealth by his faithful services in peace and war. And even though they sepulcher at the capital only a handful of dry, white dust, heaped over with a mound of grass, they should do it reverently, gratefully, in memory of John Adair, for, in the language of the immortal bard—

"On the earth there breathed not a man more worthy of a woman's love, a soldier's trust, a subject's reverence, a king's esteem, the whole world's admiration!"

> "Nor should his glory be forgot
> While Fame her record keeps,
> Or Honor points the hallowed spot
> Where Valor proudly sleeps."

A HUMOROUS PROPOSITION

To Act as Umpire in the Controversy between Governor Proctor Knott and the Hon Milton J. Durham, Controller of the U. S. Treasury.

As a peaceable citizen of Kentucky I gratuitously volunteer my services as umpire between the Governor of Kentucky and Hon. Milton J. Durham, the Controller of the Treasury. I do this in the kindest spirit, hoping thereby to prevent the shedding of much human gore, which might occur through the accidental (?) discharge of the famous Kentucky "hoss-pistol," it being quite likely that either gentleman (according to the social code) may arm himself with the said dangerous toy, forgetting, in the excitement of the moment, that there are certain stringent laws in regard to carrying concealed deadly "weepins" in this State.

This unfortunate conflict, coming, as it does, in the wake of the matrimonial alliance of the President, casts a gloom upon the hearts that desired to take joy in the general dissemination of happiness incident to the national nuptials—even as the small cloud, "not larger than a man's hand," may overcast the blue of heaven until it darkens with the wrath of the hurricane.

Governor Knott, in his first open letter to the controller, complains of the latter's murder of the king's English (or at least the stab given to it by him which may prove mortal), the cruel wound having been inflicted in a letter to Esquire Gill, of Shelby county, Ky., which was meant to be "private," but which found its way into print through means not made public—as yet.

It is apparent that the "Guvner" has taken umbrage at the Hon. Milton J.'s aspirations toward the position now filled by His Excellency, for he has unsheathed his matchless sword of eloquence, which, if not made of veritable steel, can at least create blue lightning, having been dipped in virulent satire which has endowed it with the fine quality of a first-class jack-knife—to cut both ways.

It seems that the "Guvner," with the characteristic pride of a Kentuckian, feels deeply aggrieved that a gentleman who holds so prominent a position as that of Controller of the United States Treasury should express his patriotic sentiments in bad grammar to the brave and sympathetic people of Kentucky, and, moreover, by innuendo intimated that *his* administration was not a gigantic failure, but, from an *ex parte* view, a *diminutive* failure, on account of his lack of executive ability. In ante-bellum days party leaders could be discriminately or indiscriminately discussed, their acts being praised or censured by individual or general voice; but, according to the changes in the natural order of public affairs, this course, being no longer sanctioned by custom, is no longer admissible. The Hon. Milton J. seems indeed to have regarded the administration of State affairs quite in the light of a child's toy balloon. To touch it with a needle or any sharp instrument allows the gas which has inflated its transparent proportions to escape, after which, even for amusement, it is not worth a tinker's damn. It seems that in addition to his *sub rosa* criticism of Governor Knott, Judge Durham proves himself no disciple of lazy, delightful, kind-hearted Izaak Walton; in brief, he does not allow himself to be governed by the accepted rules of all good fishermen. Big fish are allowed to take the entire reel before efforts are ever made to land them.

He seems, too, to have forgotten that he who proves too much proves nothing. In retaliation for the Punic faith with which his confidence was treated, he intimates in unmistakable terms that Governor Knott holds his office as Hayes held the Presidency, *i. e.*, by chicanery and fraud, and he suggests that if His Excellency had ceded the spoils to the conqueror, when he saw that the Hon. Thomas Laurens Jones had received the nomination, he would have forsaken his thirst for office, have stepped to the footlights on that memorable day in Liederkranz Hall, and have declined to accept a nomination obtained by strategic skill, and not by the voice of a majority of the delegates. While the honorable gentleman by these timely suggestions proves that, in his judgment, justice should be done though the heavens descend, there are those who be denizens in this "Grand Old Commonwealth" who are not slow in making acknowledgment that:

> "Of all the beautiful pictures
> That hang on memory's wall,"

The one of the distinguished representatives of the Eighth Congressional District, baptizing his pedal extremities in the wash-bowl allotted to the faces of gentlemen in the committee-room, is perhaps the most beautiful. By such act, it is true, he was a faithful exponent of the creed that "cleanliness is next to godliness," but the abhorrence and disgust of the dilettante Northern Lights taught him the sad lesson that a man may "shake the dust from his feet" in leaving his native State, but he could not dispose of alluvium in the speckled wash-basin of a committee-room without at least running some risk of cold—shoulder.

So extreme has been my anxiety in regard to the issue of this wordy warfare that it has led me—I frankly confess it—to seek a council with that intellectual giant of Oldham, General Tom A. Harris, who has traveled in every clime and been a beacon in every refined society (I hope the compositor will not make a mistake and print this word "deacon" instead of "beacon!!!"), and he has timidly suggested the intervention of some spirit willing to face the "music" of whizzing bullets, Gatling guns, and other instruments of ancient and modern warfare that may be in vogue in the way of battering rams, lances, spears, rapiers, battle-axes, tomahawks, and "sich like," and dispossessing them of these side-arms restore repose to the public mind, and peace and harmony, and above all, the usual amount of homogeneity to the Democratic party. Kentucky loves those of her sons who are capable of deeds of disinterested valor. Therefore, I offer myself, in the spirit of Curtius, the brave Roman youth, to fill this hiatus which threatens to divide the interests of the Democratic party in Kentucky.

A LONG TIME IN SADDLE.

The Longest Ride Made by Marshall's Cavalry During the War.

In the year of 1863, on the 10th day of August, the order to report at once to headquarters was received by Marshall's Cavalry which, at the time, under command of General Geo. B. Hodge, was stationed at Giles Court House, or Parisburg, as it is sometimes called (being the post village of Giles county, Va.), situated on the left bank of the New river, and surrounded by as picturesque mountain scenery as may be found anywhere in the world. Parisburg is two hundred and forty miles west of Richmond, and nearly a hundred miles north-west from Abingdon.

In response to the command, the "Cavilery," as Morey (now of the Cynthiana *News*) called it, prepared for the march that was to lead them to the gory fields of Chickamauga, thence around Rosecrans to McMinnville, which was the base of General Rosecrans' supplies, while his army occupied Chattanooga, and I believe I can truthfully assert that General Wheeler, with his cavalry (a large body at the time), destroyed more Government stores than were captured on any raid during the war. There were thousands of pounds of bacon, large quantities of flour, sugar, molasses, coffees, teas, and ordnance stores, and hospital accouterments. Bombshells were bursted by the hundreds, whose reverberations could be heard for miles around as if a great battle were being fought; everything was destroyed that could not be carried along, or sent forward in the army wagons that were captured at the same time and place. From McMinnville the march was continued to Murfreesboro, recrossing the Tennessee river at Muscle Shoals, and thence to Courtland, Ala., General Wheeler making his headquarters at the residence of a lady by the name of Miss Jones, whom he subsequently married, and in passing, it may not be inappropriate to mention the fact he still resides there, and represents that district in Congress. A lengthy and historic ride was that which began in August and brought us to the month of November of that same year. And all the while the cavalry had been constantly engaged in making forced marches and continuous skirmishes, including the three days' battle of Chickamauga, the history of which has long since been given to the world, painted in the glowing colors of victory, and the terse etching of defeat by the ablest writers in both armies; and, therefore, I forbear waving my small ensign in memory of it, preferring to call attention to those points in history which are usually overlooked by the dignified writer who hopes to enfold his equally dignified thoughts in vellum and Russia leather, and neglected by the facile pen of the correspondent who is fond of personalities in which generals and colonels are conspicuous—viz: To the poor horses and the "little Confederate mule," and the equally poor and stubborn private soldier who "fought, bled, and died" a thousand times over in the service of the "Lost Cause" they so dearly loved for itself alone. I occupied the position of assistant adjutant general at the time, and had ample opportunity to grapple the details of camp-life fully, and noting the condition of both man and beast, to sympathize with and appreciate privations they endured. The weather was excessively dry, no rain having fallen for days, and the dust would rise like moving clouds above the cavalry as they marched in column; indeed, so dense was it that each army could easily locate the other by this dusky signal in the heavens. Everywhere the country suffered from the drouth; accommodations were almost unattainable, the principal articles of food being green corn and sweet potatoes, gathered from the half-tilled fields, and sometimes eaten raw as we rode along the dusty highways or roasted when we encamped; while, to lend diversity to the entertainment, occasionally a fat hog would be murdered with malice aforethought, by some stray picket "hid in a thicket," and when the murky mantle of darkness covered the world, the brown breast of Mother Earth was the softest pillow on which her rebellious children could lay their weary heads. This paucity (to the soldier at least) of all that made life endurable was the general condition of the country from the narrows of New river via Abingdon, Va., Bristol, Jonesboro, Greenville, Sevierville, and Hamilton to Athens, Cleveland, Tenn., and Dalton, Ga.; thence to Rome, Ga., and back to Cottonport, east of the Hiawassee river, at which point the Confederate cavalry crossed to capture Rosecrans' supplies. Then the condition of affairs was changed for the soldier. Rations were drawn, and the "inner man" was satisfied, especially with the decoctions of the coffee bean that were boiled in large kettles, and made strong as "black drops," and served effectually to aid him in enduring the exhaustion to the nervous tissues superinduced by the wearisome marches on horseback, than which nothing can so wear flesh and spirit, many men sleeping in their saddles.

Amid the privations, and the wear and tear on body and soul, there still were, even then, the most amusing incidents that gave food for

THE BARREL MARCH.

merriment, to lessen the anxious thoughts summoned from the heart's recesses by the dogs of war. One picture I especially remember, which, for the ridiculous, could hardly be surpassed. About two hundred deserters had been dressed in barrels and kegs of all kinds and sizes, their heads had been closely shaven, and they were made to march through the streets of Dalton, Ga., to the music of a band, as a mark of disgrace for the abandonment of the cause of their choice and their lack of courage in a time that tried men's souls. The different sizes of these fellows, the equally different sizes of the barrels and kegs, the variety of countenances, the contour of heads peering above them, would rival the novelty of expression in the noses of a company of Baltimore Plug Uglies, and the equal novelty of coloring in a patch of hollyhocks growing in a poor man's garden. Colonel Cofer, of the "Orphan's Brigade," was Post Commandant of Dalton at the time. He was afterward Chief-Justice of Kentucky. A more ludicrous picture yet was that of the Confederate Cavalry crossing the

Tennessee at Cottonport, and confronted by Generals Minter's and Wilder's Federal Cavalry. Some of the Confederates were riding little mules that must have been first cousins to those whose histories Mark Twain recorded in the pages of "Innocents Abroad." Their little eyes looked so tired, their little legs seemed to tremble with weariness at so long bearing upon their sturdy little backs such burthens of valor. They wore upon their heads every conceivable shape of hat, the variety of which none but an old rebel could comprehend. Their garments were as varied and faded, worn and torn, as was their head-gear. Their feet were about as well covered—sometimes, indeed, not covered at all—and sticking out from the sides of their mounts, in many instances, as if with the intent of establishing a sort of natural abattis to the approach of the enemy. Thus accoutered and attired, they passed along, making the woods and hills re-echo their song:

> "We are the honest yeomanry
> From old Kentucky's soil,
> A fighting for our property
> We gained by honest toil."

The cavalry, after leaving Courtland, moved to North Alabama with the intention of going into winter quarters, but the movements of the enemy in South-western Virginia were of such a character that they occasioned our being ordered to Virginia, marching via Atlanta, Ga., to Greenville, S. C., via Morgantown, N. C., to the Yadkin Valley, where we encamped on the farm of the Siamese Twins, who treated us with marked consideration.

Referring above to the honest yeomanry fighting for property reminds me of a fist fight I witnessed near Atlanta between two soldiers. One was a Texan; the other a Kentuckian. The former had given mortal offense to the latter by saying, "I was out here fighting for your property while you were in Kentucky sleeping on goose hair!" (another name for feather).

The application of certain opprobrious epithets followed, and, as a consequence, a hand-to-hand struggle ensued, in which the Kentuckian brought "the first blood," boasting that no man should or could "throw into his teeth" that he was fighting for his property while he was at home sleeping on goose hair. The suggestion of a supine position and the languid ease of a feather bed seemed to especially incense him. I became interested in the developments of the case and "made free" enough to inquire what property he possessed when he left "God's country?"

He promptly replied, "None; I possessed none; but that fellow shall never be the wiser."

This was eminently characteristic of a soldier. I have frequently heard them, when sitting around the camp-fires, boast of their wealth and the comforts whose enjoyment they were denied because of their pursuit—as they thought—of their "rights." Indeed, the average Kentuckian is rather "frisky," to confess the truth, when it comes to reaching out for office, bragging upon his individual merit or asserting his entire independence of time, place, and circumstance. I think Kentucky can "bear the palm," even from Mississippi, as the home of "born heroes." At least, any man might thus argue who had shared their privations in camp, as I have done, and who twenty years after has the privilege (?) of sitting under the sound of their voices and listening to their tales of valiant heroism—with a few mental reservations—there stands no immediate need of flaunting in the face of an attentive and "intelligent audience." Nor is the average Kentuckian inclined to modesty wherein the subject of "self" is involved. He grows brighter with adversity, even as "fox-fire" shines best in the darkest places.

Kentucky, in the days of "lang syne," certainly had some adroit fellows in our command. They were noted, equally, for their horsemanship and courteous address. They exhibited an aptitude for accommodating themselves to almost any emergency. When the famine drove Abraham from the land of Canaan into Egypt, if he had had even one of those cavaliers as an avant courier, he would never have been driven to the necessity of claiming a fraternal interest in Sara, in order to get something to eat; for that advance guard could have won his way, and found the place of secret stores without any difficulty. To watch their insouciant grace on all occasions was, in itself, as good as a play. To win the Pass of Thermopylæ to their Spartan courage seemed mere child's play, and they could as readily have conquered three hundred Xerxes and their armies, to hear them tell it, as have died in the Pass with Leonidas and his followers.

It is pleasant to recall the amusing incidents of the war; the memory of them is like gathering roses from waste places, or hearing the song of birds amid the dust and roar of booming cannon and clashing arms.

One other reminiscence and I shall have done.

There was on a certain occasion the trial of a private soldier in the Confederate cavalry, in which the poor fellow was charged with four distinct offenses. First: That he had never brought a canteen of water to his mess since he had been in the army. Second: He had never had a blanket of his own to sleep on, winter or summer. Third: That he depended on his mess for both his smoking and chewing tobacco.

Fourth: That whenever he was placed on vidette duty he was certain to invite an attack from the enemy. A judge was selected and a jury was impaneled on a log, and two lawyers were appointed to prosecute and defend. After the examination of half the company and the conclusion of the arguments, the jury took the case and acquitted him on the ground that, while probably all the charges were true, no comrade had ever heard him utter a syllable of complaint when detailed by a sergeant for any purpose whatever, whether to go upon what was called a hazardous expedition, or to do fatigue service. There are many soldiers living in this city who remember the trial and the flaming speeches that were made on that memorable night. And comical to relate, immediately upon the return of the jury with the announcement of acquittal, the accused asked a friend for a chew of tobacco, which very nearly caused his rearrest.

"Gander-pullings" were occasions of state with the cavalry soldiers, and "shin-digs," as they were termed by us, that were given by the girls in the neighborhood of the camp, left indelible impressions on the minds and hearts of those who were participants in their enjoyment, and in some instances resulted in marriage. To-day, where families have been established, there exists co-extensive diversities in fortune and affection; but where the ghosts of memory alone people the halls of the past, and their immaterial faces bloom like the phantom flowers in the deserted hearts of the old soldiers, it can but be a source of pleasure to grow young again in the recalling of other times and other scenes amid the rush and whirl of the busy life of to-day.

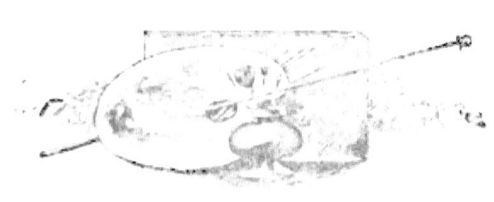

OLD PROVIDENCE CHURCH, AND THE TOMB OF GENERAL ROBERT B. MCAFEE, NEAR MCAFEE'S STATION, MERCER COUNTY, KY.

CHRISTMAS TIMES OF LONG AGO.

And How the Country Boy Celebrated Them.

The advent of Yule-tide throughout the Christian world is usually anticipated as the most prominent event of every year. It is such a holy and beautiful time—a time for wiping out old scores and beginning again—a time for little acts of kindness, of generosity, of self-sacrifice whose magnitude is recognized only in heaven. Millions of dollars are annually expended in commemoration of the birth of Christ, the Saviour of mankind, who gave His life to expiate sin and save sinners. His holy example to the children of earth was so full of loveliness, so replete with beatific gentleness and forbearance that, to the contemplative soul, the expenditure of all the world's hoarded wealth in celebration of even one anniversary would be but a meager offering to His divine memory. Only too often the sacred time is given over to feasting and merry-making, without a thought of the beloved Master or the pangs He endured, for sake of even the lowliest and least among us. For myself, I love everything that is sacred, or that has for its object refinement of the senses and elevation of the soul. The word Christ embodies the Church and its divine teaching, and haloes the heart with the rainbow of hope in eternal life. Seeing the preparations for the happy time going on in the busy world about me; watching the eager delight with which matrons and maidens and light-hearted children anticipate the day, and the zest with which men, with the burdens of business cares heaped upon their shoulders, turn aside from the thronged marts of trade, and the rush and drive at the Bourse, to form or renew their acquaintance with Santa Claus, for the sake of the dear ones at home, revives in my heart the memories of lang syne over which, waking or sleeping, shines the golden light of love, like the glow of a sun that never sets at all.

It is many and many a change that time effects on all of us; not only in a physical sense, and in point of sentiment and feeling, but in habit and in custom. The enthusiastic "craze"—for it can be called little else—for expensive automatic toys, and the thousand and one varieties of articles suitable for Christmas presents, and as mementos of the day that will outlive the transient pleasures of its celebration, recalls to my mind the primitive delights of other days when the insidious charms of bric-a-brac shops and toy stores (where Santa Claus makes his deposits of curiosities fresh from Wonderland every year, just before the advent of Yule-tide,) were less prevalent than they are to-day,—and I take pleasure in contrasting the past with the present, with the gentle hope blooming like a rose in my heart, that the reminiscences of my own boyhood may recall that lost, delicious time to the minds of other men whose enjoyments were perhaps as innocent and pure as my own, and the memory of which, also like my own, may be imperishable.

I was reared in the country. My father was a descendant from one of the Scotch-Irish ancestry, and attended the Presbyterian Church for "refreshment" in the days of Rev. Thomas Clelland, who began his sermons at half past nine o'clock in the morning, and concluded them only in time for the "flock" to get home by the going down of the sun. In those good old days the female members of the congregation almost invariably carried with them to church old-fashioned reticules filled with "rations" for the children of the flock, and there being usually a sort of recess between morning and evening service, it was the "accepted time" for refreshing the "inner man," while the religious contemplation of the soul upon supernal subjects was for the time being abstained from, only to be resumed with renewed vigor at the reopening of afternoon service. About a half mile distant from the church was a well, with an old oaken bucket, much resembling the moss-covered pail of which Wordsworth sings in immortal strains. It was worked by a pole over a post, in which a groove had been cut and a wooden pin thrust through two auger holes bored at opposite sides, allowing space for the movements of the pole. The bucket was suspended from one end of it, and a large rock fastened to the other end. A primitive and crude way of drawing water from a well, but as I remember the taste of the cool, crystal-clear liquid to-day, there was never a diviner draught quaffed by human lips. It was to this well that we sojourned to partake of refreshments for the body, and, to my mind, seen by the light of to-day, those variegated reticules were the most mysterious receptacles for the good things of earth ever invented. Surely such round, red-cheeked apples, and rich brown gingerbread, spiced to a queen's taste; such flaky biscuit and rosy ham, were never found elsewhere than in the queer, quaint reticules, with the drawstrings at the top, our mothers used to take to old Providence Church, in Mercer county, for our special delectation! What did it matter to us that the sermons had their fifteenth and sixteenth parts? We were satisfied and happy, and when we were tired we young members of the congregation went to sleep. There was no desire for slumber upon the parts of the elder listeners. The Rev. Thomas Clelland was a very popular minister. He was among the first of Kentucky's prominent clergymen, and his impassioned appeals to the hardy pioneers to look beyond the present and fear the wrath to come often brought tears to the bronzed cheeks of those who had endured the hardships of pioneer life without murmur or flinching. The evils to which the flesh was heir amounted to nothing with them, in comparison with the temptations to the soul. Temptations! In those days, it seems to me now, there were no temptations, except for little boys, in the way of playing marbles, and hookey, and stealing apples that always looked so tempting and were so sour! The difference between youth and maturity is so vast and unfathomable. It may never be bridged or crossed. Until I was fourteen years old I had never seen a Christmas toy—had never read a fairy tale. The wonderful tale of Cinderella and her glass slipper, the harrowing experience of Red Riding Hood and the wolf, and the marvelous maneuvering of Prince Fortunatus with his queer little red cap, were sealed treasures from me, nor did I ever find the door at which I could cry "Open, sesame!" until the desire to solve the mysteries beyond it had passed away.

My father's family, white and colored, numbered about twenty-two folk, and my recollection, now, is that we were all light-hearted and happy. In the month of November, every year, there is a special season recognized among the yeomanry as "hog-killing time." When it rolled around, the struggle among the boys to obtain the "bladders" was sharp and decisive enough to have delighted an Alexander or Napoleon. Never in all the year was such industry shown or such obliging dispositions displayed. Their blandest smiles and most unique compliments were gracefully bestowed upon their butcher without stint or measure. The bestowal of a "bladder" was considered by the country boy as a mark of great appreciation of his good qualities, and always exhibited by him with an air of triumph that would make the fortune of any mimic conqueror on the stage, could he at will assume it. Certain am I that the most charming toy of modern invention was never received by a town boy with one-half the zest displayed by his rustic cousin. The "bladder" was always duly "blown up" and suspended from the garret rafters to await the coming of Christmas. It was never forgotten or ignored. On the morning of the twenty-fifth of December, the sluggish and uncomely youth of the country would rise at four o'clock and climb to the loft after his signal guns, with which to offer his crude salute to the coming of the blessed day. After the quaint supply of their gaseous ammunition was exhausted, there always remained to them a still cruder way of making a noise, which was to hew a smooth place upon a log, and, spitting upon it, to place thereon a live fire coal, and then to strike the coal quickly with the bole of the ax, thereby creating a fearful blast. This sport was indulged in until the announcement that the egg-nog was ready for drinking. Talk of your French liqueurs, you who will, and of your Green Seal, and Ives' Seedling, and all that sort of thing, but the egg-nog our mothers made out of cream and eggs, sugar and good whisky, was a drink fit for the gods, whether you spelled it with a big or little " G." After the "nog" was enjoyed, came breakfast. This consumed, the dogs were called, and all hands, barring the "women folk," started for the woods and through the fields for a Christmas rabbit hunt. At night various entertainments were sought in the neighborhood, and merry-making continued throughout the week. But no fire-crackers, and no fretful and furious toy pistol played parts in those days! And when the new year dawned there were no records of accidents and deaths from the use of "bladders" and fire coals. Christmas day and the week ensuing was only a delightful dream, in which snow-clad fields and leafless forests and skittish rabbits, howling and yelping dogs, and hooting voices of care-free boys, were oddly and incongruously mixed up with roasted turkey and pumpkin pies, sweet cream and "cow butter," with a whipped syllabub of eggs and whisky. Alas! those golden days are indeed relics of a dead-and-gone forever past that take no part in the life of to-day, but are somehow sacred and set apart like the graves of the loved and lost. I take pride in the progressive features of the age, but because our nights are illuminated by electricity, and we seem to have no need for moon and stars, I love not less to recall the times when men loved to look up to them with awe and wonder as to unapproachable worlds on worlds, without knowing anything about the use of telescopes or taking a scientific view of their spheres and orbits, and all that. And although I look on and admire the brilliant exhibit of fireworks, even as does the sweet-scented dude who smokes his sugared cigarette, I sigh to recall the dear old days, now dead forever more. Even the old-time darky exists no longer. Now he is a "gem'man ob color," who carries his revolver and his razor as an evidence of his freedom. His song is no more heard at the corn huskings as of yore. His mellifluous notes that once filled the air with melody are now like the strings on Tara's harp, from which the soul of music has fled, and which now hangs mute on Tara's walls, as if that soul were dead—or something to that effect, according to the Prince of Melody, only that Tara's harp lost its harmony when Freedom died, and the darky lost his voice because Freedom was born again. However, I offer the quotation because, as "Mary Jane" would say, it chimed in as if it was the right thing in the right place.

The old-time customs, with the living of to-day, are like national cemeteries—they bear the inscription, "In Memory of — ——," all over them. The time has also passed for the horny-handed yeomanry to drink "Home-made Bitters," which was composed of pure whisky and yellow poplar and dogwood barks. In lieu thereof, they have learned the names of all the fascinating modern beverages—which, by the way, are not as "safe" for a constancy as the old time "dram." Funny, is it? but nevertheless a fact, that when the wife of one of the old time yeomen rebelled against the use of the "Bitters" aforesaid, he sought his physician, stated his dilemma, and obtained from him a recipe, which was invariably "a quart," with two dry reeds stuck down in it to induce the unsuspecting wife to have faith in its medicinal properties.

Ah, well! These were simply little frauds, indulged in for the stomach's sake, in the primitive days of the country, before the art of lying had become epidemic, and the spirit of truth was lost in the chaos of total depravity. Such stories do to laugh over. They amount to nothing.

For my part, at the inception of Christmas cheer, I would add a word of encouragement for Steve Holcombe and his good work, and would say further that I personally have no objection to the installation of Moody, Sam Jones, and "all of 'em," in our midst, unless it be Bob Ingersoll, who, fascinating as he may be in advancing his individual ideas, can never induce me to repose faith in his patent bridge as a safe pass over the river to the eternal camping ground on the other shore. I love to believe that Christ was born to save sinners, and that He died to redeem a benighted world.

"FEBRUARY 22D."

A Speech, Commemorating this Sacred Day, Delivered in the House of Representatives, February 21, 1873.

Mr. Speaker: When the gentleman from Campbell moved to adjourn in honor of George Washington's birthday, I had no doubt in my own mind but that the motion would carry without a dissenting voice, especially after the concurrence of the House in the Senate resolution providing for the firing of a national salute at midday. Had I entertained such a doubt, I should have been tempted to ask the indulgence of this honorable body even earlier than I now do, that I might have appealed to their pride as Americans—as *Kentuckians*—to defend their institutions as they do their honor, and, surely, the commemoration of George Washington's birthday is an institution which should ever be called to remembrance, and celebrated with honor and solemnity by every man whose soul is not so dead as

> "Never to himself hath said:
> 'This is my own, my native land.'"

To-morrow is the 22d of February!

From my earliest boyhood, I was taught to revere and keep holy, first, the Sabbath day, and, next to it, the 22d of February, George Washington's birthday! How the simple words carry the mind away back "down the corridors of time!" How we recall the stories of his innocent boyhood, his youth, replete with honor, courage, and intelligence, his manhood, through which he stood "first in war, first in peace, and first in the hearts of his countrymen."

The storm of the Revolution surged over us, and passed, and we are a free people, but he who was the morning star of liberty is no longer cherished in the hearts of this generation, although the nation has not completed a century of existence.

It does occur to me that we are rapidly forgetting or ignoring those time-honored customs whose observance once characterized Americans, and, most especially, *Kentuckians*. I regret, exceedingly, that any member upon this floor has put himself to record against the motion made by the honorable member from the county of Campbell, for record *lives*, while oral expressions die away upon the air like sounds from a well-strung lute.

We owe the commemoration of this day to the blood that was shed at Bunker Hill, to the first battle that was fought in defense of American liberty. And we owe it to Kentucky's illustrious dead who fell at Buena Vista, and nearly all of whom lie in your State cemetery. If it were in my power, I would bring back Theodore O'Hara, Tom Monroe, and all of Kentucky's gifted sons who proved themselves worthy of their nativity.

Theodore O'Hara sleeps to-day in the valley of the Father of Waters, restfully, as becomes so great a soul, so gallant a spirit; but Kentuckians are unjust to themselves when they leave their distinguished dead to repose forever in another State. The green graves of his countrymen who sleep "On Fame's eternal camping-ground" call for honor to him *to whom honor is due*. Those were the men who reflected glory upon Kentucky, who made her fame for prowess on the tented field and inspiring eloquence on the rostrum as wide as the roll of the seas.

The name of Kentucky is known everywhere. Henry Clay and his compatriots accomplished this much for her. Such spirits as she had embodied in her brave and gifted sons inspire song and poesy and chivalry in the hearts of the "loving and the daring," wherever the light of civilization shines.

Two of the heroes of Buena Vista—the honorable gentlemen from Anderson and Taylor—are on the floor to-day. No longer needed in the "rank and file" of the army of the republic, they are to be seen in the solemn council of the State. I would be willing to adjourn in their honor, for surely they will hold to-morrow sacred in their memories. The Senate has adjourned over.

This precedent has long existed, and it should never be ignored while reason holds her throne or memory lasts. It is a time-honored custom. It should be perpetuated through

"Cycles of ages yet unborn."

And I ask again earnestly, appealingly, is it possible that a Kentucky Legislature is the first to make the breach rather than the observance? Is it possible that a *Kentucky Legislature* refuses to respect not only the birthday of George Washington, but also the blessed memory of those whose genius and greatness, whose gallantry and goodness, have made us so proud of the "Dark and Bloody Ground?" What is so dear to our hearts, so sacred to our honor as the "dead past" our illustrious predecessors have bequeathed to us? Let us not then shame it by ignoring a custom that was dear to them and should be dear to us.

Now I am the descendant of a race of people who were the compeers of Boone. They came through Lavisa Fork nearly one hundred years ago, when this country was lonesome through the last degree of dread, and when the forests seemed too dark for a ray of sunshine to penetrate the dense, umbrageous boughs to cast its brightness even on "a sere and yellow leaf." The red man and the wild beasts of the wilderness possessed the country. They had naught to guide them on their journey but their manly courage, their strong right arms, and their trust in God. Yet, I dare say, they held sacred the anniversary of the birth of the great chieftain of the republic, and I want to follow in the wake of their fealty to liberty. I want this Legislature to remember the fame of Kentucky, and not recede from the position of honor and trust which she ascribes to every one present.

Kentucky was the first State admitted into the Union after the adoption of the Federal Constitution—the inscription upon the marble block she furnished to the construction of Washington's monument tells this much—and the motto was suggested, we believe, by the illustrious John J. Crittenden: "Kentucky, the first State admitted into the Union under the Federal Constitution, and will be the last to go out of it."

And ah! through blood and tears *did she not keep her faith?*

She has no glory that is not ours.

As a young Kentuckian, I am justly proud of all her history. She has not a landmark that is not as dear to me as the ruddy drops were that visited Brutus' sad heart. Aye, I love her as England was beloved by Pitt or as an Athenian loved the City of the Violet Crown; and I would not destroy a memory or desecrate a custom of her people any more than I, with ribald jest, would dare invade the solemn sanctity of a holy temple of the Lord.

Custom is the Al Sirat between the past and present, and the sin of forgetting an honor due to the dead, who gave us country and State, because he is dead shall never weigh upon me as a deed that would have been more honored in the observance than the breach. Let the man present, who can, look upon the portrait of George Washington,

"God-like, erect, with native honor clad." and vote against the resolution to adjourn in honor to his illustrious and glorious memory. *I can not*.

George Washington was a man who was eminent because he stood high compared with all around him; conspicuous, because he was so elevated as to be seen and observed; distinguished, for he had that about him that made him stand apart from all others in the public view; celebrated, for he was widely and universally spoken of with honor and respect; illustrious, because a splendor was, and *is*, thrown around him, and the memory of him which confers the highest dignity. To commemorate his birthday will be a token of esteem paid to worth; a mark of respect; a sign of consideration; a reverence; a veneration, and I, for one, as an American, as a Kentuckian, *as a man*, shall celebrate it.

Bishop Taylor once said: "Sermons are not like curious inquiries after new nothings, but pursuances of old truths," which I quote for the reason that it applies to my remarks. I have ventured nothing new, but I have told "old truths," and I trust this honorable body will accept them at their worth, as the solemn conviction of a man who knows, and "knowing, dares maintain," all the rites due to the memory of a knightly and chivalrous soldier, a patriot, and a gentleman.

BIRTHPLACE OF GENERAL GRANT.

GENERAL U. S. GRANT.

How sudden are the blows of fate! What change, what revolution in the state of glory! To-day we walk with head erect, level-fronting eyes, and haughty mien; to-morrow, by some untoward chance stripped of our panoplied pride, we find there are none so poor as to do us reverence. The poet of poets has written eloquently of adversity, claiming that its usages were "sweet," and that like the ugly and venomous toad, which wears a jewel on its head, out of its multiplicity of evils and ugliness it teaches us to find good in everything. For my own part I am ready to aver that although "to paint the lily and gild refined gold," may be a figure of speech which it is the province of a poet to utter in this eminently prosaic age, it is scarcely calculated to make the hungry hunger less, or those who are cold to cease repining and shivering together.

A great many of the strange stories and superstitions extant centuries ago have long since been rifled of their power to command credence, even from the credulous; and of all of them not one has been proved to be more utterly unfounded and fallacious than this one about the richly-endowed cranium of the genus Bufo. Never yet has a jewel been discovered, although the number of toads immolated upon the altar of investigation by the inevitable small boy, and the no less inevitable seeker after knowledge, would, if collected together, pack the basin of Lake Michigan as compactly as sardines fill a box. And no more are there "sweets" to adversity than there are jewels in toad-heads, unless, indeed, it be accounted "sweet" to discover the falsity of those who, professing friendship in sunny hours, help us to enjoy life, but who in dark ones forget and desert us.

History affords us many citations of the rise and fall of empires, dynasties, and States. Crowned heads have been brought low—the high and the mighty being but as dust beneath the feet of the "common herd." A prince of the blood has been a kitchen scullion, and the love'iest queen who ever wore a diadem darned and patched her threadbare linen, and had to beg for the materials with which to do that. Men, in America especially, have been millionaires one day and beggars the next. But never in the annals of any country has the fluctuation of fortune, the folly of ambition, and the fallacy of faith in human fidelity been so thoroughly exemplified as in the case of General Grant, whose misplaced confidence with its unfortunate results ought to make him an object of sympathy, as he must always be of respect and admiration, with every well-meaning, right-thinking American citizen. His misfortunes in no wise detract from his greatness as a general, his power as a political leader, or his cleverness and sincerity as a gentleman and a friend. I am very certain that in this assertion the opinions of other Confederate soldiers will bear me out. They are so wedded to the principles of chivalry by tradition, heritage, and in point of fact, that they are never slow to recognize the fine traits of true manhood, no matter where they may be seen, or by whom they may be exhibited. And because of this, it is not strange that General Grant's conduct at the close of the civil war should be kept in grateful and kindly remembrance even to this late day.

On the 9th of April, 1865, I was with the Kentucky brigade in Virginia when it was surrendered on the same terms agreed upon between General Grant and General Lee, at Appomattox: The soldiers, all commissioned officers rather, were allowed to retain their side-arms and horses. On the same day as that of the surrender we turned our faces toward Kentucky, crossing New river above Dublin (in fact, swimming it, as the Federals had burned the bridge at that point), and marching to Newburn; from thence entered Kentucky through Pound Gap, continuing our route down Robertson creek to Beaver, crossing the country via Salyersville to Mount Sterling, where we were met by General Hobson, who granted the Kentucky brigade of cavalry (which, in the beginning of the war, was organized by the lamented General Humphrey Marshall) the same terms conceded at Appomattox.

For General Grant's nobility and kindness on that occasion the memory of all Confederate soldiers must ever gratefully revert to him. Many of them were ready at the time—wearied and worn with the long and heart-rending struggle—in their joy at reaching "God's country" safe and sound of limb, with a horse "and a pistol by his side," to regard him as not only "the greatest living American, but a soldier whose intrepidity and valor should win for him the highest rank in the hearts of the people in times of peace," an admission which was made, indeed, and which was borne out by subsequent facts. Plaudits sounded,

From the mountain down to the shore,

And fifteen thousand cities and hamlets blazed with illuminations in honor of his "glorious victory" at Appomattox. But the "still, small voice" of his noble and true heart, and the memory of the look in Robert E. Lee's eyes, when he refused to see the reversed sword-handle tendered him, as was the bounden duty of the vanquished toward the victor, must have sounded sweeter notes of praise than the acclaim of multitudes. Who, but the bravest and most magnanimous of soldiers and gentlemen could be capable of such an act? One man in a million could do it. Greater than he who conquers cities is he who conquers himself, and Confederate soldiers must forever revere Grant for the nobility of that one deed, if for none other.

When the war closed, if General Grant would have accepted it, it was in the hearts of the people of the United States to present him with any one of the Western Territories, furnishing him with a clean title to the same. But now that age and misplaced confidence have deprived him of what little he had saved from his long and arduous public services, where are the clans that leaped around him at a motion of his hand, as in other days the clans of "Bonny Scotland" at the sweeping of the wind started up from the purple plumes of heather? Gone—all gone!—and now?

> An old man, broken with the storms of fate,
> Is come to lay his weary bones among ye;
> Give him a little earth for charity,

Is what his present and his future mean in comparison with the resplendent glory of his past! In other days when he filled the highest office in the gift of the American people, he moved panoplied in homage like the royalty of the Old World. Nay, his sway over the hearts of the people was founded on gratitude and esteem, but where are those myriad friends to-day? His fidelity to his friends was the marvel of the world! How do they serve him now, when adversity has fallen on him like a blight?

I, for one, appreciate what he did for me in 1865, when by the terms of the surrender I was allowed to retain "Roderick Dhu" and my old "navy" pistol (huge enough to make four "bull-dogs") as a heritage, with permission to depart from Virginia, after nearly four years' service in the Confederate army.

Now, that nearly twenty years have been numbered with the "eternal past," and the country has been restored to peace and prosperity—with an incoming Democratic administration—without a vestige of rancor in my heart, I feel proud—as an American citizen I feel justly proud of General Grant, and had I followed his "star," I could not claim for him or extend to him more respect than I do to-day for his long and distinguished services and merit as a leader of the American people. To retire him upon the pay of an army officer at $17,500 a year would be but paltry recompense to him who touched the pinnacle of greatness, and whose glory compassed its full meridian.

I fervently believe that the Confederate soldiers—who remember and still appreciate the value of his influence in their behalf just after the war, as poor and fragile as many of them are—would cheerfully contribute toward his comfort were any feasible plan indicated that would be satisfactory to him—even though it should be the purchase of a bluegrass farm in Kentucky, where he could pass the remainder of his days in peace and quiet, among those who fully appreciate valor and nobility of character in an American citizen, it matters not under what flag he fought, or what army he led to victory.

GENERAL JOHN H. MORGAN.

How the Great Confederate Cavalryman Met His Fate.

After long years, to recall memories of incidents involved in the subject defined by the above caption affords the writer a melancholy satisfaction, since it may revive in faithful and chivalric hearts an interest in that hero who, living, stood among his compatriots without a peer as the model cavalier, the ideal soldier; and who now, being dead, a mere "handful of dry, white dust, heaped over with a mound of grass," may, perchance, be lost sight of in the riotous rush of a noisy world. If the reminiscence accomplishes this much the writer will feel amply repaid for his wanderings among the graves and tombstones of the past, where the sunshine of a busy and prosperous present has stolen in and woven a golden fret-work over the cold and silent places where sleep the heroes of the Lost Cause.

No lovelier breadth of country on the globe can be found than that which lies along the route from Abingdon, Va., via Bristol and Jonesboro, to Greenville, Tenn., and the varied panorama once stretching out before the admiring eye hangs forever afterward in memory's storied hall like a rich and gorgeous picture over which long years have flung their mellowing tints.

The hills, the meadows, the dusky screen of woods, the gray rocks, the ripple and rush of waters, the pine clad heights, the cedar valleys through which the rivers run, the purple lights that lie in the distance, the whiteness of the near mists, all had put on their gala dress to welcome autumn as a royal guest, when General John H. Morgan issued orders on the 2d day of September, 1864, and "took up the line of march" along the above-named route, arriving at Greenville, Tenn., on the evening of the 3d at the hour of sunset. Ah! how that scene returns to me! I sadly muse and vividly see, as of yore, the

> Warm lights on the sleepy uplands waning
> Beneath soft clouds along the horizon rolled,
> Till the slant sunbeams through their fringes raining
> Bathe all the hills in melancholy gold.

Alas! it is a vision silent and swift to come and depart as some sweet, wandering thought, which gives eager eyes a glimpse of its bright wings, and, presto, vanishes! General Morgan's command consisted of the remnant of his old brigade, Giltner's brigade (commanded by Colonel Henry Giltner), Vaughn's brigade (commanded by Colonel Bradford), and two companies from Cosby's brigade (commanded by Captain Peter Everett). Colonel D. Howard Smith, I think, commanded probably the general's old command (when on the march) and those men who were under Captain Everett, numbering in all about four hundred. General Morgan numbered, in his entire command, about fifteen hundred effective men.

Arriving in Greenville, they were disposed of as follows:

Bradford's command was ordered to Blue Spring, nine or ten miles beyond the town, in the direction of Bull's Gap, at which place General Gillam was encamped with a force numbering about three thousand men. Colonel Giltner was ordered into camp at the crossing of the Babb's Mill road, about five miles from town, in the direction of Rogersville, Tenn. Colonel D. Howard Smith and Captain Everett, with a small force, were detailed to Arnold's place, west of the town about one mile, while the general's old command, commanded by Captain Clark (in encampment), settled down like a swarm of bees on the college lawn, north-east of the town. This last-mentioned place was not more than two hundred yards from the residence of Mrs. Williams, at whose hospitable house the general had established his headquarters for the night.

The Williams mansion was one of the loveliest homes in Tennessee. Attractive in its outside appearance—being a large, double, two-story house, with verandas, and wide, deep windows and heavy portals and breezy halls, like all the best class of Southern houses—it was doubly so within, being furnished in elegant style, and, like a good ship manned with sailors, it was kept up in a grand way by a stately hostess and a well trained retinue of competent servants—a household rarity at any time.

The house was situated in the midst of a beautiful flower-garden, where summer had already begun to gather up her robes of glory, and, like a dream of beauty, to fade away. The Williams family was rich, even so rich as to have their own church and a regularly-engaged chaplain to perform service in it. Their mode of life was not changed by the fact of war in the country or on the borders. The best the land afforded was theirs, and that, too, in no stinted measure; and, doubtless, General Morgan congratulated himself that he had found such a delightful and hospitable home, at which all the delicacies of the season were offered with lavish grace. Yet *being there* was the primitive cause of his unfortunate and unhallowed demise.

Mrs. Williams' family proper consisted of herself and three sons—William, Joel (or Joe, as he was familiarly addressed by everybody), and Tom. The last mentioned of the sons lived in what is termed "the single state." Joe and William were both married. William's wife was a Miss Broils—an exceptionally lovely and gifted lady. Joe's wife was a very pretty young woman, whose maiden name was Rumbaugh. This lady was a staunch Union woman in her political proclivities, and that, too, when her spirited and handsome brother, Captain Thomas Rumbaugh, had a long time previously donned the gray uniform and made as gallant a soldier as ever marched to the sound of a drum and the ear-piercing music of the fife.

Joel Williams lived in the country, but, as ill-luck would have it, his wife was in town on a visit at her mother-in-law's house, and she met General Morgan there when frowning Fate impelled him to make his headquarters at that special point. Naturally, she did not show any enthusiasm over the new arrivals in the household, and it was said afterward that she threatened to "give them trouble." Certain it is that subsequent events proved the truth of the rumor, although it never can be doubted that the cordiality was sincere and the hospitality genuine which the mistress of the mansion, upon her part, extended to the gallant Morgan, the prince of gentlemen, and, if treachery environed and overcame him in the splendor of his manly beauty, no stain lies on her escutcheon because of the ignoble deed!

The hours flew on apace. There were festive sounds in the mansion, for the stately dame presiding there was doing honor to a hero. Lights gleamed from windows and open doors, and now and then a golden ripple of laughter or the echoes of happy voices would float out on the breeze, winging its way through the airy halls with the sense of peaceful sweetness that the breath of blossoms brings when blown about by night winds in the new time of the year.

Heaven's blue deepened; globules of heavy dew fell; the stars—night's flying hosts, in their noiseless, triumphal cars of gold—sped onward across the trackless firmament; the flowers swung their rainbow-tinted censers; the rapt night received their fragrant souls into her embrace, and the sorrowing whippoorwill outsung the nightingale! Never did the dark come down over a happier or more hopeful set of soldiers. The light-hearted fellows—first in a battle, first in a dance, as chance might decree—fully contemplated being over the Cumberland mountains and fairly possessed of "God's country"—as they termed Kentucky—before the crimson and purple and gold of another sunset, 'broidered with marvelous fringe of glowing and harmonious colors, the horizon's line, where broad-based earth in dun repose meets the open face of the deep-blue Infinite. They were especially happy because Morgan commanded them. The keenest sarcasms, the merriest jests, went around. Did not the march promise to every one, "according to his lights," the fulfillment of his most cherished hopes, his most ardent desires? One *gourmet* declared he went with the hope of getting "a square meal;" another wit proclaimed his intention of capturing "a blooded horse," whose pedigree on his return should read: "Out of Kentucky, by a rebel." Another would be pensive at the thought of returning to the old, familiar places and seeing the old, familiar faces. Here a cheek would glow in anticipation of laughing lips and brightest eyes, that would deepen in roseate color or intensify in brilliance when a certain somebody met them again; then a dimness of vision or a sadness of expression would betray the earnest nature which, longing fervently to see the loved ones at home, lost not sight of the dangers of the expedition.

Ah! ah! "The Old Kentucky Home Far Away," to exiled hearts in those dead and gone days, had the beauty which Canaan wears to the Christian soul, and the glory which envelops ancient Greece to the meditative dreamer's pensive fancy. None but he who has been an exile can enter into *rapport* with the ecstatic feelings of these light-hearted, gallant fellows of whom I write! Hope held out alluring rewards to the brave. Alas! how often does God break to our faces the idols of our dreams!

The morning of the 4th of September, 1864, proved the fallacy of human desire, even as withered leaves speak to the contemplative heart of longings—idle longings, which many a time fill the chalice of departed hours. This is the way that, to those who rode with Morgan, disappointment and sorrow came to keep them company in lieu of gayety and plenty.

In the Williams mansion all became quiet. Greenville fell asleep. In the woods, the meadows, and the fallow fields Nature and her children kept watch together through the blessed hours of silence and repose.

Gradually the sky, hitherto so serene, became overcast; the autumn-bronzing winds began to blow; the rustling leaves made weird music on the boughs; the birds nestled closer together; the slow, intense, drizzling rain began to fall; darkness deepened and deepened. There were shadows stealing along through the gloom; there was the dull thud, thud of a horse's hoofs breaking on the somber silence; there was a swift, sinuous sound of a woman's moving draperies; then all was still. There was a soft rap at the door; there were broken sounds of whispering; there was an abrupt command, rapid movements through the night, a tramping of manly feet, the hurried urging of a horse into a gallop, and then all was hurry and excitement; not a sound, not a bustling excitement, but that still, sweeping, onward rush as of the warring elements that approach to do battle in a storm.

And then, as the lightning gores the darkness with "a vivid, vindictive, and serpentine flash," it became known that Mrs. Joel Williams had escaped the house, eluded the guards, mounted the horse, and was away over the hills, bearing blight and death and disaster as she went through marshes, swamps, dismal fens, over stony peaks and bald summits, on, on, into the dark and the deepening darkness, through wild ravines and gorges, riding straight as an arrow speeds in its flight for the camp of Gillam to betray John Morgan! And, like a sleuth hound slipped from his lashes, after her, after her, along the dangerous way, overhung by drear cliffs, drenched with the driving rain, blinded by the darkness, with the pallor of anxiety on his cheek and the energy of despair in his heart, after her, after her, under towering peaks, past meadow lands, stretching away and away, knowing not the route, not dreading the danger, following blindly the clattering of horse's hoofs in advance of him, like shadow pursuing shadow in a dream, rode the gray-coated scout to overtake and capture her. In vain! in vain! She eluded him! How well was proved when at five A. M. a scouting party from the Union camp, comprising about six hundred men, entered the little town of Greenville from the

Paint Gap road, which had been left uncovered by reason of Bradford not proceeding, as ordered, to Blue "Springs." Useless now all repinings, all reproaches—useless and vague as the echo of a heart's regrets! They surrounded the general's headquarters, captured his staff, his couriers, and some stragglers who followed ever in the golden wake of his martial glory, as the mote dances in the sunbeam and shines with reflected splendor. The general himself succeeded in eluding them and escaped from the house. He was in his shirt sleeves, not having time even to don his uniform. Into the flower garden he went, where the darkness and the rain and the mist all combined to woo him into a place of security. The winds whispered, "Hide! hide!" The drenched roses—the sweet, rain-brushed roses—whispered, "Hide! hide!" Ah! life was so precious to him!

The church before referred to was situated on the street; it ran parallel with the flower garden on the north; under it ran a culvert which opened upon a meadow lot. Major Gassett, one of his officers who had succeeded in escaping with him—indeed, who had seen the enemy approaching and quickly as he might had given warning—went with him into this culvert. They passed through it to the north side of the street. The general, led on by the shadowy and mysterious fate, whose guiding hand he had no power to avert, immediately returned, leaving Gassett, who afterward made his escape, and for a few moments he once more sought refuge beneath God's sanctuary, after which he hurriedly passed into the flower garden where his friends, the roses, hung their tear-besprent faces, and the mists were lifting themselves skyward, and crossing it, entered a vineyard, where the sun's golden fingers, touching the emerald globules of the luscious grapes, had turned them to blooming purple and pale amethyst.

Alas! alas!

It was at this point, and doubtless while awaiting the arrival of his troops, that he was discovered by the enemy, the direful, dreadful enemy, who thronged the street running from the town to the depot (the Williams house was in sight of the depot), and parallel with the yard upon the south. They fired on him. One shot took effect in the left side of his chest, felling him to the ground. Brute instinct overmatched reason and the cry of humanity. Those who had perpetrated the deed climbed the picket fence, and lifting him bodily, threw him over into the street! Here he was lifted again, thrown across a horse in front of a fiendish soldier, whose name, were it known, ought to be handed down through cycles of ages yet unborn, in a cloud of infamy, like that of him who burned the temple of Ephesus! Picture it, O lovers of justice and humanity! Picture it, O soldiers in either cause, and weep and blush for the shame and the horror of it! Through the streets of Greenville rode the fiend whose form shamed his race! with a wounded and dying man swung across his saddle bow, cursing, reviling, muttering as he galloped hither and yon among masses of horror-stricken citizens gathered in the streets!

I saw one woman pale and tremble and shudder like a wind-shaken aspen as she recounted the scene, and related how she had seen the general (with his ashen-hued, death-stricken face turned to the light of the day and the gaze of the gaping crowds) running his fingers through his hair, with his eyes lifted to heaven. O, my God! The supreme agony of that moment. Do any of the horrors of the dark ages depicted on the historic scrolls transcend it for brutality? How and when he gave up the ghost; how and when his spirit poised itself for flight, and thus eluded his ignoble tormentors, those who loved him will never, never know.

He was thus borne about through the town, and thence some distance beyond it, where the force of invaders with their royal trophy of war met General Gillam with his command, who, after a slight engagement with Smith, entered the town, Smith falling back at his approach.

Why the general was not rescued by the command which was encamped within a stone's throw of his headquarters upon the college lawn is a question I can not answer. I was with Colonel D. Howard Smith and Captain Everett one mile west of the town on the Arnold farm. Upon hearing the firing in town the command was ordered to mount and to move to the hill west of the depot.

The enemy had left town. The Confederates fell back in the direction of Jonesboro. At Leesburg Colonels Giltner and Bradford joined Smith. Giltner being senior officer here took command.

I was ordered to take a small force, and proceeding to Greenville under flag of truce, to discover, if possible, what had become of General Morgan, and to look after our dead and our wounded. At five o'clock P. M., September 4, 1864, we arrived and found General Morgan—dead! Ah! death struck sharp on life makes awful lightning.

He had been shot at daylight. Was it a wonder to us who loved him that the light was gone from the day; that the confiding roses were dead on their stems, and wore only crowns of rust in lieu of blushes? Was it a wonder to us that the rainbow-tints of autumn, sprinkling hill and dale like shattered gems, wore no beauty to our tear-dimmed eyes? How was it proved to us that believing we marched in the path of glory, we found ourselves at the last wretched pall-bearers of our brightest hopes, with sorrowful, lagging steps, tramping along the shadowed path of dreams? My heart sickens over the memory!

Through the influence of some friends of mine I was permitted to take charge of that beloved body. A neat walnut coffin was furnished by sympathizing citizens, and at my own expense I hired a one-horse wagon (none other was obtainable!), into which the coffin was placed; and thus, accompanied by a small escort, I proceeded with his remains to Jonesboro, Tenn. O glorified hearse! O mourning retinue! What a hero! What obsequies!

At Jonesboro I met General Basil W. Duke, Colonel Richard Morgan (brother of the general), and other field officers of his command, who but a short time previous had been "exchanged" at Charleston, S. C. O, such a home-coming to loving hearts!

In death, he seemed just to have fallen asleep! The crucifixion agony had gone from his face, and the same gentle, kindly smile hovered over it we had seen so often there when the glow of health and magnificent manhood vivified his form and set the splendid seal of power upon his bold and knightly brow, gemmed with his matchless eyes! So he went. So we, who loved and admired him, mourn his loss. To this day we are haunted and hunted down with melancholy surmises and broodings over his chances, had such and such things happened. If he had been left when he was shot he might have recovered of his wounds, as many another man did in that region. Had he remained in the culvert or under the church with Major Gassett, he might have escaped, as Gassett did.

And so we thread the weary sequences; but be all this as it may, thus ended the life of the boldest and most admired cavalry officer of the South! His raids were always brilliant, dashing, conspicuous. His name was thundered far and wide across the country, and will never, never be forgotten! He was a fine soldier, a splendid horseman, a thorough gentleman. No Bayard of fame ever was a braver knight or a more gallant chevalier. Indeed, may it be said that his was

> One of the few immortal names
> That were not born to die!

Singular to relate, as a closing memento, and not as a thread of the romancist woven into the warp and woof of facts, Mrs. Joel Williams' gallant brother, Thomas Rumbaugh, to whom she was intensely devoted, despite his rebellious spirit, was shot and killed during an encounter at Bull's Gap, scarcely three weeks later, almost on the identical spot where she met Gillam and betrayed to his untimely end the prince of cavaliers! Verily, verily,

> Every sin brings its own punishment
> That rings its changes on the counter of this world.

HOW TO BETTER ONE'S SELF.

The moral lever of Archimedes was earnestness; and to this day the authority of noble descent, the influence of wealth, the glory of genius can not be compared with it in power, neither separately nor aggregately. It is proven to be true every day, and from time immemorial its demonstration has remained unchanged that men of earnestness, rather than men of genius, have wrought the changes in the moral aspect of the world. We could make dozens of citations to prove the truth of our asseveration. Cromwell, Marlborough, Washington—the one earnest in his ambition for power, the other greedy for glory and greedier for gold, and the last wearing his noble love of constitutional liberty as a monarch a crown—each and all were made powerful by their earnest resolve to succeed.

The principle holds good to-day. What we do we should do with our hearts. Earnest resolution is the power that razes all obstacles; it breaks down and crushes out all opposing forces. Devoid of this inspiring principle—this necessary enthusiasm—it will forever be impossible to accomplish anything great. The man who has courage to face a difficulty, courage to do right no matter how tempting the wrong may be, courage to do right no matter if right doing requires a sacrifice, is the man to succeed; he is the man with the earnestness of character which success requires as an "open sesame" to its untold wealth and untold glories. There are many persons—and the fact is lamentable—who scorn to make an effort toward personal aggrandizement, who seem to think that their presence in the world is honor enough to the universe, and that nothing is required at their hands but existence. They come under various heads, the most useless and worthless among them all being the loafers. They may be seen on the street corners, at all public places of amusement or resort, with the same languid, "laissez nous faire" expression of countenance and conduct. To such we would say that, unless they resolve to better themselves by fulfilling the urging of the poet to

"Work for some good, be it ever so slowly;
Cherish some flower, be it ever so lowly,"

They will surely find that Time's sand-dry streamlet flows not ceaselessly through its glassy straits; for it ends where the eternal life begins, and too late, when summoned to answer to their records, they will see they have never called into exercise the strength of their manhood, but have lived as drones in a busy hive and died worthless and soon forgotten. The man who betters himself in this world is not the light-willed, half-reluctant actor, but the man who, resolving to accomplish, accomplishes. He who stands undecided whether to go forward or backward—he who half enlists himself in a cause and expects to succeed—is a loon. He can neither command nor deserve to attain success in any effort so assumed. What does it matter that a man is endowed with a rich intellect if he never consecrates it to some noble aim, but takes it with him to the grave and hides it away in the dust, like his life—a miserable failure? How is the world bettered by his having lived at all, any more than the Laplander is blessed by the fact of fragrant flowers and luscious fruits springing almost spontaneously from the loamy soil of the sun-warmed tropics, while he trudges through a land of ice and snow?

Nothing can prove an insurmountable obstacle to the man who knows how to be earnest and resolute. Poverty may be, and indeed is, always a real evil. It would be absurd to deny that fact and also the fact that it is the parent of many, indeed most, of the physical and moral evils under the sun. Experience teaches this to us, and we can not deny it, but the man with a will to succeed never remains a victim to poverty for long. The common comforts and necessities of life he soon gathers about him. No life can be pregnant with sorrow and sin that goes in the straight and narrow path that leads to the golden goal of success, and thenceforward consecrates the triumphant devotee to elegant enjoyment and ease and banishes forever from him petty cares and worldly anxieties, and leaves the time, the thought, the whole spirit, free to contemplate the attainments of energy. There must be many denials of body and soul—oftentimes disappointments—and blighted hopes of heart and brain and the bitter tears of fruitless repentance that come too late to redeem some hours that might have been happy. There may be—there will be—personal regrets for certain circumstances; there will be a lack of sympathy with other struggles up the steps—a confidence of selfishness that often marks the onward progress of the successful man; but after all, who shall say the cost is greater than the gain?

One of the great secrets of knowing how to better one's self is the strength and courage that are required to do without that which is not needed when the spirit of admiration, by a stress of will, is compelled to submit to the spirit of self-abnegation. Another is the resolution to attend strictly to one's own business and to keep one's own opinions to one's self. The courage to speak when it is necessary, and to hold the tongue when it is equally necessary, is as rare as it is desirable. And he who follows out these rules for guidance, and allies with them unfailing energy and unwavering resolution, will find there are few things of this earth that are unattainable when effort for attainment is made through these legitimate means.

But one thing should never be forgotten. And that is that

> "He most lives
> Who thinks most, feels the noblest, acts the best."

And, after all is said that can be said of false doctrines and true ones, one inalienable fact remains shining like a star on all the future and lighting all the past—the highest crown of excellence attainable in this world is in being and in doing good.

The sweetest lives are often the humblest and the happiest.

Let the aspiring take as a motto Tennyson's strong, sweet words that have the ring of a silver clarion in them:

> "Howe'er it be it seems to me
> 'Tis only noble to be good.
> Kind hearts are more than coronets,
> And simple faith than Norman blood."

KINDNESS.

There is an old proverb which runs in this wise: "Do a favor and lose a friend." We do not believe gratitude to be incompatible with other noble instincts of the human heart. We believe that persons can feel grateful forever, and cherish, with kindest memories, actions that are ofttimes only slight in themselves, but, coming as they did, at a time when they were needed, are never forgotten. There is everything in the way a favor is bestowed. If it is done with gentle smiles and kindly words, however small the service, it is more gratefully recollected than a much greater service would be, if grudgingly given. Against such actions our inner spirits rise in contradiction. Sometimes we feel almost an aversion against the donor, and however much we struggle with this sense of ingratitude, it is there, and will not down at our bidding. This feeling may always be justly ascribed to the fact that the service was rendered ungraciously. There are persons in this world who sometimes confer favors not because their feelings are kindly toward the object favored, but because they desire and expect gratitude in return, the sense of it being pleasant to the contemplation of the soul. Such persons are almost invariably disappointed.

The expectation of the sentiment destroys the beauty and grace of the kindness. And yet this fashion of doing good, that at some future time good may be done in return, is the most ordinary way of "being kind."

The true way to confer a favor is to do it so delicately that the recipient will not be oppressed by a sense of obligation; *au contraire*, will feel almost as if they are the generous ones in allowing the kindness to be bestowed. Such a way of doing good is a fine art, and one person in fifty is possessed of it! And yet there are thousands of people who take great delight in performing praiseworthy actions and acts of benevolence, but who have about them such a cold, hard way, that it seems as if they were prompted by a sense of compulsive duty, and not by generous sentiment.

But even this class is preferable to those individuals who lend to the Lord and expect usurer's interest for their charities; in other words, confer gifts graciously, and lay claim to the heart of the recipient with an air of

"So much, for so much, —
Rialto prices."

They are not unusually actuated by narrow motives; they either expect an extended reputation for goodness and generosity, or a greater benefit in return for the one conferred; or they derive gratification from the sense of assuming an air of superiority as a benefactor and a philanthropist.

Then, there are people in the world who are kind and charitable impulsively or whimsically or spasmodically. But these lapses into goodness are dependent upon the effervescing exuberance of the heart, caused by some pleasant, but transient, excitement of the mind. An acquaintance in deep distress might go to such a one to-day and find him "the friend indeed," and going to-morrow instead of to-day, might be repelled with cold indifference!

"The true way to bless is to be blessed," a sweet poet tells us, and that is the moral of it all. True kindness of heart instinctively seeks to communicate peace and pleasure to all within the circle of its influence, and the delight which is derived from the power of benefaction is all that the donor desires in return.

The purest kindness, and the noblest charity, is to love your neighbor by doing good to him first, that he may be loved as a consequence of you having had the chance to be good to him.

Genuine kindness of the soul—deep-rooted, and nourished from a holy source—is that principle which increases our love for those to whom we have been kind, and who were so conditioned as to need such goodness at our hands. Kindness does not always mean tangible and undeniable service; its most incalculable benefits are gentle actions, and loving looks, and sympathetic utterances.

So many hearts grow hard and rough in this world, because around them, in their daily lives, there is no blessed atmosphere of goodness —no soft, humanizing influence of love and gentleness and consideration. God pity such! When the heart is kind and the mind is sympathetic, it looks through the eyes, it speaks in the voice, it guides the hands, it actuates the motions, and makes one feel as if he could clasp the universe to his heart in the fullness of his love. Being kind and good is the chief delight of existence, and the bare idea of remuneration or return of benefits bestowed is painful, and lessens his sense of happiness.

Such a character is never mistaken. St. Paul exclaimed: "Ye are not your own." If we contrasted the good we do our fellowmen with the goodness of God to us—contrasted them as the finite alone can be contrasted with the Infinite—what would remain to us if God claimed from us a return for all He bestows? Life itself would cease! We would be atoms in a vast aggregate.

If we belong to God rather than to ourselves, what right have we to claim gratitude for the benefits we bestow upon our fellow-mortals, when we so seldom remember the gratitude we owe to Him, our Lord and Master? When we demand compensation for the good we are enabled to do, when a sense of doing something that may redound to our interest springs up, then we are selfish; and self-love, or a desire for gain, or a trivial whim actuates us, and not charity, not love for a fellow-being, and not kindness. Not many among us will be able always to stand the Ithuriel test.

But doubt not the purely charitable and kind are the chosen and beloved of God, and He forgets not one among them now, and will forget them not in the hereafter.

NOTABLE CHARACTERS.

Who May be seen Frequenting the Court-rooms and Other Public Places.

The public may have some curiosity to know how to apply the soubriquet of the "Wisdom Horse," the "Smart Aleck," and "The Whacker." We will try to give an explanation of them in rotation; and, after informing our readers who they are, we will conclude in a second edition with "The Tramp," "The Crank," and "The Ta Ta," and why they have been denominated by their respective *nom de plume*.

The Wisdom Horse we will first consider, as he seems to be of more importance, especially in his own estimation, than any of the other persons in the text.

THE WISDOM HORSE.

The owl is the emblem of wisdom, owing to his aplomb when perched upon a tree, with his large sapphire eyes peering into space, unconscious of any danger that may surround him. So with the Wisdom Horse, who lives, apparently, upon his own admiration, ever ready to impart his store of knowledge to those who are willing to be punished by him in the long and minute details of his information. He receives the most startling sensation with the air of a stoic, and never stoops to learn anything whatsoever, as he knows it all by intuition being the receptacle of some infinite artist, who bestowed upon him, individually, this wonderful look of the magician—this overawing, august air of the "big I" and "little u."

Secondly: The Smart Aleck is a didapper in appearance and wears clothes of the most approved styles, and very generally wears an attenuated moustache, and carries a small cane of some fancy shape and unknown material, which to explain he intrudes himself upon a party for the purpose, ostensibly, of giving its history and the manner in which he came in possession of it, etc. This opportunity is generally sought by him when he has diagnosed the hour for the party upon whom he thrust himself to be about going for some "O. P."—which means other people's whisky—a brand which the most fastidious drinker rarely fails to take. It is well-known throughout the State, and generally accepted by all who love the flowing bowl.

The Smart Aleck can hardly be distinguished from the "Ta-Ta," from the fact that he frequents all the places of public amusement

alike, takes the front seat, if possible, and looks down upon the audience as though they were, indeed, the sublunary things, and most frequently applauds at the wrong place, and if he sees his mistake he calls it æsthetic, and passes on perfectly satisfied, thinking he made a mash on the fair-haired girl on the right, whose observation was simply attracted by his ignorance and his presumptuous manner, which is always a profound blunder and never assumed, save to the disgust of the refined and well-bred folk, who are ever at ease, whether in the mansion of an aristocrat or before the footlights, where the hearts of the beautiful and brave throb in unison. Before this person the pretensions of the Smart

THE SMART ALECK. Aleck sink into oblivion, and his impressions, if any are ever made by him, strand on some unknown shore, and are finally snowed under from the eye of the living.

The "Whacker" is the person who desires, above all other things, to "stand in" with the lawyer. They belong to that idyllic class who are ever ready to tell clients who are the best lawyers—those who will stand by the cold tombstone when they are dead—such is the tenacity of the man whom they propose to indicate to the unwary to employ in their cases; but you must understand that the "whacker" is to have a portion of whatever amount the lawyer receives, as his fee. It was this class of persons who caused the Legislature to pass a bill making such "professional" business a misdemeanor. This progressive step toward the discomfiture of the "whacker," and for the relief of those lawyers who have been giving succor to such characters; who have got many of the litigants mulcted and tangled in the web of legal lore, and who are compelled to pay the

THE WHACKER.

penalty of their want of sense—this progressive step should be greeted with much joy by every honorable man. If the law should be strictly enforced, it will be a blessing to honest attorneys, and their clients alike, and will rid the country of a certain class of purveyors to avarice, for their occupation will be gone, as it should be.

As the Tramp is of the oldest origin, he will be the first considered. The tramp is likely to be found anywhere upon the habitable globe. He migrates like a bird; his location is governed by the seasons and controlled by the prospect of supplies during his rapid transits. He flees from labor and everything that bears a resemblance to labor, as a sinner is supposed to flee from the wrath to come.

He is as entertaining as he is "odd," owing mainly to his thorough knowledge of the geography of his country and his power to delineate, with graphic speech and gesture, the great railroad lines that in their intricacy puzzle a novice, and, indeed, are a matter of wonder to the intelligent; yet the "tramp" is familiar with all the crossing and interlacing and parallels of every railroad route in the Union, and he descants upon them with the easy facility that a novelist exhibits in disposing of his characters of fancy, weaving about them the wonderful meshes of imagination, and making them, to eye and heart, real as the living beings of which they are the prototypes.

THE TRAMP.

He has the names of prominent men upon the tip of his tongue, and speaks of them with that gracious familiarity, that peculiar bonhomie exhibited by those who talk of their personal acquaintances or cherished friends. He recites his travels and his experiences with a tongue as silvery as Othello's; gives accounts of great battles, in all of which he participated "during the late war," until the credulous and the romantic imagine the halo of heroism encircles his brow; and it matters not in his recountals whether two battles were fought on the same day or not—and hundreds of miles apart'—he was there!—participating in the perils of both contests; and, like the plume of Murat, he could have been seen—everywhere at the same time—in the thickest of the battle-smoke. Upon the conclusion of these impromptu historic recitations they are at liberty to give him the best their larder affords, and to slake his thirst from the choice bottle of "family bitters." That a "tramp" could gain entré to an establishment that could boast much, either to eat or drink, may seem altogether improbable to the cautious habitue of the city, but that they do mulct the unsophisticated in the country has been demonstrated too often to doubt the probability of the assertion. Some of them can repeat poetry from old authors, discuss mythological characters, displaying a thorough knowlege of ancient and pagan history; and being quite as much "at home" in the mythical ages, with the gods of imagery, as with railroad kings and the lacing lines of road that span the country from lake to gulf and ocean to ocean. These mental displays—and they are not infrequent—are potent signs of "other days"—better days—when these nomads had futures, and when loving hearts hoped for them and loving hands labored for them to elevate them in the scale of human worth and mortal intelligence.

And at last! their wonderful gifts of memory, their often brilliant flights of fancy are used simply as "entering wedges," enabling them to remain fugitives from labor.

They refuse to adopt avocations, by which means they might earn honorable livelihoods and become responsible citizens of some Commonwealth and respected members of society. If you wish to insult one of them, simply suggest to them that steady work is preferable to such precarious modes of living. The air of disdain and contempt they assume on such occasions is as good as a play. And they are almost sure to disappear on the next train, bound for parts unknown. What arrangements they make with conductors on the railroads is something of which history has not yet given strict account. One thing is certain beyond peradventure: the tramp is indigenous to every clime alike. The writer of these lines questioned Henry Clay, after his return from seeking the "Open Sea," if he met any "tramps" when in Lady Franklin Land—rather doubting, when he propounded the inquiry, whether the individuals in question could travel so far toward the frigid zone—but the conscious smile the gentleman gave to the seeker after migratory species of the human race convinced him that the northern-bound traveler had met them in his peregrinations toward the pole, and, indeed, that they abound everywhere upon the face of the earth, whether it be in the frozen land of ice and snow and whirling winds, where jagged glaciers rear their glittering and prismatic peaks toward the clouded sky; or in the tropic zone, where all day long the golden-winged sunbeams play hide and seek among the variegated blossoms, and all night long the rich aroma of their brilliant hearts is fanned about by balmy zephyrs, lulling the soul with elysian dreams of harmony and repose.

THE CRANK.

The Crank, in character and habits, is altogether unlike the "tramp." He seems to have an especial antipathy to boarding-house keepers, and cherishes an infinite delight in "beating" them out of "grub." He esteems himself capable of filling any office within the gift of the people, and proving not only an honor to himself, but a glory to the Commonwealth and a pride to the nation.

He has an absolute mania for notoriety. He loves to be seen in front of "first-class hotels;" he will stand there for hours chewing a toothpick, with his feet pointing to the east and west, and his hands stowed away in his pockets, fancying that he has the air impressive which will lead every passer-by to imagine him a "boarder." If a notable personage should chance to register at the establishment, he is the first man to interview him upon the general topics of the day, and he is almost certain to beat him "on the turn" out of a drink and a cigar. If he succeeds in obtaining a sufficient number of beverages, he is more than likely to "wind up" with an attempt to blow out the brains or sever the jugular of somebody.

He does not wait for insult or aggressive act; he is a disciple of the law of eternal antipathies, and he anticipates acts of violence and commits desperate deeds under the inspiration of momentary insanity, which is the modern manner of defining a man's disposition when "chuck full" of whisky—and, generally, whisky paid for by some one else. These violent deeds are seldom perpetrated save in some conspicuous place where there is a prospect for notoriety. "Cranks" are usually morose villains, and ought to be shunned by every class and condition. They are dangerous, and any one who admits them

THE TA-TA

to their acquaintance runs the risk of being killed the first time they get hungry or drunk. To feel a craving for food or a thirst for liquor is with a crank sufficient incentive for him to become annoying, persistent, insolent, dangerous to all mankind; for it is quite uncertain what will incite anger, or, once aroused, upon whom the lightning of violence may be hurled.

The Ta Ta, in society parlance, is a nosegay! His peculiarities are of a different character from those that belong to the "wisdom horse," "the smart Aleck," "the whacker," "the tramp," or the "crank," but they are equally distinctive, equally characteristic. The "ta-ta" prides himself upon his shape and talent, especially and exclusively. He considers every female whose eye chances—even casually—to rest on his Adonis-like form as particularly "mashed on him." He has the air of one who constantly shrugs his shoulders (as some created thing in a lower order of the universe might do who shakes off one skin to take on another of newer beauty), as if that non sequitur air rendered him more attractive to the girls. The "ta-ta" is to be seen in all cities, foreign and American, and is to be as easily recognized by his characteristic demeanor as a leopard is to be known by its spots. The manner in which he wears his attire and the style of it, the importance he assumes when he enters a place of public resort, the sly but interrogatory glances he casts—from behind his screening "gig lamps," resting lightly upon his proboscis— makes one conscious of him as a social idiosyncrasy. He has such an overwhelming air; he uses such pungent perfume upon his handkerchief and his hair that the powerful aroma about him rivals the civet cat. He never tries his blandishments on the matrons; his harmless little flirtatious behavior they disdain to notice; his specialty is to "make mashes" on the girls, and it is for them he plays the part of a modern Beau Brummel! He considers himself a heart-breaker, and that for the wounds he creates in susceptible hearts there is no known cure. Therapeutics suggest no remedy, and the skill of the physician has never yet learned how to prescribe for that perilous stuff that weighs upon the heart. The "ta-ta" is a "masher" who directs his Cupidian shafts at the innocent and unsuspecting. He is, with the credulous, simply an overpowering "stunner," who woos "on the wing," charms with his shape, and fascinates with his talents. He is as fatal to some hearts as "Rough on Rats" is fatal to the ordinary rodent. He is a Liliputian monster springing into insignificant but undeniable existence from the idiocy of man, as unaccountably as ever Minerva sprang full grown from the head of a god! He is no more to human life than an excrescence. He would be like the pendant dewdrop on the opening rose—if he could. But rather is he the canker that gathers around and fastens on the bud. Beware of him! "Maud"

OUR DEAD—PRESERVE THEIR MEMORIES—1876.

Sitting alone in my sunshiny sanctum to-day, "a sweetly solemn thought comes to me o'er and o'er." I am thinking of our dead, and that in this, the centennial year, while the world goes on with its feasting and fasting, the beautiful custom of strewing the graves of the dead soldiery, North and South, with floral offerings has been everywhere observed. The custom is a most holy and lovely one, and it should be perpetuated through all the years to come. I can conceive of nothing more Christian-like and ennobling to the finer feelings of human nature than this culling of flowers by matron and sire, youth and maiden, to strew over the green mounds and wreathe about the marble columns that chronicle in enduring stone the bravery of those who fell discharging their duty to their country's flag and in defense of their national rights.

In by-gone times, the 4th of July and the 22d of February were days anticipated long before their advent in every community in the States (for in every one were descendants of those illustrious men who fought in the American Revolution), anticipated as the days when orators would extol the chivalric deeds and the Spartan courage and daring of those who bore arms for seven long years, until the result desired was heroically attained, and as a rich heritage this vast country, replete with marvelous capabilities and wonderful resources, was left to their posterity. And the celebration of the 4th of July and the 22d of February is a beautiful custom indissolubly associated with the names of America's noblest sons. When we have summed up all that is attractive in the past to their heroic deeds we can trace the source of all of our present enjoyments.

The United States of America are the achievements of the soldiers of 1776. Led by George Washington, and imbued with patriotism and capable of long endurance, they finally wrenched independence from the British crown. War after war ensued, and, as often as the tocsin sounded, victory perched upon our banner.

And now, at last, after a fierce and bloody civil strife, when the flags of defiance are furled, and the swords are left to rust in their scabbards, it is for the noble women of the country to strew flowers on the graves of our hero dead. It is a labor of love which should never be carelessly performed. Some day should be set apart with all due solemnity for the consecration of their last resting-places, and orators should blend the blossoms of their heaven-born genius and eloquence with the brightness and sweetness of the earthly flowers, and decorating and hallowing the graves of our dead and "gone before" so perpetuate their memories, irrespective of the uniforms they wore or the cause they espoused.

All the rare and roseate loveliness Nature affords should be combined, until the many God's acres over our land should bloom in beauty like the Rose of Sharon.

Neither adversity nor ingratitude should mar this custom made holy by its observance. And we depend upon the noble women of the land to perpetuate it. God bless them! They constitute the real incentive to our noblest deeds! They fill our land with hope and joy. To them we owe much, aye, all we are and all we can ever hope to be, singly and collectively.

Floral offerings at the resting-places of the dead is one of the most beautiful of customs. And it is fitting that the fair hands of women should evince this affection and respect for those who died in defense of them and their native land, who fought for principle and perished in their endeavor to uphold liberty.

Let us scatter over their graves the fairest and sweetest flowers. Let us cherish the memory of them, and when we die let us leave it as a heritage to our children, which may not pass away while the light of reason shines, and the soul aspires to a life that is purer and more ennobling than any this earth affords.

OUR HAPPIEST DAYS.

Of all the days that dawn and darken over the life-path, those of youth are the brightest and freest from care. There are those in this world who laugh over the wild romance and wayward wanderings and fanciful flights of the imagination incident to early years and light hearts; but after all the philosophizing is done, there are halcyon memories springing in the heart, that glow with freshness and beauty, and brighten the life of their treasurer as the green oases in the arid desert delight the traveler who, through burning sands and glaring sun, has kept body and soul together with visions of the date and palm, and the cool drip of sparkling waters flowing through the shadows.

Age grows apace, and brings with it attendant cares, infirmities, sorrows, and troubles, but the oldest and the most utterly bowed down can be lifted up and strengthened by one hour's fond recollection of the past, when pleasures were unalloyed, and the juvenile heart beat in unison with the youthful emotions of hope and delight. O! who dares compare manhood's sober realities, which overtake us in the autumn and the winter of life, with the buoyancy and beauty of sunshiny, laughter-loving, mirth-making youth? Who dares weigh the pleasure of counting gains and losses with the pleasing memories of sinless, earlier years? The man's heart must be callous, indeed, whose life does not bear on some pages—tear-blotted from frequent readings—the record of celestial joys indelibly engraven upon the heart in youth to live there in silent and unfading beauty as the latent caloric lives in the eternal rock, waiting only to be smitten by the impulse of some passionately tender thoughts to start into splendor and power! O! these memories of careless joys we realized when basking in youth's rosy morning, kissed by balmy winds, and shone on by a sun in cloudless skies. Nothing can recompense us for the loss of these; for the freshness and the beauty; for the pure happiness, born of untainted thought. Cherish, all who can—however silvered and bowed and furrowed with age— cherish the memories of those lost, happy days. They are the best of all a household's transitory stores.

Gold and silver, and glittering gems and sparkling jewels, are all alike perishable baubles, and if the mind be chained to them and absorbed by them, the day will come when it will be incapable of grander or loftier thoughts, and untainted and untrammeled emotions will be foreign and undesired. Scorn be upon the man or woman whose lives, souls, minds, energies, bodies, are all alike—physically and mentally—bound up in the one isolating thought as to the wisest and quickest *modus operandi* of scraping dollars together! Scorn be upon them that they do not exhibit a disposition to take some time to cultivate the higher and holier emotions, but go plodding on to the grave's brink, thinking of nothing, caring for nothing, save the accumulation of wealth. After all they die and leave it. Their first, last, and only love! And yet it never for one instant gives to them the substantial pleasure and the measureless delight afforded those who love to revert to the unspotted joys of youth—when Hope was glad and gay as "Eden's garden bird," and Love's wings were untarnished in their gauzy gold; nor yet does it give to them the joys and sunlit beauty that are born of the day when the sun shines on our youth, even though it should afterward die down like a sweet flower when that same sun sets in darkness that may or may not be lit by the eternal stars of faith.

OUR SACRED PAST.

A Speech Delivered in Harrodsburg, Ky., July 4, 1874.

DANIEL BOONE

Daniel Boone's wife and daughter were present at Boonesboro, in Madison county, Kentucky, on the 14th of April, 1775. They were the earliest of the pale faces, it is said, who stood on the banks of the Kentucky river.

While civilization is making such strides over the length and breadth of the New World, spanning our beautiful country with growing prosperity and intelligence from ocean to ocean, from the lakes to the gulf; while the wild territories, under the same magic wand, are rapidly developing into populous countries soon to resolve themselves into States and form additional stars in the already radiant constellation of a great republic; amid the rush and roar of the world of to-day; filled with the clash of its contending armies; athirst for fame, and gold, and glory; seeking gain and emolument at the cannon's mouth; in the halls of legislation, in the arena of society, at the loom, at the printing press, in the factories, in politics, in mechanics, in science, in philosophy, and in literature, a man may excite surprise who pauses in the progressive march of life, and turns—as Adam must have turned, with sad and longing eyes, to view for the last time that blessed paradise from which he was expelled forever—turns to view the hallowed realm of the sacred past, which contains much that is dear to memory; more that is enshrined in our hearts, and most that is the imperishable record of our country and our Commonwealth.

The early history of Kentucky offers me the excuse, if such be needed, for treating upon the subject of this sacred past, to-day, rather than the life and action of the present, especially as the names of my own ancestors are indissolubly connected with those who long ago won for you and me so much of the State renown enjoyed then and enjoyed now. This is my apology, this is the incentive that stimulates me to add my appreciative voice to the chorus who cry, "Evoe!" to Kentucky and her great men.

I confess I have an imperishable fondness for the old landmarks and every incident of her pioneer history.

In the winter of 1773 James Harrod, with his compatriots, consisting of the McAfees, the McCouns, and others, while the army of the Revolution was in winter quarters, left Fort Chizel, in the Maxey Meadow Bottoms, in Wythe county, Va., passed through Louisa Fork, descended along the water-courses, westward, to the mouth of the Big Sandy river, and bivouacked at the Falls, upon the Ohio river, where the city of Louisville now stands.

From thence they ascended the Kentucky river to Frankfort, where Robert McAfee made a survey, but there they did not sink their shaft, and cry with the red man, " A la-ba-ma" (Here let us rest .

They came on to the point where Harrodsburg now stands, and here they established the first fort, attracted, it is generally believed, by the many caverns in the vicinity, and by the fine water abounding everywhere.

This was the earliest settlement of Kentucky, and from it they gave battle to the Indians.

When the spring of the same year came with the birds and blossoms, these daring spirits returned to their command, which, at the time, was guarding the lead mines upon the banks of New river, a stream which is familiar to many of my auditory.

Kentucky! "The dark and bloody ground!"

Her very name is an epitome of the early history of her dark and bloody conflicts with the savage and wily foe! Not only does it owe its name to the Indian forays upon the whites, but to its being the grand battle-ground between the Northern and Southern Indians. And thus doubly-dyed with the blood of foe and friend is almost every rood of ground that to-day is rolled out in meadow lands or well-tilled fields or forests of primeval grandeur, with the earth beneath their umbrageous boughs, green and fragrant with the feathery tufts of bluegrass indigenous to the soil.

Ah! how often, when a boy, I sat beside the old hearthstone of my grandmother, thrilled and filled with all a boy's impetuous love of danger and adventure, and with wide eyes of excited wonder and admiration, listened to her accounts (told in a quiet way, unconscious of heroism) of life dur-

HOME OF SAMUEL MCAFEE.

ing the early settlement of the State; of how she lived in a humble cabin, of how she guarded her sheep, driving wolves away at all hours of the night, from the "pen" which, for safety, was built adjoining the cabin, using her rifle as deftly as her needle, while my grandfather was navigating a flatboat upon the Ohio and Mississippi rivers, going hundreds of miles to exchange one and another species of provender for some necessary of life. Nor was my grandmother alone in this brave self-abnegation and heroism. Many and many another woman suffered and braved as much as she.

And when I look on the array of brilliancy and beauty, of wealth and culture, that meets us at every hand, in every church, on the streets, in the concert room, in all public assemblies; when I see the women of to-day arrayed in their purple and fine linen, with the peach-bloom on their cheeks, and eyes outvying the stars in their luster; when I look on these fair, social divinities of to-day, idly luxuriating in the roses and lilies of life, and remember the divinities of heart and home—the heroines of history, the true, staunch wives and daughters and mothers of a century ago, I tell you my heart swells with a pride and tenderness no words of mine can convey to you!

I am touched almost to tears to remember that my grandmother was one of them!—that reared amid the perils of the time, she did not blush to wear homespun and leathern buskins, and to stand at the helm and carry the ship safely over the rough sea of adversity, while my grandsire drifted on stormier waves of chance!

All honor to our grandmothers! Worthy are they, indeed, of our profoundest reverence, as they lie in shrouding dust to-day, for they were capable, a hundred years ago, of deeds of heroism that handed their names down, generation after generation, as imperishable types of glory and of goodness!

I have cited my own ancestors in particular, because I know whereof I speak, and because this hour I delight to do homage to their memory. My people are not given to boasting; they are proverbial for their secretiveness and modesty. They have always avoided anything like heralding their exploits to the world; but they have a history which, for charity and heroism, will compare favorably with any race of people in the Union. From the Revolution down to the present time they have fought in every war in which the United States has been engaged.

And to-day, though generally pursuing peaceful avocations amid the marts of men, or tilling their own lands, touch on their family, and not a man, not a woman, not a child among them, but will be proud of their people and their past as all the Cæsars in their palaces! I like it! I glory in it!

And if their own race is dear to them, judge how much dearer is their native State, our motto being: "God! Our State! Our people!"

No Laplander loves his polar snows; no inhabitant of the torrid zone joys in the rich blossoms and the green dells of his own tropic clime; no Jew loves the thought of re-won Jerusalem, as my people love Kentucky!

Kentucky! The very name swells my heart to childish weakness, and brings before me, like the looming figures in the vast *Fata Morgana*, the heroes and heroines who wrought out her history and established her nationality.

The county of Mercer was not slow or backward in furnishing her quota and to-day I hold up her record to the Argus eyes of the world though they turn on her like a storm of stars. I hold it up with infinite pride; I dwell on it with infinite tenderness, and recall with feelings of the profoundest pathos, the names of those who have passed from the finite things of this world to the eternal glory of life beyond the stars!

It was here that our forefathers felled the trees of the forest and kindled the first sparks of civilization, which have since spread mile after mile over the wilderness of the West with the unerring sweep of a prairie fire without its devastating effects; for now, in the waste places of the past, the lily blends its fragrance with the rose's sweet perfume; now cities and towns and villages, with their varied sounds of mirth and sorrow, of labor and merry-making, stand each and every one as monuments to the memory of the brave and the true, who lived, and struggled, and died for us!

And yet! when in the past month the centennial day of the settlement of this very town dawned, passed the meridian, and died with the setting sun, how many among us knew, or cared to know, that day a whole century ago our forefathers built the first log hut ever erected on Kentucky soil?—two years before the Declaration of Independence! Not many, I opine! This little world about us is too eager to be in the me'ee reigning in the marts of men—buying, selling, and progressing —they have the fever of the age too intensely to care for old landmarks or the sacredness of the past!

> "They pray no longer for their daily bread,
> But next centenary's harvest."

And yet, over the breadth of our State, from border to border, there are hundreds of hearts that revert with pride to the early history of the State, and pæans are sung to the honored dead who came, in the glory and strength of their magnificent manhood, to this country while it was a wilderness; a wilderness, too, in possession of hostile tribes. The commerce of the country, then, consisted in maize and fish and wild game; and the surest facility for securing the lattter lay in the rifle of the pioneer. The sources of revenue so much talked of now were undreamed of by them!

The great West, from the Alleghanies to the Pacific, spread out its varied panorama, and each sturdy hero felt that his country's glory depended on his individual hardihood, endurance, and faithful courage; and they pulled, heart and hand, together, and together dared death and courted danger.

To them: we are indebted for the greatest agricultural section of the Federal Union! *To them!* Brawny-armed braves that they were, bearing the ensign of American liberty and progression through the forest depths, where compass and chart were alike unknown to them!

In the fertility of its soil, Kentucky rivals the most favored part of the Mississippi Valley. For richness and picturesqueness of scenery it is unsurpassed by any State in the Union! "View the country," says Filson, "'round from the heads of the Licking, the Ohio, the Kentucky, Dick's, and down Green river, and you have one hundred square miles of the most extraordinary country on which the sun has ever shone!" Aye! And peopled with the descendants of the bravest, the staunchest, the truest men who ever shouldered rifles or lifted voices in the councils of a nation!

Just view the array of names handed down to posterity, and emblazoned on the fadeless scroll of history! The Breckinridges, the Marshalls, the Clays, the Hardins, the Helms, the Rowans, the Wickliffes, the Shelbys, the Logans, the Underwoods, the McDowells, the Crittendens, the Moreheads, the Johnsons, the Daviesses, the Thompsons, the Allens, the Menifees, the Glovers, the Butlers, the Owsleys, the McAfees, the Caldwells, the Headys, the Harlans, the Browns, etc. And so the list goes on, broadening and brightening with the flight of ages until it shines the envy and the admiration of the world!

Kentucky was, also, the central scene of the imputed intrigues of Aaron Burr and his coadjutors to form a Western Republic. But the Kentuckians, brave and frank in character, were not the material from which to manufacture rebels; and the State which gave Henry Clay to the National Councils was not the one to foster disunionists.

On, down, year after year, her sons (and many of them Mercer's sons, as well) added luster to the crown of glory she wore among States!

Just read Mercer's record! I call on all the counties in Kentucky to furnish an individual one to surpass it. Mercer has furnished two

United States senators (John Adair and John B. Thompson), six congressmen (John Adair, Thomas P. Moore, John B. Thompson, Milton J. Durham, Phil B. Thompson, Jr., and John M. Glover), one appellate judge (S. S. Nicholas), and four circuit judges (John Bridges, Milton J. Durham, Charles A. Hardin, and James Q. Chenoweth), two ministers abroad, two surgeons in the United States army (Able and Thompson), to the State of Kentucky three governors, three lieutenant-governors, and the president of the first convention in 1792, and the first County Court was held here in 1777, with Colonel Tom Allen for clerk! These are facts that shine on the brow of history like priceless gems. They are part of the State's glory.

John Adair was a South Carolinian, but he came to Kentucky at an early age, and became one of her most distinguished sons. He was United States Senator and member of Congress. He was also governor of Kentucky, and he commanded the Kentuckians at New Orleans.

Judge Robinson was born in Mercer county, and the county bears too freshly in mind and heart what and who he was for me to speak his praises here.

Thomas P. Moore lived here; was in Congress, was charge d'affairs to Bogota, and was a colonel in the Mexican war. Like a comet he flashed across the heaven of life, lighting the whole social sphere with his splendor. And to-day? But one man in the country knows his last earthly resting-place.

Ben Hardin, John Rowan, and John B. Thompson all filled their niches in Kentucky's history. The former was more of a jurist than a statesman, and as such I have always heard him mentioned with a degree of respect paid to him only.

Rowan was an advocate and a politician, who filled many high places with great satisfaction to the people. His diplomatic attainments were finished in the highest degree.

In mentioning these two great men in Mercer's record, I do so because John B. Thompson was recognized as their successor. As an orator and an advocate he was peerless, and he reached the next highest position in the gift of the American people. He was born, educated, and died in this county, and if he left an enemy behind him not a man among us would know where to turn to find him. For a quarter of a century he stood like a tower of strength in this State, the pride of the county and a warm friend of Mr. Clay.

Robert B. McAfee filled many public trusts; was ever remarkably unassuming and modest. He left the most enduring monument to his many virtues as a Christian gentleman in the hearts of the people. He wrote the history of the war of 1812 and 1815; he was in the Legislature; he was lieutenant-governor; he was minister to Bogota under President Jackson's administration. As a speaker, he was not eloquent, but forcible and practical. Yet he was a successful politician. His mind was mathematical in its bent rather than legal or political. He aided in the survey of Kentucky, and in fixing her boundaries.

But where are we to find the successors to these children of Fame who "were not born to die?"—these heroes who merit the highest commendation and the profoundest reverence of their descendants?

Monumental fame alone would be but a meager compliment, even though established in every county-seat throughout the Commonwealth! And yet it assuredly would be an incentive, an inspiration, to the present and coming generations to noble deeds in emulation of the past. Such a hallowed and holy past! It ought to fill all hearts with hope and ambition where sleep to-day but the idle vagaries of a goalless youth, overshadowed by eternal mental indolence—indolence which will as certainly destroy their power in the nationality of States, some day, as that terrible and deadly fire that fell upon the cities of the plain graving the record of God's undying curse forever in the wastes of the desert!

Whatever may be the feelings of the progressionists in regard to the past, I would point the youth of Kentucky to it, and bid them let their future copy fair that past until

> "One by one they cross the portal
> Of the gate that open stands;
> One by one they join the spirits
> In those far, immortal lands!"

REMARKS

Upon the Death of Hon. James A. McCampbell in the House of Representatives, at Frankfort, Ky., January 15, 1873.

Mr. Speaker: I can not resist giving expression to the feeling that fills my heart on this occasion of the reassembling of the Legislature. I look about me and see everywhere the brave, intelligent faces of my colleagues, but there is one familiar countenance that is missing from our midst. The Hon. James A. McCampbell, from the county of Jessamine, has been gathered to his fathers.

It was my pleasure and honor to have known the deceased intimately. We were schoolboys together, and the progression of time and the uncertainty of events never altered the fact of our friendship in after years, for, while we fought in different armies and were divided in politics, our social relations were never marred. No higher tribute can be paid to his memory to-day than to say he was a gentleman, whether in the councils of his State, in the *salons* of society, or in the privacy of his domestic circle. He was a thorough scholar, having at an early age received a diploma from Princeton College, and never losing in after life the love of study embraced within those classic walls.

But even then, while yet in his youth, the ravages of the disease to which he afterward became a victim commenced to prey upon him. And such was the state of his health last winter that several times he spoke to me in regard to resigning his seat upon this floor. I saw then, from every lineament of his face, that death had already laid his cold hand upon him, like an untimely frost. But I did not believe that this sad and solemn close of his career was so near at hand, as it eventually proved.

It is always melancholy to resign life even when we have few pleasures, for there is something lusty and delightful in the simple fact of living. But how much sadder it seems to go out "beyond the soundings" forever, as he did, while the Christmas bells were chiming all over the land. "Peace on earth and good will to all men," and the world was making merry and rejoicing over the new year coming up with its hopes, and plans, and energies, and its dreams, and its delights, and desires.

But there is one upon whom the infliction of his loss is sadder than we know. Let us turn our hearts toward the desolate hearthstone, where she saw the sun set—saw it set and leave behind "the good old year, the dear old time, and all her peace of mind." Alas! for her! The new year can never bring back what the old year took away; neither the dear face, the familiar form, nor yet the fond eyes and gentle voice that brought music and brightness to her heart and home.

Let the years come and go as they may, he will never more see

> "The blossoms on the black thorn,
> The leaf upon the tree."

The busy world will pass by his grave, forgetting and by him forgot; but we who admired him as a man and valued him as a legislator and loved him as a friend, we will mourn with her always, and our prayers will be, "God rest his soul forever!"

The gentleman who occupies his chair (Hon. William Brown) let us hope may wear his mantle with honor, and leave in the hearts of his brother members that feeling of regard and respect which is always the highest meed a gentleman can win and wear, and which will forever be shrined with our memory of his predecessor as priceless pearls in a casket belonging to one we loved, and who, being gone from our midst, we grieve for sincerely.

THE BLUE AND THE GRAY.

A Suggestion that Kentucky Should Lead the Van in the Matter of a State Reunion of all the Soldiers of the War.

In New York and Winchester, Va., conventions have been held by ex-Federal and ex-Confederate associations for the purpose of harmonizing the feelings and fraternizing the interests of the people North and South. A similar meeting will be held in Owensboro, Daviess county, Ky., on the 22d, 23d, and 24th of October, 1885, and a thorough appreciation of the kindly sentiments engendered by such community of interest and immunity from error prompts me to give expression to a certain individuality of opinion which is but the faint heralding of the mighty voice of the people moved by one impulse, and held firm by one principle—the love of country and of liberty.

Kentucky was the first Democratic State, after the war, to hold a convention. In May, 1866, the Democrats of Kentucky met in convention in the city of Louisville and nominated for clerk of the Court of Appeals Judge Alvin Duval, from the county of Scott. Colonel D. Howard Smith, who had been a colonel in General Morgan's Kentucky cavalry, and who afterward served as auditor of the State of Kentucky for twelve years, could have been nominated at that convention had it not been considered by the Democrats of other States as incompatible with party interests to nominate, at that time, an ex-Confederate soldier for a State office. Colonel Smith gracefully yielded to what seemed to be necessary policy, and placed in nomination the gentleman indicated above, and at the August election of 1866 he carried the flag of Democracy to victory, thereby reviving the old National Democratic party, which had in former years added luster to the country and its history. And from that day down to the present time the Democratic party has been in power in Kentucky, notwithstanding the fact that the Republicans controlled the Government and a majority of the States in the Union from 1860, when Mr. Lincoln was elected to the Presidency, to 1884, when Mr. Cleveland, of New York, who was the Democratic nominee, received a majority of the electoral vote and was inaugurated on March 4, 1885—twenty-four years! And in the interim the war was fought, not merely on the vague impulse of civic strife where a contest for supremacy of power and property was held, but it was a question of right or wrong doing—a question of principle by which the country would be judged in ages yet unknown. According to the issue of the struggle, the negro was freed, the amendments to the Constitution were adopted, and reconstruction with its attendant evils carried to a degree which was appalling to the Democratic party all over the country. But slowly and surely as the still, gray light of early dawn betokens the coming of the sun to brighten a darkened world with its refulgence, and send its quickening warmth into the heart of the earth, the signs of the times pointed to the ascendency of the Democratic party. And surely as the evolutions of time brought day and night, November 4, 1884, was the Waterloo of the Republican party. Millions of eager eyes read the signs aright, and millions of joyful voices hailed the national transformation with delight.

Kentucky was the first State which knocked for admittance into the Union after the Revolutionary war. It is but a natural sequence of her character among the States that she should be the first to call a State reunion of her soldiers—those brave and heroic spirits who buckled on their armor and defended the principles for which they were willing to die. The blue and the gray have made history for the country at large which posterity will be proud to perpetuate. It matters not under what flag these soldiers fought, their valiant deeds have become the rich heritage of the American people.

The boundaries of a common country form the mausoleum of our brothers-in-arms; and their bones, it matters not where they may be interred, whenever claimed, belong to the respective States that gave them to the cause of liberty. The question, however, of the disposal we shall make of our illustrious dead when—

> "The muffled drum's sad roll has beat
> The soldier's last tattoo,"

Was long ago settled when Colonel Theodore O'Hara, of Kentucky, wrote his poem, "The Bivouac of the Dead," and thus set, as it were, a consecrating seal upon the subject. The "gone before" are indeed beyond recall, but it rests with us, the living, to perpetuate their heroic deeds. And in such heroic reunions only can we bring close to our hearts the memories of our lost comrades, linked together like priceless gems upon a golden cord. We are growing old, and it assumes for us the importance of a duty that we shall imbue our children's hearts with the kindly feelings which engender pride in and love for our common country, and to teach them that it should be their universal boast that they belong to the greatest nation in the world, the freest, and the most enlightened. Think of the scope of populated country! Think of the immigration and the development of the United States! Why, it has been with the strong, swift, majestic sweep of the eagle toward the sun that civilization has penetrated the wilderness of the West, girdled the prairies and tunneled the mountains, and stretched the electric wires, like silver lines, even to the golden gates of San Francisco. And this wonderful progress has been made within twenty years! When we attempt with the absorbed gaze of a visionary to lift the misty veil of Isis which shrouds the unknown and the unseen, is there one among us who does not fancy the uplands of the future to be glowing in the sunshine of prosperity, peace, and happiness? Is there one among us who does not feel a thrill of deep delight when he realizes that this rich national benison will descend undivided to our children, and to our children's children?

The sons of Kentucky never shirk the issue of national affairs. They are, therefore, entitled to consideration in Governmental, State, and local matters. Her sons have fought in all the wars in which the United States has been engaged since the Revolution. The records of her services are to be found in the annals of the country. No State in the Union can produce the names of as many impassioned orators as Kentucky. The Clays, the Marshalls, the Menifees, the Hardins, the Rowans, McKenzie, and others have left an indelible impress upon the history of Kentucky. The harmony of their oratory has sung itself into our forests, and winds have wafted it from the mountain down to the shore, even as the voice of Demosthenes mingled its music with the thunder of the waves, and so goes sounding on from time to eternity. Therefore, it seems right and appropriate that Kentucky should set the example to her sister States in the matter of soldiers' reunions —and even as she once advocated neutrality, because of her love for all, does she to-day advocate fraternity and community of interest. Welcome, then, thrice welcome to those soldiers who, inspired by these sentiments of national pride and national regard, will indicate a time and place when we can hasten to take them by the hand, and look into their eyes, and listen to their happy voices, and thank God that we have "stacked arms" and that we are brothers who have learned to know that "united we stand, divided we fall!"

THE FUTURE.

THE future of life, when philosophically contemplated, is, at its best and at its worst, but little more than a journey taken through a foggy atmosphere; for the reason that we never feel sure of our knowledge of the things that surround us save those which are present and in the most immediate circle. Their proximity affords us intelligent comprehension of their color, size, and shape, and, moreover, we are able to judge of their helpfulness or harm, their balefulness or pleasantness as exactly bearing upon their relation to us; but beyond the pale of proximity everything becomes proportionally dim, vague, and shadowy, for the reason that no man among us has ever been able to penetrate the mysterious realm of the beyond, that unknown borderland of the soul. The fog of doubt veils all things, and the more conscientious among us sometimes hesitate to commit themselves to an operation of even the real nature of what is before them. The uncertain light of chance sometimes penetrates the fog of surmise, but only long enough to let us see that the poet was a philosopher who wrote—

"Things are not what they seem."

The shadow of an awful coming dread sometimes looms before us in the gloom and shuts out the prospect of probable pleasant places we may by chance discover if the sun of hope shines, and often we sit down in it and feel almost ready to abandon our life journey at once and forever. But this is a coward's reckoning. No road was ever yet so rugged, no rocks were ever so hard and gigantic that the eye of faith, if it will only look, may not see some little thread of a path of safety that will lead us on securely to the topmost pinnacle beyond the region of storms, where we may look down into the smiling and fruitful valleys that lie on the sloping side we have yet to tread. There is no fog the eye of faith may not pierce, but it so seldom cares in this prosaic age to see.

Sometimes we are cheated with false semblances of greatness. We look aloft and see some apparently impossible bold projection looking skyward, and we attempt to climb and we succeed, only to find that we have animated ourselves with a vagrant hope, for it is only a projecting cliff—not the golden summit to which the ambitious and the brave aspire.

The constant uncertainties of the future make us oftentimes impatient of our fate. We flatter ourselves that in the way of experience or toil there is some grand height from which we shall be able to descry the way of our life's journey mapped out before us. We struggle on and on, and, gaining the eminence, discover at the last that when the mists of earth are past the clouds of heaven surround us, and we still grope step by step through the shadows toward eternal light.

Sometimes we reach a low, green valley of delight, and indulge in the vague and winning dream that the rest of our journey lies over a smooth and pleasant way. The quietness and sweet peace that surround us with halcyon airs assure us that hills and mountains have been climbed and passed, and that no obstruction can again arise to bar our progress, when lo! the gray mists that veil the face of the future deepen and darken until there is total blackness, and groping through it we discover the yawning chasm of doubt or the fathomless abyss of trial and temptation yawning, wide-mouthed and horrible, to engulf our soul. In vain we endeavor to turn back in the darkness, which is so dreadful, in order to essay a search for some by-path out of chaos we may have overlooked. In vain! for the hungry horror of that chasm confronts us. We can not avoid it. We strive to penetrate its dismal shadows and discover what lies at the bottom, in order to summon requisite faith and arm ourselves with requisite courage. But this effort is also futile. The shadows do not uplift themselves; the distance does not narrow itself to the gauge of the human eye; the gloom is not dissipated. How secure and blissful and peaceful is the past, which we once thought so barren of rich or ripe results, when compared with our awful ignorance of the future—the foothold that takes us over the chasm where we have to feel for each step before we dare to essay it! It is all so dreadful! The past is dead, its realms in the land of fairy, and it is as utterly impossible to go back as it seems to go forward, and always the gray mist of the unknown lies about us. Who among us does not realize in the present or remember as a part of the past that uncertain, pitiful groping for foothold across the awful abyss of trial and temptation? Who among us does not recall the desperate spirit with which we clutched at everything that promised assistance? And, ah! how often, when we seemed to most need support, have we found ourselves grasping some frail, unsubstantial thing that has taken slight root and is worthless to aid us, or else is rotten and bitter to the core? Who among us can not remember just how we stumbled along, how the stones cut our feet, how we bruised ourselves on roots and stumps, how sometimes our bodies grew almost breathless with weariness, how our limbs trembled, how we tore our flesh, how our hands bled and our heads swam around and our hearts ached, and how, when the last atom of strength and courage and endurance seemed exhausted, we suddenly found ourselves near the River of Life, and the silver mists of the Valley of Happiness rising heavenward, and everywhere, far and near, the harvest fields of faith and courage, golden and fruitful, and everywhere the blossoms of truth and beauty filling the air with fragrance and color.

This is, after all the horror of the awful abyss, the glory of the future that awaits every noble and courageous struggler up the steeps.

The ultimate source, the eternal foundation, is forever wooing us from the dull commonplace to loftier heights. With humility softening the soul, with faith beaming from the eyes, with the lips blooming into praise of the infinite delights that await the pure in heart, the true in principle, the ecstasy of a life well spent, when the future shall become the present and finally resolve itself into the imperishable past, is within the reach of every human heart, every human life.

THE INGRATITUDE OF THE MASSES.

THE heart is forever out-reaching for the "far off, unattainable, and dim"—the mind is ever struggling up toward the light of universal knowledge, which it can never reach. There are mediums of attainment, and the proudest attain the loftiest—that is, when pride is the synonym of ambition. But let a man—be he whom he may—dedicate his life, his heart, his brain for the good of the people—the masses—and the day will come to him when he will see that he has spent his years in following a chimera and a dream. When in the flush and flower of his glory and his life he is gathered to his fathers, his fate may be brighter (?)—he may be mentioned in a complimentary notice as a "great luminary gone out," and anecdotes of his boyhood and early manhood will be told over the walnuts and wine in after-dinner talk. But should he be unfortunate enough to attain the zenith of his fame, and still hold fast to health with a long lease on life, he will eventually discover the fact that the gems in his crown of immortality are spurious, that the gold is glitter, and those who once sung his praises on tuneful lyres are many of them LYRES of another type. The public is essentially fickle. Paris is not the only city under the sun that should bear the palm of that reputation. Our city—Louisville—can vie with it for that honor (?). We know of a great man—great by birth—great by education—great by genius, who did public service for this city that honored him and honored it. He was once her feted son, a distinguished statesman, a peerless lawyer, a public servant, who was incapable of a dishonorable action; holding high positions, he conferred honor upon them all. Yet, to-day, he's in a grave, lowly and forgotten, "unwept, unhonored, and unsung." None so poor as to do him reverence. Monuments are reared over the dry dust of those who have lain for a century dead; but when the wound of such a public loss ought still to be bleeding afresh, the cicatrice on the public heart is not visible. Verily, fame to him was as "sounding brass and tinkling cymbal!" Yet there seems little need to reproach the public heart that it has ceased to remember him; for, while the post-office building stands—it is a monumental pile!—while the canal serves the usages of trade. Humphrey Marshall can not be forgotten. The man who forgets SELF—the man who serves others

and scorns to lie, to cheat, to bribe, to pander—is the man who fails to attain glory and gold and to keep it, in this essentially prosaic age. We have noticed it since we gave thought at all to the subject that, in this century, Dis-honesty is the best policy, especially in the public walks of life. Men may whisper among themselves—may secretly condemn corruption and fraud—but when the perpetrator passes by, be he clothed in rich vestments, be he generous in the matter of fine wines, and truffles, and bribes!—and his train of worshipers cast themselves down before him, as the eastern men of old cast themselves in the dust when the king passed by. The heart of the people lusts after glitter and gaud and the flesh-pots of Egypt, and the wise and the brave and the beautiful, unless they offer it these "good things of earth," receive not its homage. After all, the untaught heart of the savage, which is won by a red blanket, a string of shining beads, and a drink of fire-water, is very like the educated (?) heart of the civilized people, only they demand—these good people—that those who dance shall pay the piper well. We have seen the brilliant go to unregretted graves; we have seen the incorruptible trampled in the dust; we have seen virtue fall in the race; we have seen vice win the goal; we have seen the honored dishonored, the distinguished forgotten, and all this by the people they entertained, honored, defended, loved, and served. And the conviction was born in our soul that those who care for themselves first, and other people afterward, are always the ones to succeed. It remains for circumstances to prove to us the contrary. We are open to a new conviction like the masses, whose power of comprehension and worship of popular idols reminds us of what Vibeur says of women: "They are like a pendulum whose motion is a continual reaction; after going to the right it must return to the left, and then again to the right, and so on. Suppose, therefore, virtue is on one side, passion on the other, and the feminine pendulum is between the two, the chances are after striking violently on the right, it will return with no less force to the left." M'lle de la Vallière became Soeur Louise of Mercy after fondling upon her lap the head of Louis XII. Can we have enough admiration for these sublime lunatics? Thus is it with the masses; they crown a head to-day which they would morally guillotine to-morrow. They sing "Io Triompe" in the brain to-day, which to-morrow they will turn into a funeral cortege and sing no Te Deum. Let the man court public homage and applause who wishes it. He is fortunate if he dies young. In brief, like Iganarelle's wife, if he wishes to be whipped, may they whip him? There was an old sign that read, "Hair dressed according to people's own ideas." We are much of this opinion, and the people pull it any way.

WHITE HOUSE, WASHINGTON, D. C.

THE THIRST FOR OFFICE.

Kentuckians and Hibernians alike have a wonderful thirst for office. Whether it be the brief authority they crave, or the public pelf, it would require a more thorough knowledge of the situation than the undersigned possesses in order to decide; but it stands as a point of fact that, so far, the thirst has been unquenchable. Divers epidemics have devastated countries and States, but this bids fair, under the present political *régime*, to slaughter whole hecatombs of office-seekers. President-elect Cleveland will have an opportunity now of studying this singular phase of Kentucky character, which amounts almost to an idiosyncrasy with many of the *genus homo* within her borders. They will doubtless generally and particularly be seeking office at his hands, and, as a prelude to the subject-matter, will very learnedly descant upon the "blooded horse" and the "bluegrass region," and exhaustively treat of their untiring individual service to "the party!" Each one will discuss the products of his section, concluding always with a peroration upon his own fitness for the respective offices desired —of course to the advancement of every social, political, and individual interest in the State. They resemble locusts—do these office-seekers. When they pounce down on a new public incumbent of high station—like the orthopterous insects who, settling down on the earth, remain until they devour every green thing—they go to put in their claims, and get what they think their dues or—" to stay all summer."

In 1862, when General Bragg returned from his Kentucky campaign, there were many Kentuckians who returned with him, fully equipped with   booted and spurred, and ready to conquer nations—"domestic and foreign." The amusing part about the uniforms was, that each one bore the insignia of rank the wearer had selected for himself, according to his imagined qualifications and his distinguished pomposity. Captains, majors, colonels, and lieutenant-colonels could be picked up by the hatful, as one would gather chinquapins after the frost falls. How many generals—"brevet," "brigadier," and "major"—"deponent saith not." History renders no account of them, nor yet of the wounded and slain, but it is an incontestible fact that, when an order was issued from the war department requiring them to join some command, there were scarcely sufficient "gaps" in the Cumberland mountains to grant them egress into Kentucky.

Without office, many of them are mere fugitives from labor—any sort of labor, unless it be very light work and the intervals flitting between drinks. So many of them exist that they represent a "general public" among themselves, and it is respectfully suggested that the sooner they are given to understand that they must rely upon their individual efforts for a support, the sooner will they be considered well-off in this world's goods. Many of those who seek office in this republican Government of ours are totally unqualified, except in conceit, yet they pant for "place" with a grim persistence which is amusing to the public eye—and their "ways and means" of obtaining it depend entirely upon the recommendation of those who occupy prominent positions in the respective civic offices of the State.

We take it for granted that Mr. Cleveland is well versed in human nature, having contended with the lightning calculators of New York and held his own; besides, he has proven himself an executive officer of marked ability, and we are forced into the conclusion, as a consequence, that many applicants for office will be sadly disappointed. Doubtless, about the 4th of March, the tide of applicant immigration from Kentucky to Washington will exceed that of the '49ers who seized their grip-sacks, and in defiance of all obstacles, rushed frantically "Westward ho!" from the States to California in search of gold. Where some succeeded many failed. So will it be with the brilliant cortege that moves on Washington in "panoplied array." There will they remain to be dallied with by other office-seekers in turn, even as the balls which are tossed to and fro by the muffled foot of the show man—until, seized and decimated by an inflammatory epidemic called "Despair," they turn their serried ranks toward the Ohio river, and, reaching their various abodes, settle down upon their "native heather" wiser and, if possible, (?) better men than when false ambition "fed upon their damask cheeks" and led them to believe they were "most excellent timber" for governmental positions.

It would be a source of general delight if all those who thirst for fat offices could be accommodated. It is suggested that the only fair outlook presented is to petition the Congress of the United States to increase the army and the navy, and allow those to select their rank to whom it is not given. If the petition fails they can again return to the "sacred precincts of home." The arms of Kentucky are always outstretched—the heart of Kentucky is always ready to enfold her "wandering heroes" to her breast, and to "bind up their wounds," won, with their laurels, upon many a sanguinary field of glory.

The Hibernians should not be overlooked in respect to office. They love position with deep devotion. They are a high souled, generous race of people. History bristles with their noble deeds, both in war and in literature. The modern Hibernian, though modest (sometimes) reaches out—like Rembrandt's shadows absorbing the light—for distant places that are to be had for the asking. The party must be fully represented. It must extend its imperial ægis over all nationalities alike, and equal rights under the law, "regardless of race, color, or previous servitude," must be respected wherever the flag floats, be it over land or sea.

Let us keep an eye on the victors in the coming contest for place. Let us trust with all the sincerity that hope holds out to the brave, that each applicant may receive his reward according to his merits, that none may go away unsatisfied or unfed; and, above all, beyond all, let us pray that the Democratic administration will be crowned with the laurels of a record as peerless as that of the past, on which the names of Washington, Jefferson, and Jackson are enrolled.

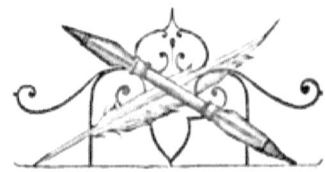

HARROW ON THE HILL.

THOUGHTS ABOUT BOYS.

"Our early days, how often back,
 We turn on Life's bewildering track,
To where o'er hill and valley plays
 The sunlight of our early days."

Boys who turn deaf ears to the kindly admonitions of good mothers can never promise themselves or any one else comfort or pleasure in the fact of their existence. Show me a boy who disregards the advice of those who love and care for him, and I will show you, in return, a lad who may one day be visited (and wept over) by his mother either in the work-house or in the prison cell. He will not only wring her heart, when he is young, by his waywardness, but he will bring her to her grave in sorrow and bow her faster than age, when he attains his maturity.

Many of our greatest men were guided in their youth by their mothers. Washington, Jackson, Douglas, and Clay were all alike left to the tender mercy of God and the fostering care of their widowed mothers.

What shining lights to the world were they! What statues to fill niches in the halls of Time!

In this city there are boys who could scarcely be controlled by a good-sized standing army. I can not conceive what they promise themselves! What hope can they have for the future when they refuse to accept the admonition of praying mothers? How can they ever expect to become useful and respected members of society if they refuse to turn from their evil associates and make never an effort to be or to do better? Why do they not attend the free schools or, if not that, study at home? Every boy should make it the hope of his youth, the pride of his manhood, to be an honorable member of society. They should prepare themselves to follow creditable pursuits in life, and, our word for it, they will be happier.

Good sons make pleasant homes and happy mothers. No gloom ever shrouds the heart's haven which their presence may not dispel.

Our republican institutions require that we should all have education enough to be capable of self-government, and happily, this privilege is within the reach of all, through the magnificent system of free schools.

Ignorance is the cause of a large percentage of the crimes which are committed. Civilization does away with much of the sin and suffering born of the stultification of soul. Culture of the mind is like inspiration. Genius that lies dormant is of as little worth to the world we live in as the jewels that sleep in unsunned splendor in the cavernous heart of the Ural mountains. Without enlightenment of the intellect no life reaches its highest and its best. These are earnest words. They are written with a desire to inspire the embryo statesmen and presidents of our New World to learn early to dedicate their hearts, their thoughts, their whole lives to the development of good in the world.

There are better ways of spending one's time than loafing on the corners, or playing games on the open street, or building bonfires and hallooing along the squares as if Bedlam were let loose and chaos had come again.

Mothers and fathers should alike realize the old maxim: "As the twig is bent the tree inclines." Never spare the rod and spoil the child. If gentleness and firmness fail of success, then use more rigorous rules, but, at all events, do not allow the young lives, dedicated to you for superior guidance, to grow like tares in a wheat-field or poppies amid the corn, only to be trampled under foot at the harvesting, or uprooted to die under glaring sun and biting frost.

Home influence is potential as fate. And with the mothers lies the labor through the heat and weariness of life's long day.

But after all the years that come and go, when the aged look back and the youthful look forward, no love is like the patient hope, the abiding faith, the tender trust of a mother!

Look to it, my boys, that you cause yours neither heart-ache, nor pain, nor tears. When the time comes, as it surely will come, soon or late, to all, when she, who guided your tottering steps and trained the lisping tongue of infancy, shall be no more, it will afford you unspeakable consolation to know that you were good, obedient sons, and that you were a comfort and source of pride to her who would have given her heart's blood at any time to serve and save you.

Whatever else we may attain in this world of grandeur and glory, of honor and wealth, we never have but one mother, and when we lose her, we lose our best and most faithful friend, and nothing can ever fill the void she leaves, even in the coldest and most callous heart.

TRUTH—A LOST ART—A SUNDAY MUSING.

There was a time, in the primitive days of this country's civilization, when a man's word was his bond, for then truth was regarded as an established principle, as a fixed law, but the attrition of mind and the forceful necessities of existence, brought into active consideration by the struggle amid the marts of men, which engrosses the attention of every other person one meets, have long since evolved the fact, from the chaos of question and doubt, that truth has, at last, come to be considered in the light of a lost art, an obsolete acquirement, a pleasant myth, which, like many another charming fallacy, has been consigned to the dust of forgetfulness and the darkness of oblivion. Blackstone's deductions of right and wrong, made after a profound study of human nature, and the laws governing it, were compressed into an aphorism which runs: " Act honestly, live honorably, and render to every man his dues."

Those who can recall to mind the life of a half century ago can well remember that the judgment of Blackstone was the active principle governing man's dealings with his fellowmen, and that the sincerest regard was paid to the truth by all who respected the institutions of our social and political government, and who felt that their personal welfare was involved in their perpetuity ; but the multiplicity of interests and the ambition among men to accumulate money at whatever cost has completely metamorphosed society, and cut in twain the only artery which gave life to the Church and upheld virtue—the underlying sill of the pulpit. How different the consideration awarded even the word "truth" in the present day in comparison with the reverence its simple utterance evoked in the past! Then it was a benign and questioned principle whose existence meant only good. Now, by many, it is looked upon as an isolated term in the vocabulary, meaning less than nothing when brought in opposition to the devices of the magician. Chance, which are offered as substitutes, whose rise insures the gaining of gold, with which they will be enabled to buy the paltry things of earth, whose glitter and gaud will vie acceptably with the gilded trappings of those vain and senseless creatures who crave all else but that which elevates the mind and beautifies the soul. Show me the man whose ambition prompts him to develop in his family a love of the truth, and I will lead you by paths of pleasantness to the home of happiness and peace, where respect for sacred things is held more dear than all the jewels that are or ever were set in the kingly crowns of earth. There is an eloquent passage in St. Matthew which reads in this wise: "For what is a man profited if he shall gain the whole world and lose his own soul?" And, thinking of it to-day, I wonder how the millionaires of this country can read of the great suffering of even the little children, hidden amid the shadowy *cul de sacs* of cities, shut out from blue skies and blooming plants, from whispering winds and God's own sunlight, with little food and less raiment, and scarcely a roof to protect them when the frozen blasts of winter shall pierce their wan and shivering forms like darts from Death's quiver, without themselves feeling the keen stings of remorse penetrating their stultified consciences and shattering their self-esteem! Ah! what a blessed boon is it that the pen and press alike afford facilities for the expression of one's feelings and the upholding of one's sentiments without fear or favor, whatever the floating problem of life which elicits sympathy or enchains interest! To me, it has always been the cause of wonderment how a man could legitimately accumulate a million of dollars when there are so many destitute souls in the world pleading through their tired eyes and with their tongues, parched with famine and fever, for meat and bread, the simplest nourishments that form the staff of life; and how, after he has obtained that sum, he can, by any possibility, hold it and believe in the sublime lessons of charity and love for our fellowmen, taught in the divine pages of the Holy Bible, is a still greater cause for wonderment. To understand the "true inwardness" of such a soul would make even a pitying angel weep over its unhappy knowledge! His miserly hand, like Ishmael's, must, indeed, be turned against the world; but can the fact be doubted that he feeds upon the vitals of the world he despises? The burning sands of the desert to such a soul would be like the curled petals of full-blown roses in comparison to the fires of the infernal regions, which he merits, and which we can see burning forever through the eyes of Dante's genius. If a surplus of riches brings its consequent evils, so does poverty, like Sisyphus, bear about the burden of a curse. When a man becomes so careless and slovenly as to forget the amenities due to himself individually, and society in general, he is the scoria of what was—nothing more—and he has become repulsive to his own sense of refinement, as well as to that quality in others, a quality which bolsters spirit and heart in hours of the darkest depression, so long as it exists at all. Such a being, to the world in which he lives, is as harmless as the dew without its humid breath. He certainly is not of as great consideration to Nature, who is our universal mother.

The poor are spread like poppies all over the face of the earth, and that this is true seems but a fulfillment of the divine Master's words, when he said: "For the poor ye shall have with you always!" Why the affliction is visited upon the world is better known to the Infinite Will than to any one among us. If riches ofttimes beget an indifference to truth and honesty in their accumulation, so does the lack of them augment the disregard of one and a paucity of the other. Yet, for all this, I aver that truth is as essential to the happiness of man as food and air are essential to the maintenance of his corporal being, and when you have stripped the body of that spiritual ornament called truth, which is reflected through the eyes, "the windows of the soul," with a light that outshines the glory of planets, you have nothing left but the sightless stem upon which hung the most beautiful and fragrant flower that ever unfurled its loveliness amid the starry splendors of Paradise. Above all things, then, the parents of to-day should guard the instruction imparted to their children. In the end, they will aggregate greater gain to them than earthly endowments

Riches take the wings of the morning and fly away whither and thither they list, but true, pure knowledge, imparted for the soul's sake, prepares those who drink at the immortal Fountain of Truth to so live that their dying will be cause for the mourning of multitudes. For the safety of the church, for the dignity of our national character, and the eternal welfare of our souls, let us look to it that the lost art of truth-telling is revived, and money-getting is forgotten in the development of those finer impulses of soul that make life beautiful and death holy.

www.ingramcontent.com/pod-product-compliance
Lightning Source LLC
Chambersburg PA
CBHW021344230426
43666CB00006B/405